No Child Left Behind Goals (and more) are obtainable with the Neurocognitive Approach: Vol. 1

Kirtley E. Thornton, Ph.D.

BookSurge Publishing Co.,2006

This book is dedicated to my wife
Monika
for all that she has endured with
patience, grace and dignity
throughout these many years
and
to all the children who deserve the
best that we can offer them
and
to all the professionals working in
this area who are striving to help
these children
and
to my family who have supported
my goals and desires

Table of Contents

Web Address:
chp-neurotherapy.com
Email:
ket@chp-neurotherapy.com

No Child Left Behind goals (and more) are attainable with the Neurocognitive approach: Vol. 1

Introduction

Presented below is one parent's report on her reading disabled child's status following Neurocognitive treatment.

"Her change in abilities and feelings is nothing short of phenomenal! She is actually reading proficiently and for sustained periods of time. For the first time in her life, she asked me to wait a few minutes until she finished the chapter of a book she was reading. Before your intervention, it was a battle of wills to get her to read even a paragraph!

There has been a basic change in her ability to act as an independent, self-regulating individual in the world, which has been remarked on by everyone who has worked with her, and especially by those who have spent extended time with her. It is truly the difference between health and developmental disability.

The Neurocognitive treatment is the ultimate in "NO CHILD LEFT BEHIND!"

In the words of another parent;

"His vocabulary has tripled. He now reads books. Before treatment he wasn't able to even read a chapter and remember what it said. He reads for pleasure now that it isn't a huge chore like it was before. His short-term memory has greatly improved. I seldom have to repeat instructions to him. His self-confidence levels has improved 100%. He used to be a boy who hardly spoke to anyone; now he will come up and introduce himself to strangers. He is even teaching a children's Martial Arts class. His grades keep improving, he has gone from an F student to a C and B student. He has lots of catching up to do and I believe if we had started this treatment sooner he would be an A student by now."

Scientific revolutions and discoveries have changed our world forever. The first and last great revolution in education was the printing of a book. The next revolution will bring modern neuroscience discoveries into the classroom and will change how the mind reads the book.

The evolution of the human brain stopped some 300,000 years ago - until now. Genetics and environment no longer can dictate how we learn and our brains work. The Neurocognitive approach can effectively change how our brain functions. The implications for society and the human species go far beyond the educational process and reading, yet that is where we need to start.

To learn to read is to light a fire; every syllable that is spelled out is a spark.

Victor Hugo

Man ceased to be an ape, vanquished the ape, on the day a first book was written.

Yevgeny Zamyatin

Education is the most powerful weapon which you can use to change the world.

Nelson Mandela

In 1789, Benjamin Franklin wrote,

"Nothing can more effectually contribute to the cultivation and improvement of a country, the wisdom, riches and strength, virtue and piety, the welfare and happiness of a people than a proper education of youth" (Brown & Moffett, 1999).

In the words of former Senate Minority Leader Tom Daschle's (Democrat - South Dakota).

"Let me suggest one final goal that could occupy the best efforts of scientists from every discipline for a generation to come. Now that we have surveyed the map of human life, let us turn our attention to that which makes human life unique: the mind. What challenge would be beyond our reach if we truly understood how we learn, remember, think and communicate? What could we accomplish if our education policy was bolstered with a new understanding of how children learn? How much safer could our neighborhoods be if neurophysiology solved the puzzle of addiction? What industry would not be strengthened by a more complete picture of the workings of the mind? There is perhaps no field in which major advances would have more profound effects for human progress and health than that of neuroscience. If the American scientific community could come together and communicate to the nation the kaleidoscopic possibilities that could result if we unlocked the secrets of the mind, we could not only achieve untold advances in science, we could open a new chapter in the story of America's support for science." (Daschle, 2004)

These quotes provide the purpose for this book – the need for the integration of education with modern neuroscience to improve the human condition with respect to the lives of our children.

With the advent of No Child Left Behind (NCLB), there has been considerable pressure on the educational system to increase the reading and math levels of our students. The title of this book states that the NCLB goals are attainable with the Neurocognitive approach. NCLB's goal is 100% basic reading abilities in our children by the year 2014. The author, as well as other professionals in the field, believes that this goal is totally impossible to attain with current intervention models. The author believes that the NCLB goals are **mostly attainable** if the physical problems in brain functioning are addressed with the Neurocognitive approach.

The Neurocognitive approach precisely defines the relationship between effective cognitive activity and electrophysiological variables and increases the cognitive effectiveness of the human mind with operant (rewarding/inhibiting of spontaneous behavior) conditioning methodology of the brain's electrophysiology. Central to its application is the existence of a quantitative EEG activation database, which is employed to define a subject's deviation from the norm on relevant variables. The activation database is the quantitative EEG data collected on a large sample of normal subjects engaged in a diverse set of important cognitive tasks. These concepts will be explained further in chapters 10-12.

Several qualifications and limitations of the approach will be addressed in Chapter 16 (The Questions). These qualifications and limitations render the NCLB 100% goal as unattainable and the title of this book as an overstatement. The logic and evidence provided, however, make it clear that our current approaches are woefully inadequate to the task. We can obtain significantly better results in considerably less time with the Neurocognitive approach with resulting significant positive effects on a number of other societal problem areas.

Reading problems in our children need to be understood in the general context of developmental and brain functioning problems such as learning disability, reading disabilities, ADHD and math disabilities. The basic tenet of this book is that problems in the physical functioning of the brain underlie these conditions and the most effective way to improve these conditions is with a physical intervention.

There are five main purposes of this book.

1)   To examine the problems of NCLB from a political, economic and realistic assessment of the attainability of

NCLB's goals.

2)   To examine the scientific research on how effective our psychoeducational interventions have been in this area during the past 80 years.

3)   To examine what Neuroscience has taught us about brain functioning and how this affects the NCLB goals.

4)   To examine the context in which the reading problem exists and how problems in brain functioning affect more than just reading ability. Brain functioning problems have considerable effect on the lives of the people who are affected as well as society in general.

5)   To explain, describe and document how a particular simple physical intervention model, Neurocognitive treatment, can effectively address these problems and have significant and positive consequences on the individuals affected and on major societal institutions.

The book will be presenting a considerable amount of information in the pursuit of integrating information across a diverse set of fields. Many of the "facts" presented are rough estimates and should be viewed in that light, as the "real" numbers are sometimes hard to discern from the data and difficult to obtain for many reasons. There are also conflicting numbers in some cases as different research methodologies can result in different numbers. We would like to caution the reader not to get bogged down in the specific numbers but appreciate rather the global extant of the brain functioning problem as it manifests itself in multifaceted ways. Behind the wealth of data presented are 3 simple concepts:

1- Many of these societal problems are intimately tied to problems in brain development and functioning.

2- Major personal and societal problems can be effectively addressed by relying upon the capacity of the human brain to respond to our requests to change how it functions.

3- The improved results of the Neurocognitive approach to these problems would have major financial, health and social implications for our society and the individuals affected by these problems.

We will be discussing relevant scientific information on the underlying brain functioning problem which is a major contributor to several major societal problems. We will present complex appearing concepts and explain them in easy to understand language while maintaining the integrity and meaning of the concepts. This discussion will not gloss over important issues but rather delve into the details of the problem when relevant to the overall purpose of the book. Our societies and the future of our world are totally dependent upon the abilities of the human mind. To understand how it functions and how to improve its functioning should be and is a major thrust of modern science. The discoveries reported in this book offer one perspective and insight into this broad area.

The United States is presently spending an estimated **$157 to $590 Billion dollars a year** for problems in brain functioning. This number is based upon estimated special education costs ($54 billion in 2004 – Washington Times, 2004), traumatic brain injury (TBI) costs ($62 billion in 2001 – Thompson et. al., 2001), and prison costs (24.5 billion in 1996 – Bureau of Justice Statistics, 1996). Estimates of the costs of crime vary but were $17.6 billion in 1992 (Klaus, 1994). Violent crime estimates (including drunk driving and arson) are $426 billion annually. Estimates of property crime are $24 billion (Miller et. al., 1996). The TBI estimates includes physical problems.

These estimates do not include other potential costs (automobile accidents, medications, drug abuse, etc.)

The discussion in this book will make it clear that our present solutions are woefully inadequate to meet these challenges. Neurocognitive intervention is the alternative approach that has been scientifically demonstrated to obtain superior results across major societal problems: education, criminal justice, traumatic brain injury rehabilitation, medical costs and drug rehabilitation. The implementation of this approach into the educational system during the early years of a child's educational experience would have a significant and positive effect upon the child, the child's family and the educational, health and prison system of the United States. The estimated cost savings for special education alone is some $327 billion dollars over time (Thornton, 2004).

This book will present a scientific argument for a solution to some of the problems facing our society. There are millions of children and their parents who are experiencing considerable difficulty in life and emotional pain as a result of the problems in brain functioning. This group would include the parent of the ADHD child who runs into the street and is killed because of his inattentiveness and impulsivity; the reading disabled child who knows something is wrong, feels inferior to his peers and cries at night; the adult ADHD person who can't maintain a job or pay his bills because no one wants to hire him or promote him; the soldier who experienced a concussion during a roadside bomb blast and isn't getting better in the VA system; the thousands of children who think they are stupid because parts of their brains don't work well.

If the reader is a parent who is not interested in all the political, economic and social issues presented in this book, but merely wants to understand how the Neurocognitive technology can help their child, we would suggest just reading Chapters 10 thru 16 and Chapter 23. These chapters provide the basic science, evaluation and treatment results and clinical updates, summaries and comments from individuals who have undergone the program.

The following brief chapter descriptions will provide the reader with the narrative and logical flow of the book and argument.

Chapter Headings

Chapter 1 - Chapter 1 - No Child Left Behind (NCLB) – Politics, Economics and Efficacy Results

Reviews the current political and economic controversies surrounding the NCLB act and the inevitable failure of the program.

Conclusion: The situation is a briar patch with no clear easy resolution.

Chapter 2 - What is the Scope of the Problem?

Discusses the prevalence of the reading disabled, learning disabled and traumatic brain injured population. These groups are the most problematic population for NCLB goals.

Conclusion: The subject population is quite large and pervasive throughout society.

Chapter 3 - Efficacy Research on Educational Intervention Programs for the LD/ADHD and TBI Student.

Reviews the historical research on what interventions have been attempted to improve these conditions.

Conclusion: The current programs are, by and large, minimally effective, costly and time consuming in comparison to the Neurocognitive option.

Chapter 4 – Causes of Non-Optimal Brain Development/ Functioning.

Examines the numerous possible causes of non-optimal brain functioning and two broad categories of interventions.

Conclusion: There are a plethora of possible negative

effects on brain functioning.
Chapter 5 - Neuroscience of Reading/Learning Disability/ ADD /
ADHD / TBI
> Provides a somewhat superficial view of modern neuroscience
> and what it has been discovered about the physical nature of
> these problems.
> **Conclusion: We are beginning to have some idea of the
> nature of the underlying physical problems.**

Chapter 6 – Behavioral Manifestations of Brain Functioning
Problems Which Relate to Reading Problems.
> Examines the behavioral manifestations of brain functioning
> problems in terms of the DSM IV classification system.
> **Conclusion: The problem is more than just a reading
> problem.**

Chapter 7 - Comorbidity Relationships in the ADHD condition
> Examines the ADHD condition, which is the most researched
> of all of the conditions in terms of what we know about
> comorbidity issues.
> **Conclusion: There are significant comorbidity issues in
> the ADHD child.**

Chapter 8 – Cost Issues
> Examines the costs of having the ADHD condition, for the
> family, the subject and society.
> **Conclusion: There is a high cost, financially and
> emotionally, for all concerned.**

Chapter 9 – Drugs and the Quality of Life
> This chapter examines this most common treatment approach
> to the ADHD situation, describes the side effect problem and
> the possible effects on the subject.
> **Conclusion: Drugs are not very effective. There are
> substantial side effect problems and "Black Box"
> warnings. Medications are not a viable option.**

Chapter 10 - What is the EEG?
> This chapter describes the basic concepts of the quantitative
> EEG.
> **Conclusion: There is a relevant science to the problems
> discussed.**

Chapter 11 - The quantitative EEG (qEEG)
> This chapter reviews the logic and research literature on the

ability of the qEEG to differentiate clinical conditions and its usefulness in reference to NCLB.

Conclusion: The approach has shown its usefulness in improving clinical conditions and cognitive functioning, which is particularly relevant to NCLB.

Chapter 12 - The Development of the Activation Database Guided Neurocognitive Interventions.

This chapter outlines the development of the activation qEEG approach in terms of its logic and database development.

Conclusion: There is an alternate way to look at the qEEG.

Chapter 13 -The Activation qEEG Evaluation Procedure

Conclusion: The activation qEEG evaluation procedure is a viable and logical approach to examine the brain.

Chapter 14 – Evaluation Examples

This chapter provides examples of evaluation results of the brain.

Conclusion: We can evaluate individual brains and obtain meaningful results.

Chapter 15 – Treatment Examples

This chapter goes through clinical examples in detail to show how the brain responds and the resultant changes in cognitive functioning which result.

Conclusion: The Neurocognitive intervention model has obtained far superior results to all other intervention models in existence and at a considerable savings in cost.

Chapter 16 – The Questions

This chapter discusses some overall questions raised by the procedures and approach as it is currently practiced.

Conclusion: There are some important clinical and scientific questions which require an understanding to maximize the effectiveness of the intervention.

Chapter 17 - Implications for Society

This chapter discusses the implications of the approach for our position in the world community with respect to intellectual and educational standings.

Conclusion: Despite our world status in many respects, the US is having problems being competitive in the

educational arena.

Chapter 18 - Education – Potential Effect

This chapter discusses the relationship between IQ, SAT scores, achievement levels for individuals and the Gross Domestic Product (GDP).

Conclusion: There are powerful relationships between scores on IQ tests, an individual's success in life and societal productivity.

Chapter 19 – Prisons, Drugs and Special Education

This chapter discusses the implications of the approach upon our prison population, drug problem and special education problem and reviews research in these and other areas.

Conclusion: The approach has produced positive results in a number of clinical conditions.

Chapter 20 – Other Clinical Applications: Alcoholism, Autism, Asperger's, etc.

This chapter examines the EEG biofeedback literature related to alcoholism, autism, asperger's, post-traumatic stress, sports, peak performance, and the military

Conclusion: The technology is relevant to a number of behavioral areas.

Chapter 21 - The Future of the Technology – The Final Frontier

This chapter discusses the future of the technology.

Conclusion: The implications are quite significant.

Chapter 22 - The Problem of Change – The Politics of Change and the Failure to Respond

This chapter reports the results of efforts to change the system and the lack of response of the bureaucratic and political systems.

Conclusion: It is very difficult to change a bureaucracy.

Chapter - 23 – Client Reports

This chapter provides clinical updates from individuals and the parents of students who have engaged in the interventions.

Conclusion: Clients and their parents are very happy with the results and note diverse effects across a wide category of behavior.

Chapter 1 - No Child Left Behind (NCLB) – Politics, Economics and Efficacy Results
The Standard Deviation Effect Size Measure

The statistical concept of standard deviation will be employed throughout this book. It will be the basic measurement value by which all intervention effects will be examined. Therefore a brief description of the meaning of the statistic is relevant before any discussion of the issues.

Figure 1

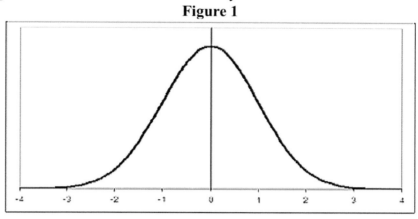

The Bell Curve

The concept of a distribution of values precedes the concept of standard deviation. Any trait, behavior or phenomena we wish to examine will have a set of values associated with the population we are examining, e.g. weight. If we examine the weight of thousands of people, we can obtain an average weight and a distribution of the weight values from the low end to the high end. How these values are distributed can be graphically represented. The x-axis (the horizontal one) is the value in question... weight, for example. The y-axis (the vertical one) is the number of data points for each value on the x-axis. Most data follows what is called a normal distribution that is exemplified by the bell curve, as shown in Figure 1. The standard deviation measure is a statistical way of understanding how these values are distributed from the mean value or how tightly all the various examples are clustered around the mean in a set of data. A distance of one standard deviation from the mean (above and below the mean) represents about 68% of the people in the weight distribution bell curve. A distance of two standard deviations (above and below the mean) represents 95%

of the people. A distance of three standard deviations represents 99% of the people. The average weight of the American female is 164 pounds according to the National Center for Health Statistics (2004). The standard deviation of the weight of the American male and female is 30 lbs. Thus, 68% of US women are between 134 pounds and 194 pounds. If a male or female were to put on 2 standard deviations of weight, he/she would gain some 60 pounds. Whatever measure we employ will have its own mean and standard deviation, which is defined by the data and the constructs we are employing.

The means and standard deviation of IQ tests are defined statistically as 100 and 15 respectively. Thus 68% of the nation will score between 85 and 115 on a standard IQ test. If we had an intervention that could raise the normal IQ score by 15 points, we could effectively move the mean of the US population from 100 to 115 or one standard deviation. Such a change would represent a major shift in the intelligence of a nation, with far reaching consequences.

For an individual to qualify as a member of Mensa, they must have an IQ of 133 or above. Mental retardation is defined as an IQ of 70 or below. Thus a two standard deviation difference from the mean (100) has a powerful implication for an individual's life.

Some educational writers have contended that a .25 SD improvement can be considered educationally significant while others have argued for a .50 SD number. All would agree that the larger the effect size is, the better. Most current intervention strategies average about a +.50 SD improvement on the measures employed. The Neurocognitive approach averages greater than a +3 SD effect, more then 6x the effect size and in considerably less time.

To determine the relative effectiveness of the different programs we will examine the standard deviation (SD) effects of the interventions when the authors provided sufficient information to calculate the effect. The SD effect is determined by the following formula (post treatment mean – pretreatment mean)/ (standard deviation of pretreatment group).

The NCLB Program – Efficacy Issues
Efficacy Reports to Date
The NCLB goal is to obtain adequate reading and math ability in 100% of our children by 2014. However, from an epidemiological perspective, reading disabilities affect at least 80% of the learning disabled (LD) population and thus constitutes the most prevalent type of LD (Lerner, 1989; Lyon, 1995). Thus NCLB is a program whose subject population

is predominantly the LD child. Unfortunately, despite the considerable governmental and public attention devoted to this problem, the results have been singularly unimpressive and have resulted in considerable political and economic turmoil.

State of California - API shows +.18 SD improvement.

The state of California summarized (2005) the Academic Performance Index (API) of the 9,300 schools reporting results and indicated an average 20-point increase on the API. The standard deviation of the initial values was 111, thus the change represents an average of +.18 improvement in SD scores. (California AYP, 2005)

Northwest Evaluation Association report

NEA reports .01 to .05 SD effect of NCLB.

The Northwest Evaluation Association (NEA) (2005) studied the effects of the NCLB program on student's achievement levels. The report covered over 300,000 students in 200 school districts in 23 states between grades 3 and 8. In comparing the fall 2001 data with the fall 2003 data, the study reported effect sizes ranging between .02 to .10 standard deviations (SD) with an average of +.05 SD for the math achievement scores. For the reading achievement scores, the average effect size was +.01 SD. Every aspect of the study confirmed the greater effect on math achievement levels over reading achievement levels. The authors conclude "the rate of improvement... **is not sufficient to create any reasonable prospect that all students will achieve proficiency by 2014.**" (pg. 57) One hundred percent reading proficiency by 2014 is the goal of NCLB. (NWEA report, 2005)

National Assessment of Educational Progress Report (2005)

NAEP reports a .05 SD improvement over 13 years.

In December of 2005 the National Assessment of Educational Progress report was issued (NAEP Report, 2005). This report is referred to as "The Nation's Report Card", as it focuses on achievement scores of the nation's students. The report focuses predominantly on the 4th and 8th grade results of nationally standardized testing and reports the results in terms of proficiency ratings (below basic, basic, proficient, advanced). Table 1 presents the distribution of these percentages for the below basic category. Table 2 presents the numbers for the proficient and advanced levels. These values as well as the values presented in Table 1 make it clear that the United States does have a problem with reading ability in its children.

The report indicates that 38% of 4th graders and 29% of 8th graders are at the below basic level in reading. In mathematics, the 21% of the nation's 4th graders and 32% of the 8th graders are below basic levels. The federal government has insisted on including the LD population's performance in these figures. Of the children who are classified as disabled 67% of 4th and 8th graders are classified as below basic levels in reading while 44% of 4th graders and 69% of 8th graders are below basic levels in mathematics.

Table 1 - NAEP Report Figures - 2005

	Below Basic Levels Reading	Below Basic Levels Mathematics
Nation		
4th Grade	38%	21%
8th Grade	29%	32%
Students with Disabilities		
4th Grade	67%	42%
8th Grade	67%	69%

Table 2 - NAEP Report Figures - 2005

	Proficient / Advanced Levels	**Proficient/ Advanced Levels**
	Reading	Mathematics
Nation		
4th grade	30%	35%
8th grade	29%	29%
Students with Disabilities		
4th grade	11%	16%
8th grade	6%	7%

The national progress on these reading measures has increased from 215 in 1992 (standard deviation of 36) to 217 in 2005 (4th graders) (NAEP Historical Data). The resulting standard deviation improvement is +.05, which is not an impressive improvement over a 13-year period. **These figures make it clear that the goal of NCLB can never be attained with**

current technologies, no matter how much money and time is spent.

To calculate what would be required to approximately obtain the NCLB's goals, let's look at the standard Bell Curve. If we could move the bell curve to the right (Figure 1) so that the mean is 2 SD above where it is presently, then only 2.5% of the population would be at or below the previous mean.

The average standard deviation for 4th grade reading scores on the NAEP is 36.8 (from 1970 to 1999). (NAEP Historical Data) Very roughly, this shift would be equivalent to moving the NAEP reading scores from 217 to 290.6. **At the current rate of 2 points in 13 years, it would take us some 474 years (year 2479) to move the bell curve to the right, assuming (of course) that the trend continues.** The goal might be possible if the Neurocognitive approach was employed in every school system.

Let's go back to the 2005 results and look at the numbers a little closer. The report indicates that, on average, about 10% of the school population is labeled disabled. Therefore, if we have a school with 100 children, 10 will be labeled disabled and 90 will not. Of the 10 disabled children (4th grade), 6.7 (67%) are reading below basic level. Of the 90 not disabled children, 38% or 34.2 children will be reading below basic level. Therefore, the total reading below basic level group will number 40.9 (41%) of the 100 children. Only 17.6% (6.7) of the group will officially be classified as disabled. Therefore 82.4% of the total reading below basic level group will be composed of children who are not classified as disabled.

Somewhat problematic in these numbers is the concept of a disabled child who is reading at advanced levels. If the child is reading at advanced levels then what is the nature of his disability? It is clearly not reading. To answer this question would require delving into the data and how the children are classified and is beyond the focus of this book. Following this classification and logic, the primary cause of the reading problem (82%) is a cultural/environmental one and not a brain functioning problem (children labeled disabled).

Yet this interpretation is problematic. To simplify the problem, a sample school of 100 children is reporting 34 "normal" children who are reading at below basic levels and 7 "disabled" children at the below basic level as well. Assuming no brain functioning problems, there are two cultural/environmental possible causes (home or school) to the reading problem for the 34 "normal" children who are at or below basic levels. As the school is presumably exposing all the children to the same curriculum and hasn't isolated the 34 children in a different room where no teaching occurs, the cause of the reading problem would appear to reside in the home environment. The children are in school about the same number of hours during the day as they are at home. While it is certainly self-evident that parents have a considerable input into the child's cognitive development, it is very problematic to blame the nation's reading problem on poor parenting and then try to solve the problem in the school setting with the same approaches we have always used, were using as the child was attending school for years, and were using when these assessments were being conducted. To put it another way, if a house is burning down why are we sending our half-filled pails of water to a bush fire down the street which has been burning for years and which we've never been able to put out?

The more credible and realistic way to look at this problem is to understand that there are wide variations in individual abilities and backgrounds and when these individual variations reach a certain level the child becomes classified.

Cause, Effect and the Intervention Problem

It is necessary to place this problem in the broader context of the causes of a reading problem. To understand this problem in depth will require some discussion of the issues involved. We will examine this problem with some hypothetical students who all failed English reading tests. This analysis will be a somewhat simplified version of the major issues.

Student A, a feral child named Saturday, was born with no genetic "wiring" problems and no environmental assaults upon his brain functioning. However, he grew up in the forest where there were no educational experiences to help shape his brain development.

Saturday was discovered (on a Saturday) when he was about 5 years old and was in the company of monkeys in the Kwazulu-Natal province of South Africa. He was captured and taken to a school for the disabled. He was very violent during his first days here. He used to break things in the kitchen and get in and out through windows. He didn't play with other kids and instead he used to beat them. He liked uncooked red meat. He didn't like blankets. He wanted to sleep naked and he hated clothing. Ten years later, Saturday was still unable to speak. He had been taught to walk, but was still refusing to eat cooked food and preferred raw vegetables instead. Bananas were his favorite fruit.

Feral children, also known as wild children or wolf children, are children who have grown up with minimal human contact, or even none at all. They may have been raised by animals (often wolves) or somehow survived on their own. In some cases, children are confined and denied normal social interaction with other people. The lack of a human social and language environment during critical learning periods has severe implications for brain development.

Another famous example involves the Indian Wolf-Girls. Two young girls (age 8 and 18 months) were discovered under the care of a she-wolf in India in 1920 and were taken to an orphanage. They behaved exactly like small wild animals. They slept during the day and woke by night. They remained on all-fours, enjoyed raw meat, and were given to biting and attacking other children if provoked. They could smell raw meat from a distance, and they had an acute sense of sight and hearing. The older child did acquire a small vocabulary.

Tarzancito is another example with a more positive outcome. Tarzancito was discovered by wood-cutters living wild in the forests of El Salvador. When he was found towards the end of 1933, he was about five years old. He had survived by eating raw fruit and small fish and slept in trees to avoid the wild animals. He was captured only after the usual struggle. Once he returned to civilization, Ruben (the name he was given) made considerable progress, and was eventually able to attend a normal school.

Student B, Albert, was born with no genetic "wiring" problems, was exposed to a highly enriched educational environment but was never taught English.

Student C, Tom, was also born with no genetic "wiring" problems but suffered a number of environmental physical assaults upon his brain functioning (TBI, malnutrition, pregnancy and birth complications, etc.)

Student D, Dick, was born with genetic "wiring" problems but no environmental physical assaults upon his brain functioning.

Student E, Harry, was born with genetic "wiring" problems and environmental physical assaults upon his brain functioning.

Student F, Jane, was born with no genetic "wiring" problems and no gross environmental physical assaults upon her brain functioning, but was raised in a family that did not actively stimulate her intellectual/reading development.

There are 3 issues in this problem:

1) What is the cause of the reading problem?

      a)   From a scientific viewpoint there is an inherent value to understanding the cause. The assumption behind the scientific viewpoint is that if we can understand the cause, we can then intervene appropriately. There are two causes – 1) a brain functioning problem or 2) a cultural/educational background problem.

From an educational perspective, the cause is of some intellectual interest but will have no effect on the intervention decision, which will involve either tutoring or some form of psychoeducational intervention or restructuring the learning environment (Chapter 3). These are the only available options to the schools at present.

2) What is the effect of the cause on the brain's functioning and test scores?

    a)   The question here is whether and how the two possible influences have their effect. It is self-evident that genetics or a physical assault (TBI, Toxins, etc.) can have a physical effect on the physical brain. The relevant questions are "What is the effect?" "On what structures?" "What functions?" and "To what degree?" This question addresses the problems of Tom, Dick and Harry.

    b)   It is less obvious, though documented in research (Carmody et al., 2006), that the educational or cultural background can 1) have a physical effect on the brain functioning and 2) the effect can be different than the effect of a deleterious physical event. Carmody et al. (2006) demonstrated in an fMRI study of attentional ability (15-16 year olds) that medical risk (pre term birth) and environmental risk differentially affect how the brain physically responds to a cognitive task (to be discussed further in Chapter 4). This would be the relevant question for Jane. How has Jane been affected by a "poor" environment.

This research begins to answer the relevant questions...."What structures?" "What functions?" and "To what degree?" This would be the relevant question for the feral child and Jane.

3) What is the most appropriate and most effective form of treatment?

    a)   For Albert, educational interventions alone would be most appropriate, as he has never been exposed to

English but has an excellent brain to work with.

b)   Tom, Dick and Harry all have some sort of physical damage to brain structures and functions.

    i. Educational evaluations, by themselves, would only tell us how the problem is manifested on tests and not what physical structures/functions are affected. Interventions would be directed towards the tested deficit with tutoring and individual instruction in the deficit area. For example, for an individual with a math deficit the tutoring intervention would merely address the problems in algebra (for example) with repetitive exercises in algebra and individual instruction. Generally, there would be no attempt to focus on the underlying cognitive dysfunction such as internal spatial addition or mental rotation. The assumption behind this approach is that if we do it long enough, the student will eventually "get it". There is some evidence (Chapter 5) that, in the case of reading interventions, physical changes in brain structures and functions result from this type of intervention. If Tom, Dick, and Harry all showed a reading problem they would receive approximately the same intervention. The cause would be irrelevant, as well as the effect of the cause on the brain's physical functioning. Only the effect on educational testing would be relevant to the intervention.

    ii.   Physical interventions, as defined by an activation quantitative EEG would provide specific information on what is not physically functioning properly during a reading task. The reading problems of Tom, Dick and Harry would be addressed differently according to what is revealed in the evaluation. In this situation, the cause is somewhat irrelevant and the main concern is the physical result of the cause upon the electrophysiological functioning of the brain. Once the physical basis for the reading problem is repaired, educational interventions can proceed at a much faster pace.

iii. For the feral child and Jane, the diagnosis becomes a little more problematic, as it would be uncertain what was the brain functioning problem or whether it was a strictly a problem in educational/cultural background. An activation qEEG evaluation would readily solve the problem and determine what is the best course of treatment. For the feral child, the massive deprivation would clearly have significant physical effects upon brain functioning. Whether Jane would show problems in the physical functioning of the brain would be a relevant question.

Table 3 presents these subjects and the appropriate options available. Presently, in our school systems the only available option is the psychoeducational one. As the research in this book has demonstrated, the approach is limited due to effect sizes and the problems just discussed.

Table 3 - Tom, Dick, Harry, Albert, Feral Child & Jane

Cause	Effect	Effect	Intervention	Intervention
	Brain Function Problem	Lower Test Scores	Educational	Physical
Poor Brain Functioning				
Genetics	Dick	Dick		Yes
Environment				
a) active assaults - toxins, etc.	Tom	Harry		Yes
b) poor genetics & active assaults	Harry	Harry		Yes
c) Passive - Lack of Enrichment	Feral Child Jane	Feral Child Jane	Yes Yes	Yes ?

Good genetics & educational background		Albert	Yes	No

NCLB Cost Issues

Public spending on K-12 education was $422.7 billion in 2001-02. (NCES, 2004) One author reasoned that if we use a conservative estimate of 20% added costs for the nation as a whole to accomplish the goals of NCLB, the national increase would be about $84.5 billion. An estimate of 35% additional costs yields a national increase of $148 billion. (Mathis, 2003) The current federal Title I appropriation is $11.3 billion, and the Administration's budget request of $12.3 billion is below the authorized amount of $18 billion in NCLB. (Schemo, 2003) Thus federal under funding of the NCLB program is between $72 and $136 billion dollars below the estimates of what is required and $6 billion below what has been authorized.

Several authors who have looked into the conflicts and problems in this area have described the following analysis of the situation with NCLB.

"President Bush said in his weekly radio address of January 4, 2003 that the additional $1 billion was "more than enough money" and that "we are insisting that schools use that money wisely." (Bush, 2003) It would appear, however, that Bush's additional 1 billion dollars is somewhat short of the $84 to $148 billion that would be conservatively required, assuming that the interventions actually worked. The author of this book maintains that these interventions don't work sufficiently well enough to obtain the goals. This financial structure puts the states in an awkward financial position; they have to pay the extra funding required and they have no options to sue the government for the money, which they can't. Legal scholars as well as the Secretary of Education (Richard Riley in a letter dated 19 January 2001) have stated that the states have the responsibility of providing educational resources to meet new standards. The alternative for the states is to reject the money and the mandates. If the states take the money and require local districts to meet state standards, then these same local districts can legally demand that the state provide adequate money to meet these standards. Local districts can cite a growing number of financial adequacy studies to support their case in the courts. Presently (National Governors' Association) the states face a total fiscal year 2003 deficit of $58 billion.

The withdrawal of states from the NCLB regulations and funding has been gaining wide support in the past few years. There are currently 47 out of 50 states that are rebelling against the NCLB mandates either by withdrawing (15 states) from the NCLB program or have enacted legislation to counter its mandates. (Washington Partners, 2005)

"In Utah, the Republican-majority House of Representatives voted to reject NCLB implementation "except where there is adequate federal funding." State officials are currently negotiating with the Department of Education to allow Utah to use an adjusted version of its own U-Pass accountability model for calculating NCLB. If an agreement is not worked out, the state legislature is likely to approve a proposal rejecting NCLB at an April 20 meeting. Republican legislators in both Minnesota and Arizona introduced "opt-out" legislation that essentially allows states to reject certain NCLB stipulations. This legislation has moved forward in Minnesota. At least 10 other state legislatures have passed resolutions highly critical of the law.

Connecticut officials have requested an exemption from annual testing of all students in grades 3 through 8, arguing that additional testing will not provide additional information about students' achievement and that the cost of administering these additional tests is $41 million above the $23 million Connecticut has received to do so. The Department of Education has rejected this request. According to the National Education Association, there are currently 18 states considering legislation on NCLB. Of the 18 states, New Mexico is the only state to have actually passed legislation; it urges Congress to ensure students are not left behind because of a lack of funding. Thirteen states have legislation being debated in committee; five states have passed legislation through one or more legislative bodies; and three states have defeated and/or withdrawn legislation that would have called for changes to NCLB.

Twenty-one states considered bills critical of the No Child Left Behind (NCLB) Act.

Fifteen states, Arizona, Colorado, Connecticut, Georgia, Hawaii, Illinois, Louisiana, Maine, Minnesota, Nevada, New Mexico, North Dakota, Texas, Vermont and Wyoming, considered legislation to opt out of NCLB.

Four states, Maine, New Hampshire, Vermont and Wisconsin, considered legislation that would prohibit the use of state resources on NCLB implementation.

Seven states, Colorado, Connecticut, Hawaii, Maine, New Mexico, Utah and Virginia, passed resolutions critical of NCLB through both chambers of their legislature.

At the state level, Utah and Colorado have led the way in opting out of NCLB. Utah has passed a law that gives state education law priority over NCLB, despite the threatened loss of more than $76 million in federal funding. The law has received unprecedented popular support in the state Colorado passed a law that permits local school districts to opt out of NCLB without facing state penalities. In other states, the legislative proposals range from assessing the state and local costs of NCLB implementation (Nevada), to directing education officials to seek waivers of particular requirements (Virgina), to directing the Attorney General to file suit if NCLB is underfunded (Maine), to opting out of NCLB (Nevada)." (NCLB Left Behind, 2005)

The conflict is on two levels; 1) money - the states can't afford to spend the type of money that they some authors think is required to accomplish the goal and 2) feasibility of the goal - the states know they cannot accomplish the goal no matter how much money is spent, given the lack of improvements to date noted in this book by assessment agencies.

The Regulations and Consequences

Although the press releases regarding NCLB focus on reading, the regulations really focus on two areas (reading/language arts and math). The NCLB program compels schools that are not maintaining adequate yearly progress (AYP) to provide part of their federal funding to outside providers (Supplemental Providers) who will provide tutoring or other services to raise the child's achievement levels. Of particular interest to note in the regulations are the long-term consequences. If a school fails to meet AYP four years in a row, the consequences are quite severe in that the district must implement certain corrective actions to improve the school, such as replacing certain staff or fully implementing a new curriculum. At the fifth year of failing, the school district must initiate plans for restructuring the school. This may include reopening the school as a charter school, replacing all or most of the school staff or turning over school operations either to the state or to a private company with a demonstrated record of effectiveness. As the act was signed into law in 2002, the year 2007 becomes the fifth year for many of these schools. George Bush will be out of office in Jan., 2009, leaving considerable time for the NCLB regulations to have a strong effect on the under performing schools.

Controversies regarding NCLB

In Massachusetts

The Boston Globe ran a story (11/20/2005) on the results of the

Massachusetts's efforts in the No Child Left Behind program. The story focused on whether all the money flowing into the program really has had any effect and quoted the executive director of a national education organization as declaring it "a national scandal". All involved in the program acknowledged that no one really knows how the children were doing on the states relevant exam. The report also indicated that U.S. Sen. Edward Kennedy, a supporter of the No Child Left Behind Act, said he has heard so many complaints about the quality of tutoring nationwide that he has asked the Government Accountability Office to review the performance of tutoring providers.

On the Web

A critical analysis of NCLB on the Education News web page (Solomon, 2004) reported:

"In a misguided attempt to strengthen public education, the No Child Left Behind legislation will actually damage our schools.

Under NCLB, all children are required to reach academic proficiency, or acceptable academic levels established by each state. While states have defined minimum acceptable standards for regular students, they never envisioned that disabled children would also be able to attain those levels. But the NCLB law makes no exceptions---disabled children, which now make up 10-15% of all school kids, must pass the same tests as regular students.

The impact of this requirement will result in states needing to lower standards for all children because states are not allowed to have a different standard for disabled youngsters. Yet those lower standards will still be too high for most disabled kids. So the unintended consequence of a mistaken attempt to "raise the bar" will actually result of a lowering of that same minimum level of accomplishment for most students while being still too high for the learning disabled. Finally, under NCLB, if children attend a failing school, they are eligible to transfer to another school with transportation provided, if space is available. The implication of this is astounding. The best schools in any town are generally those in the highest priced neighborhoods. Why? Because the most educated people, on average, have the best jobs and the most money. They buy in upscale neighborhoods. Their children are "learning ready" when they start school. Those neighborhoods have the best schools because they have the best students.

"Failing" schools will generally be those with the poorest and minority students and those are the kids that will be bused to the best schools. Does this sound familiar? It should because it is deja vu. The same busing plan destroyed our inner cities in the 60's and 70's because poor children were bused to more affluent neighborhoods where those homeowners fled to the suburbs. This provision of NCLB will result in busing all over again. But the untold "gotcha" is that when there is not enough room in other public schools to accommodate all students who want to transfer, the next version of NCLB will mandate vouchers to private schools. That seems to be the real, underlying rationale for NCLB in the first place."

Support for this statement resides with the NCLB regulations themselves that state that after 5 years of failure to maintain AYP "the school district must initiate plans for restructuring the school. This may include reopening the school as a charter school, replacing all or most of the school staff or turning over school operations either to the state or to a private company with a demonstrated record of effectiveness."

The Baltimore Sun (March 29, 2006) ran an article reporting that 11 of the Baltimore schools will be taken over by the state due to their continued low performance. This is the first state takeover of school systems under the NCLB act. More may follow.

The problem with this solution is that the charter schools are no better at solving brain functioning problems then the regular school system as they employ essentially the same intervention methods. They also will fail. **And then what?**

The 2003 report of Charter School progress (Nelson et al, 2004) indicated that the there was a 5% to 9% greater percentage of students who were below basic levels in the Charter schools than in the public schools (4th and 8th grade levels in reading and math). Table 4 presents the results of this research study. This table makes it clear that the Charter school approach is not the answer for the same reason the public school approach is not the answer: the interventions are not obtaining the results we need. There are approximately 3,000 Charter schools in the US (2003-2004) with about 700,000 students (GAO, 2005a).

Table 4 - Charter vs Public School NCLB Comparison - Nelson et al. 2004

	Below Basic	At or Above Basic	At or Above Proficient	At Advanced
Grade 4 Math				
Charter	33%	67%	25%	2%
Public	24%	76%	32%	4%
Grade 4 Reading				
Charter	45%	55%	25%	5%
Public	38%	62%	30%	7%
Grade 8 Math				
Charter	42%	58%	24%	8%
Public	33%	67%	27%	5%
Grade 8 Reading				
Charter	33%	67%	29%	4%
Public	28%	72%	30%	3%

In the Newspapers

Part of the preceding prediction as already become true, as evidenced by a report in the New York Times Education section on November 26, 2005, which reads as follows:

"After Tennessee tested its eighth-grade students in math this year, state officials at a jubilant news conference called the results a "cause for celebration." Eighty-seven percent of students performed at or above the proficiency level. But when the federal government made public the findings of its own tests last month, the results were startlingly different: only 21% of Tennessee's eighth graders were considered proficient in math. …. In Mississippi, 89% of fourth graders performed at or above proficiency on state reading tests, while only 18% of fourth graders demonstrated proficiency on the federal test. Oklahoma, North Carolina, Alabama, Georgia, Alaska, Texas and more than a dozen other states all showed students doing far better on their own reading and math tests than on the federal one…. the report by Standard & Poor's, which has a division that analyzes educational data, also noted some states' tests are just easier."

Other legal attempts to circumvent the problem have been attempted. A federal judge in Michigan dismissed an attempt by the National Education Association, the nation's largest teachers' union, to sabotage the No Child Left Behind education act. The ruling validates Congress's right to require the states to administer tests and improve students' performance in exchange for federal education aid. Unfortunately, it will not put an end to the ongoing campaign to undermine the law, which seeks to hold teachers and administrators more closely accountable for how their schools perform. (A Victory for Education, New York Times, November 29, 2005)

The next playout in the drama is the effort by the teacher's union to stop the voucher program and thus the Charter School system.

The Wall Street Journal (Sunday, January 29, 2006) reported on the teachers' union's efforts. "Teachers unions keep telling us they care deeply, profoundly, about poor children. But what they do, as opposed to what they say, is behave like the Borg, those destructive aliens in the "Star Trek" TV series who keep coming and coming until everyone is 'assimilated'."

We saw it in Florida this month when the state supreme court struck down a six-year-old voucher program after a union-led lawsuit. And now we're witnessing it in Milwaukee, where the nation's largest school choice program is under assault because Wisconsin Governor Jim Doyle refuses to lift the cap on the number of students who can participate.

Milwaukee's Parental Choice Program, enacted with bipartisan support in 1990, provides private school vouchers to students from families at or below 175% of the poverty line. Its constitutionality has been supported by rulings from both the Wisconsin and U.S. Supreme Courts.

Yet Mr. Doyle, a union-financed Democrat, has vetoed three attempts to loosen the state law that limits enrollment in the program to 15% of Milwaukee's public school enrollment. This cap, put in place in 1995 as part of a compromise with anti-choice lawmakers backed by the unions, wasn't an issue when only a handful of schools were participating. But the program has grown steadily to include 127 schools and more than 14,000 students today. Wisconsin officials expect the voucher program to exceed the 15% threshold next year, which means Mr. Doyle's schoolhouse-door act is about to have real consequences. "Had the cap been in effect this year," says Susan Mitchell of School Choice Wisconsin, "as many as 4,000 students already in the program would have lost seats. No new students could come in, and there would be dozens of schools that have been built because of school choice in Milwaukee that would close. They're in poor neighborhoods and would never have enough support from tuition-paying parents or donors to keep going."

There's no question the program has been a boon to the city's underprivileged. A 2004 study of high school graduation rates by Jay Greene of the Manhattan Institute found that students using vouchers to attend Milwaukee's private schools had a graduation rate of 64%, versus 36% for their public school counterparts. Harvard's Caroline Hoxby has shown that Milwaukee public schools have raised their standards in the wake of voucher competition....

The unions scored a separate "victory" in Florida three weeks ago when the state supreme court there struck down the Opportunity Scholarship Program. Passed in 1999, the program currently enrolls 700 children from chronically failing state schools, letting them transfer to another public school or use state money to attend a private school. Barring some legislative damage control, the 5-2 ruling means these kids face the horrible prospect of returning to the state's education hellholes next year.

The decision is a textbook case of results-oriented jurisprudence. The majority claimed the program violates a provision of Florida's constitution that requires the state to provide for "a uniform, efficient, safe, secure, and high quality system of free public schools." Because "private schools that are not 'uniform' when compared with each other or the public system" could receive state funds under the program, the majority deemed it unconstitutional. This is beyond a legal stretch." Not only have courts in such states as Wisconsin and Ohio rejected similar bogus "uniformity" challenges to school voucher programs, but so have other Florida courts. The logic of the ruling could also apply to charter schools, which are public schools that are able to live by non-uniform rules. That's the entire point of school choice--to break out of the stifling monopoly that traps so many poor children in "uniformly" awful schools.

What the Milwaukee and Florida examples show is that unions and their allies are unwilling to let even successful voucher experiments continue to exist. If they lose one court case, they will sue again--and then again, as long as it takes. And they'll shop their campaign cash around for years until they find a politician like Jim Doyle willing to sell out Wisconsin's poorest kids in return for their endorsement. Is there a more destructive force in American public life?"

Problems of measuring achievement levels

There are other problems in interpreting improvements, even if they are obtained. About 70% of the year-to-year change in test scores for grade levels or schools is simply random variation. (Kane and Staiger, 2002) Differences in the student body from one year to the next, combined with the statistical error in the tests themselves, make it impossible to know whether the tests are measuring real gains (or losses) or whether the changes are merely random noise.

Similarly in Massachusetts, those schools that received a medallion for large gains in one year saw those gains disappear the following year. (Haney, 2002) In Florida, the same pattern emerged, with 69% of the schools that posted gains in the first cycle of testing falling back in the next cycle. (Figlio, 2002) In Maine, J. Lee found the same phenomenon and noted that the random fluctuation, not surprisingly, increased as the size of the school decreased. (Lee, 2002) More problematic, however, is that the increase in test scores was not accompanied by increases in an underlying goal of NCLB...increased high school completion or college attendance. (Carnoy et al., 2001)

There have been many estimates regarding the number of schools across the U.S. that will probably turn out to be failing under NCLB. The Center for Assessment says 75%, North Carolina estimates 60%, Vermont calculated 80% over three years, and Louisiana reports 85% -- even though two-thirds of their schools show improved scores. (Fletcher, 2003)

In conclusion, NCLB appears to be suffering from unrealistic expectations, fluctuating and self-serving standards, inadequate funding, massive statewide resistance, and minimal effect sizes, which are all reflective of the virtual impossibility of achieving the stated goal. Although the goal is to improve our students' skills, the failure of the program resides more in our current intervention models than in the politics and funding. Current intervention methods are inadequate to the task and expensive to implement, as this review will indicate. Until there is a basic change in these approaches, neither the federal plan nor any state plan will have a real chance of achieving any significant results on a cost and intervention effective basis. The assumption behind both federal and state plans is that if we spend enough money and time the problem will be fixed, despite 80 years of research to the contrary.

Apparently President Bush's scientific and educational consultants did not provide him this perspective on the problem, or he ignored it.

Why any NCLB program is doomed to failure.

The federal government mandates cannot create an effective intervention, only scientific research can. If the states realized that they might be able to accomplish the goal at a fraction of what they are presently spending on interventions, their attitudes would probably be less confrontative and legal.

Schools face legal & financial pressures from parents wanting results

As if federal pressure to produce results wasn't enough, the parents of the disabled child are putting increasing legal and financial pressures on the schools to produce results. If the child isn't improving the parents put their child in expensive alternative schools and force the school to pay for it. An article in the San Francisco Reporter highlighted these problems (Feb. 19, 2006) when it stated "Expensive legal judgments and confidential settlements add hundreds of millions of dollars to already soaring special education costs across California, while taxpayers are kept in the dark about how the money is spent.

Meanwhile, California school districts shift more than a billion dollars a year out of their regular school budgets to pay for it all. "This is not sustainable," said Paul Goldfinger, a California school finance expert. 'Special education is a growing portion of budgets in many districts, squeezing out services for other pupils.'... Last year, 3,763 children with disabilities were the subject of formal complaints over educational services, triple what it was a decade ago. Parents open the vast majority of cases, and districts have a built-in financial incentive to settle them because it can cost up to $40,000 to go to a hearing. And then there's the possibility of an expensive judgment against the district. So districts try not to let a case go that far. Last year, districts participated in 386 full hearings -- just 10% of cases opened. The rest -- 90% -- were resolved through secret settlements.... Since 1993, the number of students in public special education programs rose 27%, to 681,969 from 539,073. But special education students placed in private schools at public expense rose nearly five times faster -- 128 %, to 15,926 from 6,994."

Sometimes these disagreements can become very expensive to the school system. In the Manhattan Beach Unified School District and the California Department of Education decision (Aug. 18, 2005, Porter v. Board of Trustees of Manhattan Beach Unified School District et al.) the schools were ordered to pay more than **$6.7 million** to a child with a disability and his parents for their failure to appropriately educate the child for more than five years.

A Supreme Court Decision (Nov. 14, 2005, Schaffer vs. Weast) may change the legal quagmire that the schools have been in. The decision stated that people who demand changes to their children's special-education programs have the burden of proving those programs inadequate.

The Neurocognitive Program's Results

The Neurcognitive program has been able to achieve what is sought in the NCLB mandate. One of the students engaged in our Neurocognitive program increased their percentile ranking on the reading scale of the Terra Nova some 48 points (from the 27th to the 75th percentile level) and maintained the gains on the Terra Nova for the following 3 years. The student's vocabulary score increased from the 21st percentile to the 72nd percentile (51 percentile points) and their reading composite score increased from the 22nd percentile to the 75th percentile (53 percentile points). His overall percentile increase was 33 percentile points across the 11 subtests.

Another student, who had been classified as having reading problems, increased their percentile rank on the school administered California Achievement battery as follows, after 20 hours of intervention: Vocabulary (57 points increase), Comprehension (32 points), Total Reading (40 points), Language Expression (49 points), Total Language (17 points) for an overall average of 39 percentile point increase. On the math sections, she increased 6.5 grade levels on the school administered California Achievement battery Total Mathematics score. The nationally administered test was administered some 9 months after the treatment ended. A third student doubled their score on a nationally administered reading test (from 350 to 720) after about 30 intervention hours. The special education teacher dismissed the gains. The response of "too good to be true" is fairly typical when individuals examine these types of results. What has been occurring, over and over again, is that the results are dismissed based upon the "too good to be true" concept and the system returns to its noneffective interventions because the personnel are more comfortable with their "tried and true" approach.

These types of results have been supplied to every state special education department, many special education schools, etc. The list is provided at the end of the book. There has been no attempt on the part of the school systems to implement this type of program. Only Minnesota has reportedly come close by providing some $450 million dollars to implement a rudimentary program in reportedly about 50-60 of its New Visions schools. The results were in line with other research at the time, which was reporting a +.50 SD improvement on attention and related measures (Joyce, 1997), similar to standard psychoeducational results and not reflective of the potential of the technology. Efforts made by the author to improve the Minnesota intervention approach and results were rebuffed.

Why aren't these results accepted?

One explanation for the lack of acceptance of the results comes from research in social psychology. There is a psychological phenomenon called the "halo" effect. When person A meets person B and forms an impression of B, that perception will be incredibly resistant to change. Let's suppose that person A thinks person B is a wonderful individual. When person B goes out and robs a bank and steals candy from children, person A does not change their opinion of B. Person A explains "away" the inconsistent behavior by saying to themselves that person B must have had a good reason or was being forced to do it. The explanation for the behavior is made consistent with the perception, rather than the perception changing to be consistent with the behavior. The opposite of this phenomenon can be called the "devil" effect. Person B is perceived as a horrible person but gives lots of money to some charity. Person A now has to explain the inconsistent behavior. Rather than change their judgment of person B, person A says "there is something in it for him...he's after something else..he's not really a good person."

This is similar to the special education teacher who couldn't accept the results of the student who doubled their score on a school administered reading test. The results were probably dismissed as "not possible....students can't change that much...something must be wrong with the test...it's a fluke." A more rationale response would have been "the neurocognitive treatment he is receiving is working."

The "devil" effect is going to be a major problem for the Neurocognitive treatment approach to overcome. Well meaning school officials and special education teachers will say "No, that's not possible... we know these children can't get that much better...look at all our results for the past 70 years...these results are wrong...there is something wrong with the data...the test was wrong...I don't believe it...redo the test....my mother always told me that if it looks too good to be true, then it probably isn't true." Educators are use to minimal results and have accepted these results as the only ones possible. A major mindset shift is required to accept this new possibility.

Unfortunately, the human mind does not change its cognitive set very easily. There is a concept in the field of Neuropsychology called perseveration. The concept refers to the tendency for the mind to apply a previously successful solution to an old problem to a new problem despite evidence that the previous approach doesn't work with the new problem. In our computer age, this type of behavior is evidenced when the computer operator keeps hitting the mouse button and the computer has locked up. Yet the operator keeps clicking on the mouse, waiting for the previous solution to work. Finally, the operator reboots the computer and the mouse works.

In the educational arena, we know that the current approaches don't work well but they do work better than the previous no intervention approach, so educators continue to hit the phonic mouse button or whatever intervention mouse button that they have been employing.

The Paradigm Shift

What the Neurocognitive approach represents in this area is the classic scientific paradigm shift. The paradigm shift refers to a basic conceptual change in how a phenomenon is approached or understood. For the past 80 years, the educational system has been operating under the concept that we can somehow verbally / non-verbally interact with a brain that isn't developing or functioning well and somehow make it a normal or better brain. Educational interventions have been pursuing the best way to talk to the brain for decades. Unfortunately, in the author's opinion, the psychoeducational approach hasn't worked very well. It has only been recently that some research studies have indicated that it might be possible to change the brain's physical response with such approaches. However, the results beg the question that if the goal is to document that the interventions work both on both the educational and physical level then wouldn't it also make sense to work the other side of the problem (e.g. seeing if the direct physical intervention on the brain's response pattern results in achievement gains and what is the difference in effect size). The tenet of this book is to demonstrate that the gains are significantly better if the approach is directly on the brain's physical response pattern. The data provided support this assertion. The approach is called a paradigm shift, as it represents a basic change in approach. In this case it is the approach to the problem from the inside – the brain itself – not from the outside with verbal methods. The results obtained to date strongly argue for this paradigm shift; it works better and it works a lot faster. What right do we have, as professionals and as educators, to offer less than what we are capable of to these children?

CHAPTER 2 – What is the Scope of the Problem?
Reading/Learning Disabilities & Traumatic Brain injuries

An understanding of the scope of the problems in this population as well as the costs to society is an appropriate place to start this discussion. The population involved is quite large and very expensive to service and there is no evidence that a Darwinian spontaneous genetic advancement will solve the problem of brain functioning for us.

Prevalence and Costs

It is estimated that the prevalence rate for learning disabilities is 15% of the student population (Learning Disability Association of America). The Office of Special Education estimated that 6.5 million children required special education in 2002. Sixty-three percent of these children have specific learning disabilities or speech/language problems without a concomitant physical disability. (Office of Special Education)

The rate of growth has been accelerating and shows no sign of slowing down. Approximately 6.5 million children (ages 3 to 21) have been diagnosed with special needs. This is an increase of nearly 40% in 8 years, according to the U.S. Education Dept. "Learning disabled is our No. 1 area of growth, and it is inappropriately used as a catch-all diagnosis", says Troy Justesen, acting assistant secretary of Special Education & Rehabilitation Services for the Education Dept. "We are working very hard to place a stronger emphasis on early and better identification." (Business Week -October 19, 2005) Identification, however, is not rehabilitation.

There are several reasons for this growth rate. It has been attributed to improvements in medical technology, which have resulted in deinstitutionalization of children with serious difficulties, increased childhood poverty rates (Finn et al., 2001), the advent of high-stakes testing, and the financial incentives created by special education funding in the US (Greene, 2002). High-stakes testing refers to the use of a test to make a major educational decision about children, teachers, schools, or school districts.

The debatable causes of the rise in enrollment do not negate the enormous cost of interventions for this population. Special education for students with disabilities is the largest categorical program in public schools. (Packard Foundation, 1996).

Table 5 - Special Education Costs by State and Federal Government

FY	$ Per Pupil	Spec. Ed. #, in millions	IDEA Auth.in Millions	Actual IDEA Millions	IDEA Rec. Millions	%Paid by Feds	%Paid by States
1991	$5023	4,761	$9,566	$1,845			
1992	$5160	4,941	$10,198	$1,976			
1993	$5327	5,111	$10,890	$2,050		9%	91%
1994	$5529	5,309	$11,741	$2,150		8%	92%
1995	$5689	5,378	$12,238	$2,320		8%	92%
1996	$5923	5,573	$13,204	$2,320		7%	93%
1997	$6168	5,729	$14,135	$3,110		10%	90%
1998	$6407	5,903	$15,128	$3,800		10%	90%
1999	$6584	6,055	$15,946	$4,310		10%	90%
2000	$6821	6,118	$16,629	$4,989		13%	87%
2001	$7066	6,138	$17,348	$6,340		15%	85%
2002	$7320	6,153	$18,015	$7,529		17%	83%
2003	$7583	6,163	$18,693		$9,978	21%	79%
2004	$7856	6,171	$19,391		$12,428	26%	74%
2005	$8138	6,176	$20,104		$14,878	30%	70%
2006	$8431	6,174	$20,821		$17,328	33%	67%
2007	$8734	6,162	$21,527		$19,778	37%	64%
2008	$9048	6,143	$22,232		$19,778	40%	60%
2009	$9373	6,129	$22,978		$22,978	40%	60%
2010	$9710	6,124	$23,785		$23,785	40%	60%

Table 5 represents some estimates reported by the National Education Association (NEA) in 2002 (NEA Report, 2002) of the rising costs, population and breakdown of federal versus state funding for this population. The table indicates that the states funding requirement to the Individual Disability Education Act (IDEA) was 83% of the 2002 budget, while the federal government chipped in 17%.

The Washington Times (Nov., 20, 2004) reported that federal spending for the Individual Disability Education Act (IDEA) had increased from $2.1 billion in 1994 to $10.1 billion in 2004. A congressional bill calls for Congress to reach a 40% federal share for special education costs by 2011.

The federal share now (2004) stands at 18.6%. If $10 billion represents 18.6% of the total cost of special education, then the 2004 cost of special education was $54 BILLION DOLLARS. This is close to the $48.5 billion estimated by NEA.

Different reports on the costs of IDEA for the special education have been generated over the years. The federal government has spent between $460 and $500 billion on special education since 1975 (Wood, 1998). If the $460 billion is an accurate number and represents an estimated 10% of the total cost during this period (as Table 5 indicates is a estimate during this period), then the states were contributing the remaining 90% of the $460 billion dollars or $414 billion dollars during this period. No matter who is examining and reporting the numbers, the values are always quite large.

The question that remains is: What has been the result of this huge expenditure of money? The NAEP improvement from 215 in 1992 (standard deviation of 36) to 217 in 2005 (4th graders) (NAEP Historical Data) is not an impressive result. If the intervention programs aren't working very well then why are we spending these vast amounts of monies? Our modern technology can take us to Mars and breakdown the DNA code, but it has been unable to change the basic abilities of the human brain. There have been only minor improvements in the conceptualization of the treatment approaches to the problem in 80 years, with minimal (at best) improvements in results. Only in the past 25 years have we begun to understand the underlying brain development problems inherent in these conditions and have begun to develop a technology that can effectively address these problems.

Additional Costs – Prison Population

Beyond the immediate educational cost issue of these students reside the long-term societal effects, especially in our prison systems. Between 28% and 43% of inmates require special education in adult correctional facilities (vs. 5% in normal population) and 82% of prison inmates in the U.S. are school dropouts. New York City spends $55,300 a year for each incarcerated youth (Winter, 1997). We will delve into the prison population problem in a later chapter in the book (Chapter 19).

Traumatic Brain Injury
Incidence / Prevalence and Costs of TBI

Of the 1.5 million cases of TBI annually in the United States, 75% are classified as concussions or mild TBI (MTBI) and over 235,000 cases are hospitalized (Langlois et al., 2004).

One source (National Dissemination Center for Children with Disabilities, 2004) estimates that more than one million children experience

26

brain injuries each year.

It is estimated that 5.3 million people (2% of the population) live with disabilities caused by TBI. In addition to the 50,000 deaths from TBI, some 80,000 to 90,000 cases have lifelong disabling conditions (Thurman et al, 1999). The causes of TBI leading to emergency room visits are motor vehicle accidents (20%), falls (28%), assaults (11%), other (32%), and unknown (7%) (Langlois et al., 2004). The costs of managing TBI have risen from $48 billion in 1991 (hospitalization costs of $31.7 billion dollars and fatality costs of $16.6 billion dollars) to $62 billion by 2001 (Thompson et al, 2001).

Thus, the LD and TBI population constitues about 4% of the population and cost the US about $375 Billion dollars a year. In 2003, the US defense budget was $417 Billion dollars.

CHAPTER 3 - Efficacy Research on Educational Intervention Programs for the LD/ADHD and TBI Student

Despite the enormity of the social and educational problem, the interventions currently employed have largely been unsuccessful in obtaining significant and meaningful results. In 1988, Lyon & Moats concluded: "It is difficult, if not impossible, to find any evidence beyond testimonials and anecdotal reports that support the assumptions, treatment methods, and stated outcomes associated with medical and psycho educational models … [T]here is overwhelming empirical and clinical data indicating that medical and psycho educational models, as they are presently conceived and used, are inadequate for determining what and how to teach learning disabled students." (p.225) Oakland et al. (1998) reaffirmed this opinion when he stated that a review of the treatment literature on dyslexia "reveals a limited number of scientifically sound and clinically relevant reports of significant treatment effects." (p. 336) More recently, Birsh (1999) concluded, "despite the widespread inclusion of multisensory techniques in remedial programs for dyslexic students and a strong belief among practitioners using these techniques that they work, there was little empirical evidence to support the techniques' theoretical premises." (Pg 7).

Individual Intervention Approaches

Orton-Gillingham Method (+.34 standard deviations after 350 hours).

One of the more widely used programs is the Orton-Gillingham method, which was developed in the 1920s and assumes that dyslexia is caused by neurophysiological-based disabilities. In this technique, multisensory teaching technique provides linkages between the visual, auditory and kinesthetic senses and concentrates on the fusing of the smaller elements of letters, sounds and syllables into the complexity of words. Over the past 80 years additional elements have been added, such as phonics. Despite the popularity of the method, there have been only two research studies with adequate control groups, with a combined treated sample size of under 50 experimental subjects, that have examined the effects of the intervention.

The Orton-Gillingham program was reported (Oakland et al., 1998) to be superior to gains obtained with standard reading instruction provided by teachers in a classroom setting on reading comprehension, word recognition, and polysyllabic phonological decoding. There were no significant differences on spelling measures and monosyllabic phonological decoding. The average improvement was +.34 Standard Deviations (SD) on standardized testing after 350 intervention hours (N=48, control group). However, the Orton-Gillingham videotape obtained the same results as individual tutoring with this method. Guyer & Sabatino (1989) reported positive results for the treated group (size of 10) (in comparison to a control group) of a summer program with the Orton-Gillingham method. The study did not provide the data necessary to calculate a standard deviation effect.

Wilson Reading Program (SD effect not available)

The Wilson reading program is a derivative of the Orton-Gillingham method. The Wilson website describes its program as "teachers incorporate a 30-minute daily foundations lesson into their language arts classroom instruction. Foundations lessons focus on carefully sequenced skills that include print knowledge, alphabet awareness, phonological awareness, phonemic awareness, decoding, vocabulary, fluency, and spelling. Critical thinking, speaking and listening skills are practiced during Storytime activities" (Wilson reading website) The website also indicates "The Wilson Reading System (WRS) is a research-based reading and writing program. It is a complete curriculum for teaching decoding and encoding (spelling) beginning with phoneme segmentation. WRS directly teaches the structure of words in the English language so that students master the coding system for reading and spelling. Unlike other programs that overwhelm the student with rules, the language system of English is presented in a systematic and cumulative manner so that it is manageable. It provides an organized, sequential system with extensive controlled text to help teachers implement a multisensory structured language program."

Only two research report were available on the Wilson website. (Wilson Research) The original study (McIntyre, C. and Pickering, J. (eds.) 1995) reported that some 220 students in grades 3-12 had an average growth of 4.6 grade levels in Word Attack (from a pretest average score of 2.85 to a post-test score of 7.44) and an increase of 1.9 grade levels in Total Reading (pretest average score of 3.38 to a post-test average of 5.24) on Woodcock Reading Mastery Test after 62 lessons. In the area of passage comprehension, the average gain was 1.6 grade levels (from a pretest average score of 3.46 to a post-test average of 5.05). (Woodcock Reading Mastery Test-Revised (Forms G and H) or the Woodcock Reading Master Test (WRMT, Forms A and B). An additional report (unpublished) indicated that 168 students selected were in grades 2-5. These students made an average grade-level gain of 3.8 in the word-attack subtest and 1.6 in total reading on the WRMT after an average of 64 sessions.

Summarizing across both studies, the website indicated that "a total number of 419 students with significant reading deficits spanning grades

3-12 were evaluated following 60 sessions of instruction. The Woodcock Reading Mastery Test-Revised yielded an average gain of 3.5 grade levels in Word Attack and 2.0 grade levels in Comprehension." The lack of means and standard deviations provided render the results not amenable to effect size analysis. Potential maturation and practice effects were not discussed or appeared to be controlled for. A request was mae to the Wilson website to obtain the information necessary to calculate the effect size. No response was ever received.

Lindamood-Bell Program (+.95 SD after 89 hours)

The Lindamood-Bell intervention model follows the five components of reading – phonemic awareness, phonics, fluency, vocabulary and comprehension as specified in the No Child Left Behind Act (Lindamood-Bell website). The program is conceptualized as a sensory-cognitive approach, which involves imagery as well as other exercises in the interventions. Results of the Lindamood-Bell treatment approach have been published on their website. A recently web published report (Burke et al., 2005) reported the following standard deviation changes (Table 6) for a sample size of 180 students who underwent an average of 89 treatment hours. The overall average SD improvement was +.95 SD (employing the SD of the students who withdrew and those that did not withdraw in the calculation of change).

Table 6 - Lindamood-Bell Results - Burke et al, 2005

	Pre Mean	SD	Post Mean	SD Change
Peabody Picture Vocabulary	78.8	8.85	86.6	.88
Oral Directions	4.8	2.4	6.9	.88
Woodcock Word Attack	85	9.39	99.2	1.51
Wide Range Reading	79.6	8.45	88.5	1.05
Wide Range Spelling	77.1	7.25	81.6	.62
Gort Rate	5.3	1	6.0	.70
Gort Accuracy	5.4	1.7	7.4	1.18
Gort Fluency	3.6	1.55	5.1	.97
Gort Comprehension	5.2	2.15	6.8	.74
			Average SD	.95

Tutoring

Sylvan Learning Centers (+.50 SD after 1 year program)

Sylvan learning centers employ a tutoring approach (Hattie, 1992) and reported a +.50 SD improvement on achievement score measures. Cohen et al. (1982) reported that volunteer tutoring obtains a .40 SD improvement on the measures employed. One well designed study of tutoring intervention documents improvements in reading to appropriate grade level as a result of 75 hours of intervention with children in the middle to upper middle class school districts in Albany, New York (approximate ages 9-14) (N=1407) (Vellutino et al., 1996). The tutoring was tailored to the individual's needs and typically included 15 minutes (of each session) devoted to reading connected text. The interventions were directed towards fostering deliberate use of a variety of strategies for word identification, sentence or thematic contexts for prediction and monitoring, external aids, phonetic decoding, as well as a variety of other commonly used techniques (develop a sight vocabulary, etc.).

The authors demonstrated that impaired readers could be brought up to grade level following the interventions (70% were reading within or above the average range) while 3% of the subjects remained moderately to severely impaired. The results were presented in terms of improvement slopes. It was not possible to calculate the standard deviation changes, as the necessary information was not provided in the article. As the approach was an individual tutoring method, it would be reasonable to assume that the SD effect was similar to other tutoring methods, a +.50 SD effect.

Phonics (+1.02 SD after 1 year program – confounding effects limit conclusion – limited to no effect on reading comprehension)

Phonologic and Orthographic Processing

Research has shown that phonological processing is strongly correlated with reading (Wagner & Torgesen, 1987) and spelling development (Schulte-Körne, 2001). The ability to identify and manipulate phoneme-sized elements of spoken language is a significant predictor in pre-school years of later success in reading and spelling development (Bradley & Bryant, 1978; Cossu et al., 1988; Lundberg et al., 1980; Näslund & Schneider, 1996). Orthographic processing (the knowledge of the specific word structure) (Hultquist, 1997) is the second component of spelling ability. Orthographic knowledge refers to the awareness of the probability of a particular letter following a given letter in any syllable. Some letter combinations (e.g., th) occur with great frequency (Hultquist, 1997). There has been very limited research done on the role of orthographic knowledge on reading and spelling disability. These two components are statistically related in children (Juel et al., 1986) and adults (Stanovich & West, 1989), but make independent contributions to performance on word reading tasks (Barker et al., 1992).

Results from longitudinal studies suggest that the early precursors of reading and spelling disorder are present even at 3 or 4 years of age. Speech perception (McBride-Chang, 1996) and phonological awareness in the pre-school years (Näslund & Schneider, 1996) are significant predictors of reading and spelling. (Stevenson et al. 1987)

Since the research had indicated these relationships between phonics and reading ability, it became a logical inference that if we could improve phonics ability, reading improvement would follow. Thus, popular phonic intervention programs were developed. Debates regarding effectiveness of different types of phonic interventions ensued. One such debate addressed the differences between analytic phonics and synthetic phonics.

Analytic phonics:

This approach suggests that by using onset and rime - paying attention to the beginning and ending of words, and by working at word level - relating whole to part - children can successfully learn to read.

Synthetic Phonics:

This is an approach in which children decode the word 'cat' by building it up from its separate letter sounds. They are taught to identify letters in the initial, middle, and final position in words and to sound and blend words.

Sight words: This approach focuses on the words that occur frequently in text. Having a bank of sight words releases a reader's attention needed for comprehension and for figuring out more difficult and less frequent words. Words that should be recognized "on sight" are those that are most useful whether they are regular (those that can be sounded out) or irregular (those that do not follow word analysis rules). Sight words are memorized as whole words even if they can be sounded out. Dolch Basic Word list is comprised of 220 words that are high frequency words that the child learns.

Foorman et al. (1997, 1998) studied children at risk for reading failure (eligible for Title 1) and had the children engage in phonological approaches for a full school year, resulting in improvements in phonological analysis skills. The authors examined the different phonic approaches.

The authors concluded "the results did not support the hypothesized superiority of analytic phonics. ...when SES, ethnicity, gender and VIQ

32

were added to the models, the only treatment effect that remained significant was the superiority of synthetic phonics compared to sight word in phonological processing. (pg. 272)…this facilitation does not appear to transfer to gains in word reading." They also noted that "differences in outcome between treatment groups were evidenced, but these cannot unambiguously be attributed to the treatment themselves." (Pg. 272) Table 7 presents the SD effects of the different approaches.

Table 7

	Phonological Analysis	Orthographic	Word Reading	Avg.
Synthetic Phonics	.62	1.11	1.42	1.05
Analytic Phonics	.75	.74	1.2	.9
Sight Word	.65	1.02	1.64	1.10
Average	.67	.96	1.42	1.02

The authors concluded **that improvement in curricula, teacher training, and an explicit focus on reading instruction were not sufficient to result in major gains over 1 year in a traditional public-school service delivery format." (Pg 274) "Hence, successful interventions with the type of child with reading disabilities served in public schools will require major changes in public policy and intervention approaches."** (pg. 274) This statement was made some 7 years ago and nothing has changed, as there have been no perceived options available. However, there have been options available.

This research result also suggested an interpretation problem with the results of all intervention programs that do not control for pre-intervention IQ, SES, ethnicity and gender. Almost all of the research reported does not control for these variables.

Let's use IQ as the example to understand why this is a significant problem. Suppose we're teaching piano to two groups. The first group has "natural musical ability" while the second group has none. The first group learns quickly and is proficient at the end of the training, while the second group is still struggling. Is it legitimate to claim that our music program is a success in teaching piano? If most of the success can be attributed to preexisting levels, then the program cannot be promoted as an effective intervention program for all students, as the results are highly qualified to the higher ability students prior the intervention.

Some authors (Olson & Wise, 1992) have noted difficulties in maintenance of gains and problems of generalization to reading ability and other skills. Since the goal of the intervention was to teach reading and phonics is assumed to be a critical part of reading, why hasn't the improvement in reading been consistent? For an intervention program to claim to be successful at improving reading ability it must be able to demonstrate that it improves reading ability on a consistent basis and works with all levels of abilities in the students. Would we buy a car that only runs some of the time?

The problem resides in the fact that phonic ability is only one part of reading ability and therefore really can't be expected to uniformly and consistently increase broad reading abilities. The previously referred to orthographic analysis is part of the reading picture as well. These components of reading refer to the ability of the child to read the word accurately. However, that is only the first step in the reading task. What follows after pronouncing the word correctly is the issue of word meaning, understanding context, comprehension, etc.

The discrepancy between phonic ability and reading comprehension was highlighted in a recent article in Literacy Today.

"However, evidence from 'Probe' (1999), an in-depth reading comprehension assessment from New Zealand that we introduced in 2001, highlighted an extraordinary discrepancy between the children's ability to read and their overall comprehension. The evidence showed that many had very impressive decoding skills but alarmingly poor understanding of the text in comparison. Ongoing assessments throughout the school the following two summers revealed the same discrepancy between decoding and comprehension; although the children with good decoding skills were "reading for meaning and sense" (Clay, 1990), they seemed unable to gather information effectively and accurately with regard to comprehension - and in some cases seemed quite disengaged with the whole comprehension process."

FastForWord (+.60 SD after 100 sessions – 3 independent research results indicate no effect)

The Fast ForWord program is a recent computer based reading intervention consisting of seven adaptive exercises to improve auditory and language processing by using nonlinguistic and acoustically modified linguistic speed (rapid frequency transitions in speech are slowed and amplified). Typically the treatment involves 100 sessions occurring over a 4-6 week period.

The web site provides numerous results across a number of locations. There were 26 reports, which provided standard deviation statements, and all are reported in Table 8. A few of the reports examined and indicated stability of gains at the 6-12 month time period.

Table 8 - Fast ForWord

Report	Measure	SD Change
9(24), 1-6	Reading Fluency	.20
9(7), 1-10	Reading Subtest	.25
7(6), 1-4	Comprehension	.33
8(15), 1-5	Language Fundamentals	.33
9(18), 1-5	Oral Language	.33
9(17), 1-6	Reading Ability	.33
8(24), 1-4	Reading Achievement	.33
7(6), 1-4	Total Reading	.33
8(16), 1-8	Language	.50
8(18), 1-6	Language Skills	.50
9(1), 1-5	Phonological Awareness	.50
9(25), 1-5	Phonological Awareness	.50
8(30), 1-4	Phonological Awareness	.50
8(34), 1-4	Reading Comprehension	.50
9(8), 1-4	Reading Fluency	.50
9(16), 1-7	Reading Skills	.50
9(13), 1-4	Vocabulary Skills	.50
8(19), 1-4	Oral Language	.58
9(24), 1-6	Phonological Awareness	.58
9(13), 1-4	Comprehension	.66
7(2), 1-4	Listening Comprehension	.66
8(26), 1-6	Early Reading	.67
8(6), 1-4	Total Language	.67
8(35), 1-4	Language & Cognitive Skills	1.00
8(10), 1-4	Vocabulary Skills	1.35
8(20), 1-4	Total Language	2.50
	Average	.60

Many of the reports included control groups in their analysis with result generally indicating a 5-10 point advantage for the treatment group (based on test scores which had means of 50 or 100). The SD effects were generally not reported.

No significant effect in 3 independent studies of FastForWord

Three independent studies have recently been reported which have indicated that the FastForWord program does not improve reading ability. One study enrolled 512 (3rd through 6th grade) students reading substantially below grade level in 4 elementary schools in an economically disadvantaged, urban school district (Rouse & Krueger, 2004). Just under half of the students in the intervention group fully completed the program. The authors concluded there was no significant effect on students' reading achievement (assessed by standardized reading assessment and researcher-administered standardized tests.)

The second study, recruited 415 (141 2nd grade and 274 7th grade) students who were reading well below the national average in eight Baltimore schools (Borman & Benson, 2005). Students were randomly assigned within each school and grade into either a group that used Fast ForWord as an add-on to their regular reading instruction, or a control group that did not. The authors concluded that there were no significant effects on students' reading comprehension or language skills (standardized tests) after two months of intervention. They surmised that long-term effects are not likely possible in the absence of short-term effects.

The absence of long-term effect was confirmed in the Hook et al. (2001) study that found that their Fast ForWord group showed significant gains in phonemic awareness. However after 2 years, the children's spoken language and reading were no greater than the control group. In conclusion, the results of the FastForWord intervention are conflicting and don't appear to hold.

School Interventions

Resource Room (a negative -.28 SD effect on IQ and reading measures)

Resource room interventions have been historically employed by school systems to address learning problems. One study has addressed the issue of the comparative effectiveness of resource room interventions versus EEG biofeedback (Orlando & Rivera, 2003) and obtained improvements using EEG biofeedback across a variety of reading measures. The interventions were based upon the subject's deviation from an eyes-closed database. Wechsler Individual Achievement Reading Test basic reading measures increased +.41 SD, comprehension measures increased +.84 SD, composite reading increased +.47 SD with verbal IQ gains of +.67 SD and full scale IQ score gains of +.37 SD (WISCIII). The overall average SD gain was +.55 SD.

The resource room control scored significantly lower than the EEG treatment group in basic reading (-.48 SD), reading comprehension (-.22 SD), and reading composite (-.36 SD), and had significantly lower verbal IQ scores (-.12 SD) and full-scale IQ scores (-.20 SD). **Therefore resource room allocation lowers a child's abilities in reading and general intelligence.** The overall SD change was -.28 SD. The author noted that re-evaluation data often indicates that cognitive functioning of these children frequently decreases in the re-evaluation process, especially at the six-year follow up period from the initial evaluation. As resource room assignment is a major intervention tool of the school system, this result strongly challenges its use in a school setting.

Other intervention (SD effect not available)

Selected students (Torgesen et al., 2001) identified with learning disabilities in the public schools who had reading scores below the 6th percentile in word recognition were followed in the research study. The researchers provided the students with intense, research-based interventions (not described). Using a word reading benchmark, 30% of the sample did not read in the average range at the end of intervention.

Similarity between programs

The International Dyslexia Society (IDS) (the major organization for the Orton-Gillingham method) defines dyslexia as "a specific learning disability that is neurological in origin. It is characterized by difficulties with accurate and / or fluent word recognition and by poor spelling and decoding abilities. These difficulties typically result from a deficit in the phonological component of language that is often unexpected in relation to other cognitive abilities and the provision of effective classroom instruction. Secondary consequences may include problems in reading comprehension and reduced reading experience that can impede growth of vocabulary and background knowledge." (International Dyslexia Society website). It's intervention methods involve: Phonology and Phonological Awareness, Sound-Symbol Association, Syllable Instruction, Direct Instruction, Morphology, Syntax, and Semantics.

Wilson's reading program addresses phonemic segmentation, alphabetic principle – sound/symbol relationships, decoding, encoding (spelling), advanced word analysis, vocabulary development, sight word instruction, fluency, comprehension with visualization and metacognition. The Wilson Reading system uses a unique "sound tapping" system early in the program to help the student learn to differentiate the phonemes (speech sounds) in a word. This technique is used for both segmenting and blending sounds. Throughout the program, there is less emphasis on overwhelming students with the language of rules and more emphasis on the understanding and fluent application of the rules. Wilson includes extensive controlled text (wordlists, sentences and stories) for application practice of skills. Fluency and comprehension are emphasized from the beginning.

The Lindamood-Bell program focuses on phonemic awareness and phonics by addressing sound awareness; establishment of the rules for letter-sound organization; sensory stimulation; articulatory feedback; imagery strategies to visualize and manipulate letters and words. Additional interventions address fluency, vocabulary and comprehension.

Fast ForWord Language Basics software is a series of computer-delivered exercises for young children, four to six years old, that uses fun activities to develop the basic skills necessary for language and reading development. (FastForWord website)

Fast ForWord Language Basics "consists of three exercises that develop visual attention and auditory discrimination skills as well as sustained auditory attention. Through the use of their patented technology this program improves: Sound sequencing skills, Fine motor skills, Hand-eye coordination, Pattern recognition and Color/Shape identification."

Fast ForWord Language Basics software claims to: 1- Improve memory by having the student hold a pair of sounds or a sequence of sounds in working memory while comparing them and/or identifying their order. 2- Improve precise visual attention and sustained visual/auditory attention by developing their ability to focus attention, ignore distractions, and respond quickly when a stimulus changes. 3- Strengthen visual processing skills for matching shapes and sensory-motor integration for using the mouse to position shapes. 4 – develop sequencing skills through exercises that require identifying and reproducing the order of a two-sound sequence.

The game interactive software are advertised to focus on 1- Phonological awareness 2- Color, shape and size identification 3- Working memory 4 - Letter name and letter sound correspondence. (FastForWord website)

One tutoring method (Vellutino et al., 1996) employed strategies for word identification, sentence or thematic contexts for prediction and monitoring and external aids in their program.

Over the years controversies regarding different methods have reigned in the educational world, which are reflected in the overlaps and dissimilar elements of the programs currently being offered. However, they all seem to obtain about the same result in terms of effect sizes (+.30 to +1.00 SD) on whatever measure they are employing to assess progress.

Many of these programs have overlapping areas of focus. Almost all employ some variation of phonic interventions in a one-to-one situation and emphasis upon deciphering the structure of the English language in written form (reading) or spoken (speech). Measures employed are generally educational / achievement label type testing. None of the popular intervention methods focus on improving ability measures, such as memory, intelligence or problem solving. FastForWord's description of its focus on working memory, memory and attention is not matched by any Neuropsychological measure that assesses these constructs.

Figure 2 - SD effects of major intervention programs

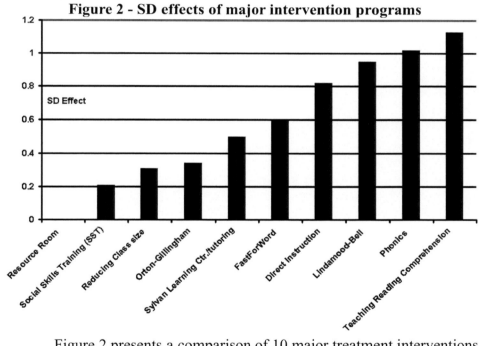

Figure 2 presents a comparison of 10 major treatment interventions reviewed (and others) to the qEEG approach. There are some necessary qualifications regarding this figure. The Wilson program did not report information, which could be translated to SD units. The results presented are on the generous side. For example, the FastForWord results employ only the results reported by in-house data while not incorporating the three studies which indicated no effect. The phonics report relies on the Foorman et al. studies (1997) and ignores the qualifications of the authors regarding the effect size and problems of preexisting IQ.

Figure 3 - Comparison across diverse set of treatment interventions - SD Effect

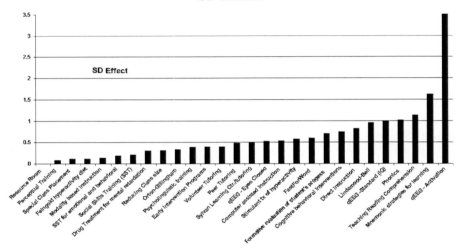

Despite the appearance of substantive effect of the mnemonic strategy approach, reliance on this type of intervention program is problematic because, generally, people do not continue to employ a strategy approach spontaneously. In addition, the results of this type of intervention program with the traumatic brain injured subject (Figure 4) has not shown these type of results. The same effect size wouldn't necessarily be expected in this impaired group.

Figure 3 incorporates some previous metaviews of this area (Forness et al, 1997; Lloyd et al., 1998) with the qEEG data. The reader is referred to these articles for a more in-depth discussion of these alternate intervention models and how these SD effects were calculated. The results of the qEEG and Neurocognitive approaches are also presented, but discussion regarding these approaches will occur in a later chapter. The figure demonstrates quite clearly the superior results that can be obtained with the Neurocognitive approach.

Broad Institutional Interventions
Chicago Annenberg project

The Chicago Annenberg project was a $49.2 million dollar project conducted during the late 1990's. It was part of a nationwide $500 million dollar campaign to improve results in the educational system. The interventions focused on many different areas of school organization and practice, including curriculum and instruction, student learning climate and social services, teacher and leadership development and the involvement of parents and the community in schools and student learning. The results of the research indicated that the schools directly involved in the project did not obtain significantly better results with the student's achievement levels than the regular Chicago Public School system. (Smylie & Wenzel, 2003)

Class Size

Stecher et al. (2003) found no strong association between achievement and exposure to class size reduction for the K-3rd grade groups studied, after controlling for pre-existing differences in the groups. California enacted SB 1777, providing a substantial incentive for school districts to reduce their class sizes from an average of roughly 30 students per class to 20 or fewer. With the signing of this bill, districts in 1996-97 were provided with nearly $1 billion in education funds to reduce class size in grades K-3. The funding then increased to roughly $1.5 billion in the second year (1997-98), and it has continued at this level in subsequent years. In addition to the state initiatives, the federal government invested more than $1 billion annually in the reduction of class size during the Clinton administration.

Stecher et al. (1999) and Stecher et al. (2000) found that students who were exposed to Class Size Reduction (CSR) in third grade performed better than those who were not. This was true in 1997-98, when both groups of third grade students had little or no prior exposure to CSR. It was true again in 1998-99, when both groups had one to two years of prior exposure. The differences in scores were equivalent to effect sizes

41

of about 0.04 to 0.1 standard deviation units. The question is, however, is whether a .04 to .10 SD improvement is worth 2.5 billion dollars a year.

School Size

Cotton, K., (1996) reviewed the effect of school size across a broad array of research reports and concluded:

1- About 50% of the studies showed no difference while the other 50% showed an advantage for the small school on achievement measures, with particularly stronger effects on the minority students and students of low socioeconomic status.

Other research reports have generally pointed to a negative relationship between size and academic achievement. All else held equal, small schools have evident advantages for achievement, at least among disadvantaged students (Friedkin & Necochea, 1988; Huang & Howley, 1993).

However, finding research data reflecting a standard deviation effect size proved elusive. One report from the Center for Collaborative Education (2001) showed that the Boston small pilot schools scored 2.3% above the Boston public schools in language arts on the Massachusetts Comprehensive Assessment System (MCAS), -.5% on the Math and -1.4% below on the science tests, as reported by Chicago Public School report on small schools.

2- The small school has significant reduction on a number of social behavior measures including: truancy, classroom disruption, vandalism, aggressive behavior, theft, substance abuse, and gang participation. The small school has also a number of positive effects on the students which included: increased extracurricular participation, positive attitudes and social behavior, higher attendance rates, lower dropout rate or higher graduation rate, much greater sense of belonging, personal and academic self-regard, and favorable interpersonal relations as well as higher entrance examination scores, higher acceptance rates, higher attendance, higher grade point average and greater parental involvement. The effects are strongest on the social behavior of ethnic minorities and low Socio-economic-status (SES) students.

Teacher Improvement

Education levels

Darling-Hammond's (2000) reviewed the research with respect to the educational level of the teacher. He reported that measures of teacher preparation and certification are by far the strongest correlates of student achievement in reading and mathematics, both before and after controlling for student poverty and language status. For example, the students of fully certified mathematics teachers experienced significantly larger gains in achievement than those taught by teachers not certified in mathematics.

When student characteristics are held constant, the relationship of teachers' qualifications to student achievement is even more pronounced. A study of high and low achieving schools with demographically similar student populations in New York City found that differences in teacher qualifications (educational degrees, certification status, and experience) accounted for approximately 90% of the total variation in average school-level student achievement in reading and mathematics at all grade levels tested (Armour-Thomas et al., 1989).

Professional Development

School districts and states often use in-service teacher training to improve student learning. Seventy-two percent of teachers nationally report having participated in training in their subject area and a comparable number in training on implementing new teaching methods. Despite widespread use, the intensity of the training is typically low. More than half of the teachers had eight hours or less of such training per year. When this intervention was studied the result was that moderate increases in teacher training had no statistically or academically significant effect on either reading or math achievement. The results did not vary across race, gender, socio-economic background, or student ability. (Jacob & Lefgren, 2002) Given these results and general tightness in school budgets, it is questionable whether this practice should continue.

Diagnosis

The educational and neuropsychological fields have been very thorough and clever, at times, in developing assessment tools which can delineate the student's educational or neuropsychological problems. The medical model implicit in this approach is that if we can correctly diagnose the problem we can apply the appropriate intervention technique. The assumption is that if we find deficit X we apply treatment X to address the problem. This was the assumption behind the Luria-Nebraska battery in Neuropsychological evaluations. However, the diagnostic sophistication is not matched by treatment sophistication, as most approaches employ the same intervention modality. The phonic intervention model is, at least, somewhat tied to the diagnostic assessment. For example, the diagnostic conclusion that a subject has a auditory memory or processing problem is not tied to any particular intervention model which has shown to be particularly effective with an auditory memory problem. The situation is very much different in the case of the qEEG technology. We can define what an auditory memory problem is and precisely define what the appropriate intervention is. And it works.

In the case of phonic pronunciation in children, the activation of the right temporal lobe is critical to successful pronunciation in terms of beta values (relative power beta2, peak frequency beta1, magnitude beta1 and beta2, peak amplitude beta2) as well as T5 (peak amplitude beta1 and beta2, magnitude beta1). (Thornton, unpublished) In adults, the successful pattern changes as the T3 left temporal (peak amplitude beta1 and beta2, magnitude beta1 and symmetry beta 1) and peak frequency beta1 at T5 and O1 become the critical components. (Thornton, unpublished) This type of developmental pattern (a move from the right to the left temporal areas), however, is not discernible with present methodologies.

Early Identification

The importance of early identification has been highlighted in recent research by Torgenson. Children who are poor readers at the end of first grade almost never acquire average-level reading skills by the end of elementary school (Francis et al.,1996; Juel, 1988; Shaywitz et al., 1999; Torgesen and Burgess, 1998).

Cavanaugh et al. (2004) reviewed the effect sizes of early intervention programs reported during the past 20 years in the scientific literature. Employing strict criteria they lowered the initial selection of 2,300 studies in 12 major journals to 27 studies for kindergarten reading interventions for children at risk for reading problems. Overall the effect sizes ranged between -.74 SD to +4.39 SD with the mean being +1.27 SD. The number of intervention hours ranged from 5 to 140 hours. However, there were many variations in approach, number of treatment sessions, personnel administering interventions, etc. Of special interest to note was the greater effectiveness (+.95 SD) of the interventions in the kindergarten group than the 1st graders (+.48 SD) or the second thru sixth graders (+.70 SD).

Espy et al. (2004) underscored this desirability of early identification and researched the early identification of the reading disabled child in the ERP (event related potential) response pattern. Event related potentials (ERP) refer to the initial electrophysiological response pattern of the brain to a stimulus. The N label refers to negative and the number label refers to the time element.

Molfese and Molfese have demonstrated, with a longitudinal sample of children, that newborn infants can discriminate phonological contrasts such as place of articulation (e.g., Molfese & Molfese, 1979b, 1985), evidenced by different ERP waveform characteristics reflected in both left hemisphere and bilateral hemisphere responses to specific consonant sounds. By the age of 2 months, infants discriminate between voicing contrasts (Molfese & Molfese, 1979a). There are continued age differences in these abilities that stabilize between age 3 and 4 years (Molfese & Molfese, 1988). Further, Molfese and Molfese (1985) found that certain components of the ERP collected within 2 days of birth to specific consonant sounds and their nonspeech analogues predicted language performance at age 3 years. Group differences (high versus low language scores) were reflected in a large initial negative peak, N1 (peak latency = 220 ms.). A second negative peak, N2 (peak latency = 630 ms.), also discriminated between these two groups of children although it accounted for less variance. These same ERP regions also discriminated between different Stanford Binet verbal scores at 5 years of age (Molfese & Molfese, 1997). Finally, differences in neonatal ERP waveforms were related to reading scores on the WRAT-R at age 8 years in normally developing children and children with reading disabilities (Molfese, 2000; Molfese, Molfese, & Modglin, 2001). The Nl peak latency at the right temporal recording site and Nl peak latency at the left frontal site for the speech syllable /gi/ were related to the WRAT-R reading subtest score. In hierarchical discriminant function models, newborn ERP components accounted for nearly 10% of the variance in WRAT-R Reading subtest scores at age 8 years, and successfully discriminated between poor and normal reading groups. The same right temporal Nl latency to /gi/ was previously identified at 5 years as predictive of the Stanford-Binet verbal scores at age 5 (Molfese & Molfese, 1997).

These results tie in very nicely with the involvement of the right temporal lobe in phonic pronunciation in children. Thornton (unpublished).

Cognitive Rehabilitation Intervention Models with the Traumatic Brain Injured (TBI) patient

Most of the research in the area of cognitive rehabilitation addresses the adult population. There are two intervention models which are currently employed…computers and strategy instruction. Computer interventions have focused on improving attentional abilities in a similar manner to a video game but can also be used to teach cognitive strategies in recalling information or problem solving. Cognitive strategy interventions teach the subject to a) organize the information to be recalled; b) visualize the information; c) engage in bizarre imagery; d) associate the information to relevant personal information (i.e. tying the information to one's birthdate, etc.). We will draw from this research to discern what treatments work in this area.

Figure 4 documents the relative standard deviation effectiveness of the currently available cognitive rehabilitation intervention approaches with the TBI patient. The interventions for the 15 TBI patients were directed towards auditory memory (paragraph recall). The values reflect the subject's scores on different paragraphs of information and thus cannot be considered learning one story very well due to repetition. When a normal (control) group is administered these types of stories, there is no overall gain in memory ability. We can't expect our memory system to work better just because we use it. This results rules out the possibility of a practice effect, i.e. practicing recalling information will get you better at recalling. There is also evidence in the research literature that practice does not improve memory abilities. Generalization effects were obtained on attention, problem solving and word list recall measures. These skills were not directly addressed in the treatment program. This figure reflects the greater relative effectiveness of the Neurocognitive approach compared to those presently being employed.

The conclusion from the preceding analysis is that for all these groups (LD, RD and TBI) the most effective overall intervention program is the Neurocognitive approach.

Figure 4 - Standard Deviation Effect Sizes of Different Cognitive Remediation Approaches to the TBI patient

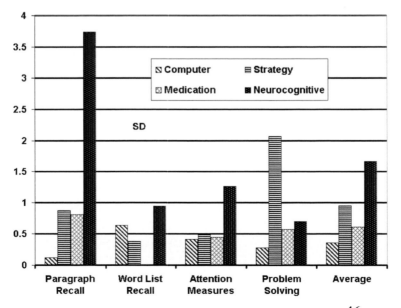

Chapter 4 – Causes of Non-Optimum Brain Functioning

It is the central tenet of this book that the problems of the special education student is one of the physical functioning of the brain. Educational interventions which are premised upon verbal interactive attempts will always be limited in their effectiveness. We are pouring billions of dollars into an educational strainer that holds very little in terms of results. Decades of scientific research support these statements.

We will be examining the functioning of the physical brain from the point of view of modern neuroscience imaging technologies. First, in order to understand how these conditions arise, it is important to relate some of the reasons for non-optimal brain functioning.

There are three major causal factors in the physical development of the brain such as a reading disability.

a) **Genetics** (Pennington, 1994, Hohnen and Stevenson, 1999)

Scientific advances in the past several decades have made the American public very aware of the role of genetics in our development. This discussion will not go into depth on these issues, but merely skirt over some of the overall findings that are relevant to understanding the broad picture.

As an example of genetic influences, twin studies have indicated that 50 to 60% of reading and spelling disorder variance could be explained by genetic factors. (Stevenson et al. 1987).

The genetic localization of reading disability has been linked to chromosome 1 (Rabin et al., 1993), chromosome 2 (Fagerheim et al., 1999), chromosome 6 (Smith et al., 1991) and chromosome 15 (Grigorenko et al., 1997).

For the ADHD condition, twin studies have indicated heritability correlational indices of approximately .75 for ADHD (Silberg et al. 1996; Levy et al., 1997; Willcut et al., 2000).

When a child has been diagnosed with ADHD in a family, over 30% of siblings will also have ADHD (Welner et al., 1977; Biederman et al., 1990; Biederman et al., 1992). When a parent has been diagnosed with ADHD there is over a 50% chance that there will be a child with the same diagnosis (Biederman et al., 1995)

b) **Non-genetic environmental factors which affect brain development.**

There are a host of environmental factors that contribute to the problem of brain development.

Pregnancy and Birth Complications: Research examples of some non-genetic factors affecting brain development would be pregnancy and birth complications, (Colletti, 1979), pre-term birth (Carmody et al., 2006), low birth rate (< or =2500 grams) or very low birth weight (<1500 grams) in males only (Johnson and Breslau, 2000), nutrition (Grantham-McGregor et al. 2000), pre- and perinatal factors such as hypoxia (lack of oxygen in tissues) or hypoxia–ischemia. Hypoxic–ischemic encephalopathy is caused by brain hypoxia (decrease of oxygen supply to the brain even though there is adequate blood flow) and ischemia (insufficient supply of blood to an organ) from systemic hypoxemia (insufficient oxygenation of the blood) and reduced cerebral blood flow (CBF). Between 20–50% of newborns born with this condition die within the newborn period, and up to 25% of the survivors will exhibit permanent neuropsychological handicaps, including mental retardation, cerebral palsy, epilepsy or learning disability. (Vannucci and Hagberg, 2004)

There are additional non-genetic risk factors which occur during pregnancy and include maternal smoking, pesticides, aspirin use during pregnancy, drug abuse, alcohol, coffee, fluoride, MSG & aspartame, anesthesia, cosmetic chemical exposure, mercury exposure, exposure to fragrances, artificial food additives, marijuana, exposure to ultrasound, damaged sperm and the heart arrhythmia drug "Amiodarone" (AMD), exposure to lead and hyperbilirubinemia (a medical condition where abnormally high concentrations of the bile pigment bilirubin are found in the bloodstream. This can result in jaundice. Hyperbilirubinemia sometimes occurs in premature babies. Thus there are many physical environmental influences that can affect brain development.

A recent issue of the Journal of Pediatric Psychology (2006, Vol. 31, #1) devoted an entire issue to the effects of Prenatal Substance Exposure: Impact on Children's Health, Development, School Performance, and Risk behavior. The issue reported negative effects on heart rate, head circumference, aggression, symptoms of oppositional defiant disorder, ADHD, IQ scores and mathematics scores.

Traumatic Brain Injury

As stated previously, about 1 million children experience a brain injury every year. How these brain injuries affect cognitive functioning will be addressed in a later chapter. Predominantly, the injury affects attention, memory and problem solving ability but can have a host of other emotional and cognitive problems depending upon the individual cases.

c) **Interactions between genetics and environmental factors.**

Caspi et al. (2002) examined how genetic factors contributed to why some maltreated children grow up to develop antisocial personality disorders, whereas other maltreated children do not. In this longitudinal investigation of males who were studied from birth to adulthood, it was discovered that "males with low monoamine oxidase (MAOA) activity who were maltreated in childhood had elevated antisocial scores, whereas males with high MAOA activity did not have the elevated scores even when they had experienced maltreatment. Overall, 85% of the males with both the low MAOA activity genotype and severe maltreatment became antisocial. Neither the low-activity gene alone nor the environmental maltreatment alone is enough to create antisocial behavior,"

Environmental effects resulting in diagnoses of Learning Disability or Reading Disability

Environmental reasons such as culture and poor educational background, which are not directly related to the physical development of the brain, can result in low-test scores and consequently be identified as a learning disability.

In addition, however, environmental issues can contribute to the physical functioning of the brain. Carmody et al. (2006) separated the effects of medical vs. environmental risk on the brain's physical response patterns (15-16 year olds) in a simple attentional task. Medical risk was determined by pre-term birth, while environmental risk was assessed with a combination of measures relating to parental education and occupation, family status, life stress, social support, minority status and the mother-child interaction. The locations (T3-P3-T5) we will be referring to are displayed in Figure 14. Further discussion of these locations will occur in a later chapter. Success at the task was related to activation of the temporal (T3) and left parietal locations (P3).

The combination of medical and environmental risk resulted in reduced activations in these areas, but in a differential manner. The higher the medical risk factors the lower the activation of the parietal (P3) areas while the higher the environmental risk factor the lower the activation of the temporal regions (T3 and T5). Medical risk did not relate to temporal activations nor did environmental risk relate to parietal activations, thus providing a clear separation of medical vs. environmental affects.

Intervention Categories

There are two broad categories of possible interventions.

1) Genetic

Genetic interventions bring a host of scientific and ethical issues, which will not be discussed in this book. Appropriate treatments for many of the additional causes of learning disability are self evident in the linked cause (not smoking or drinking during pregnancy, etc.).

2) Environmental

If the problem is strictly an environmental one (culture, poor educational background) the intervention choice is self evident – increased educational opportunity, unless there has been a physical effect on the brain's functioning. Some non-genetic causes are amenable to obvious interventions – e.g. poor nutrition.

a) Non-physical

However, once the brain has been affected by any one of these multiple genetic or non-genetic causes and the intervention is not self-evident, then there are only two possibilities. The first intervention model that has been pursued for the past 80 years has been a psychoeducational one, as exemplified by the Orton-Gillingham method, phonic interventions, tutoring, etc., which have yielded disappointing results from the author's point of view.

b) Physical

The second, and most appropriate intervention would be one that directly and effectively addresses the physical problems in brain development.....Neurocognitive interventions.

This book presents an approach that effectively addresses the physical problems underlying the cognitive and behavioral problems of the ADHD, traumatic brain injured, and the reading and learning disabled child and adult. The approach is called the Neurocognitive quantitative electro-encephalographic (qEEG) system approach. In terms of psychological conditioning paradigms, it is an operant conditioning of the cortical electrical patterns of the brain via the rewarding and/or inhibiting of spontaneous neuronal behavior.

The results obtained are dramatic improvements over previous approaches in terms of reading and auditory memory ability with generalization to diverse cognitive functions. Clinical cases and research results have been accumulating for the past 25 years on the effectiveness of a simple EEG biofeedback approach for a number of clinical conditions. The Neurocognitive approach is a more precise and broader intervention model than currently employed approaches in the field, as it employs a broader frequency range and interventions are based upon a cognitive activation evaluation procedure. This difference will be explained in Chapter 13.

CHAPTER 5 - Neuroscience of Reading/Learning Disability/ ADD / ADHD / TBI

This chapter will delve into some detail regarding our neuroscientific understanding of these problems. This chapter is a technical discussion that some readers may want to review at a later time. The main points of this chapter are:

1)   There have been significant advancements in our ability to visualize and observe the physical functioning of the brain.

2)   The conditions we are discussing have different and specific physical parameters which we have just begun to understand.

3)   EEG interventions can affect the physical functioning of the brain.

There has been numerous and important developments in medical neurodiagnostic techniques in the past several decades. Of particular importance to brain imaging studies has been the development of magnetic resonance imaging (MRI), functional magnetic resonance imaging (fMRI), positron emission tomography (PET), single positron emission tomography (SPECT), diffusion tensor imaging (DTI), magnetoencephalography (MEG) and the quantitative EEG (qEEG). These are technical medical tools that will require a short definition to understand their relevance to the LD, ADHD and TBI subjects. Each of these technologies allows us to look at the brain from different physical viewpoints. We can now examine the brain in its resting state and compare it to other brains as well as activate the brain with different cognitive tasks and examine the response pattern in terms of the locations that become active.

The MRI employs radio-frequency (RF) waves and intense magnetic fields to excite atoms in the object under evaluation (Figure 5). A powerful magnet generates a magnetic field roughly 10,000 times stronger than the natural background magnetism from the earth. A very small percentage of hydrogen atoms within a human body will align with this field. When focused radio wave pulses are broadcasted towards the aligned hydrogen atoms in tissues of interest, they will return a signal. The subtle differences in that signal from various body tissues enables the MRI to differentiate organs, and potentially contrast benign and malignant tissue. Patterns in this excitation are observed on a display. MRI can provide three-dimensional views of body organs, muscles, and joints without invasive surgery.

Figure 5 - See insert at end of book - page 311

The functional MRI (fMRI) relies on the paramagnetic (small and positive susceptibility to magnetic fields) properties of oxygenated and deoxygenated hemoglobin (hemoglobin is the red pigment in red blood cells that transports oxygen) to see images of changing blood flow in the brain associated with neural activity. This allows images to be generated that reflect which structures are activated (and when) during performance of different tasks.

Positron Emission Tomography (PET) measures emissions from radioactively labeled chemicals that have been injected into the bloodstream and uses the data to produce two or three-dimensional images of the distribution of the chemicals throughout the brain. The positron emitting radioisotopes used are produced by a cyclotron and chemicals are labeled with these radioactive atoms. The labeled compound, called a radiotracer, is injected into the bloodstream and eventually makes its way to the brain. Sensors in the PET scanner detect the radioactivity as the compound accumulates in different regions of the brain. A computer uses the data gathered by the sensors to create multicolored two or three-dimensional images that show where the compound acts in the brain. The greatest benefit of PET scanning is that different compounds can show blood flow, oxygen and glucose metabolism in the tissues of the working brain.

Single Positron Emission Tomography (SPECT) (Figure 6) is a technique similar to PET. But the radioactive substances used (Xenon-133, Technetium-99, Iodine-123) have longer decay times than those used in PET, and emit single instead of double gamma rays. SPECT can provide information about blood flow and the distribution of radioactive substances in the body. Its images have less sensitivity and are less detailed than PET images, but the SPECT technique is less expensive than PET.

Figure 6 - SPECT - See insert at end of book - page 311

The quantitative EEG (qEEG) (Figure 7) is a digitization of the standard analog EEG signal. Digitization is performed by sampling at discrete intervals. The digitization of the EEG signal, involves measuring a wave's amplitude many times per second and then storing that information to a hard disk for future analysis.

Figure 7 - qEEG - See insert at end of book - page 312

Magnetoencephalography (MEG) (Figure 8) is similar to EEG, but magnetic fields are measured instead of electrical fields. Once the magnetic field has been imaged, it can be overlaid onto the MRI image.

Figure 8 - MEG - See insert at end of book - page 312

Loreta imaging (Figure 9) combines the EEG with a source localization method that permits a truly 3-dimensional view of the brain's electrical activity. Source localization is a method to determine where is the origin of the electrical patterns.

Figure 9 - Loreta - See insert at end of book - page 313

Diffusion Tensor Imaging (DTI) (Figure 10) is a magnetic resonance imaging technique that provides directional information of water diffusion in the white matter of the brain. It is the only technique other than the qEEG that can directly measure activity in the long myelinated white matter that connects different regions of the brain.

Figure 10– DTI - See insert at end of book - page 314

Thus, with all these techniques, it is now possible to understand many aspects of what is the difference between the ADHD, LD, and TBI brains and a normal brain. To aid the reader in the understanding of this discussion, we will need to provide a very brief neuroanatomy lesson and some labeling conventions of the qEEG, as we will be discussing the qEEG in more depth in later chapters. Figure 11 is the view the human brain viewed from the left side.

Figure 11- human brain left side

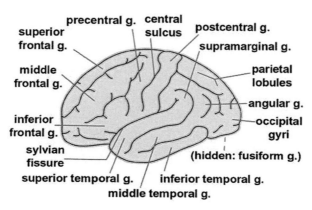

Figure 12 is a view of the brain looking down from above from the point of view of the qEEG. The nose is between the Fp1 and Fp2 locations. The left ear is next to the T3 location and the right ear is next to the T4 location.

Figure 12 – qEEG locations Standard 10-20 system and nomenclature for Locations

Left Side   **Nose**   **Right Side**

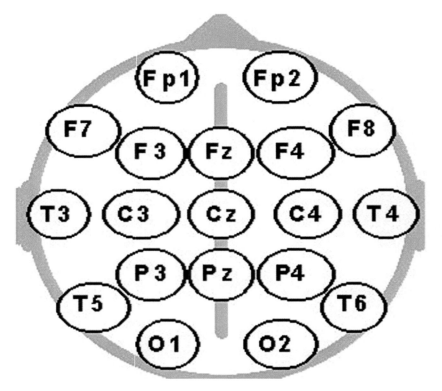

In the 10-20 system the first letter (e.g. F, C, T, P, O) is employed to indicate the location. The letter F refers to frontal, T refers to temporal, C to central, P to parietal and O to occipital. The odd numbers are used to indicate left hemisphere and even numbers to refer to the right hemisphere.

Physical Properties of the Human Brain – How our understanding has changed.

The human brain is the most complex organ on the planet. Its physical properties and how it has come into existence have fascinated scientists and humanity since man could think. It wasn't very long ago that what we knew about the human brain was defined by a "science" called phrenology.

The German scientist Franz Joseph Gall (1758-1828) proposed the initial ideas on phrenology. He thought that pickpockets possessed the desire to own things because of excessive development of an area on the side of the head. Johann Spurzheim (1776-1832) identified 35 different mental faculties, which could be identified by examination of the bumps on a person's skull. Spurzheim's goal was to reform education, religion, and penology in the US using principles of phrenology. He died shortly after arriving in the US.

British phrenologist George Combe (1788-1858) wrote a popular book, Constitution of Man, and was elected to the National Academy of Sciences. At one point he was asked to justify slavery on the grounds that people of African descent had "inferior" skulls. Combe refused, noting that educated slaves were the intellectual equals of white people. The Fowler brothers published a Journal of Phrenology between 1840 and 1911 and set up clinics to assess people for self-improvement based upon the bumps on their skulls. We have progressed in the last 200 years.

How is the human brain different than other brains?

The most important anatomical distinction between the human brain and the brains of other animals is the frontal lobes, as they are distinctly larger in humans. Human brains weigh an average of 1,300 grams, a squirrel brain weighs six grams. The brains of our nearest relatives, the great apes, weigh only 300–500 grams, even though their body size is similar to ours. Relative to body size, whales and dolphins have the next biggest brains to us, bigger even than chimpanzees.

Recent research may have uncovered why the human brain is so much larger than the chimpanzee brain. The gene, ASPM, was linked in 2001 to a disease called microcephaly, which can cause a 70 per cent reduction in the size of the human brain, and associated mental retardation. Researchers (Zhang, 2003, Evans & Anderson, 2004) have hypothesized that the human brain may have tripled in size over the last 2.5 million years due to a gene called ASPM (Abnormal Spindle-Like Microcephaly).

The genetic defect causes a massive reduction in the cerebral cortex, creating a brain similarly sized to that of our 2.3 to 3 million-year-old ancestor Australopithecus afarensis, of which the fossil known as Lucy is the most famous example. Lucy may have had a brain less than 450 grams compared to the normal human weight of 1300 grams.

The fossil record suggests that the main period of expansion started

2 to 2.5 million years ago and ended around 200,000 to 400,000 years ago. The episode of rapid evolution in ASPM had ended by 100,000 years ago, and the gene is currently stabilized in modern humans (Zhang 2003).

Of additional interest in this area are the discoveries by neurobiologist John Allman (California Institute of Technology, Pasadena, California) and his collaborators have discovered that a special type of large spindle-shaped neuron, first described in the early 20th century by Constantin von Economo, is unique to apes and humans and much more numerous in humans. These neurons are found in brain areas that are implicated in decision-making in uncertain situations (Holloway et al., 2004).

Interesting and important physical facts about the brain

The following facts are provided to the reader about the human brain to provide some appreciation of what is being discussed.

Average number of neurons in the brain = 100 billion

Ratio of the volume of gray matter to white matter in the cerebral hemispheres (20 yrs. old) = 1.3 (Miller et al, 1980)

Gray Matter: A general term given to tissue of the central nervous system rich in neuronal cell bodies.

White matter – neuronal tissue containing mainly long, myelinated axons that transmit information electrically between brain structures.

% of cerebral oxygen consumption by white matter = 6%

% of cerebral oxygen consumption by gray matter = 94%

Average number of glial cells in brain = 10-50 times the number of neurons; Williams and Herrup (1988) or 100 billion X 30 = 3 trillion

Glial cells, commonly called neuroglia or simply glia, are non-neuronal cells that provide support and nutrition, maintain homeostasis.

Number of neocortical neurons (females) = 19.3 billion (Pakkenberg et al., 2003) Pakkenberg and Gundersen (1997)

Number of neocortical neurons (males) = 22.8 billion (Pakkenberg et al., 1997; 2003)

Average loss of neocortical neurons = 85,000 per day (~31 million per year) (Pakkenberg et al., 1997; 2003)

Average loss of neocortical neurons = 1 per second (Pakkenberg et al., 1997; 2003)

Number of synapses in cortex = 0.15 quadrillion (Pakkenberg et al., 1997; 2003)

Difference number of neurons in the right and left hemispheres = 186 million MORE neurons on left side than right side (Pakkenberg et al., 1997; 2003)

Total number of synapses in cerebral cortex = 60 trillion (Shepherd, 1998) However, Koch (1999) lists the total synapses in the cerebral cortex at 240 trillion.

Percentage of total cerebral cortex volume (human):
frontal lobe = 41%; temporal lobe = 22%; parietal lobe = 19%; occipital lobe = 18%. (Caviness Jr., et al. 1998)

Number of cortical layers = 6 (refers to the layers in the thin gray matter just below the scalp)

Thickness of cerebral cortex = 1.5-4.5 mm
Thickness of cerebral cortex (Bottlenosed dolphin) = 1.3-1.8 mm (Ridgway, 1985, p. 221)
(data obtained from brain facts website).

These facts indicate that the human brain is, indeed, a very complex organ with the greatest percentage of its resources being allocated to the frontal lobe and more in the left hemisphere than the right hemisphere. The thin layer of cells just below the skull bone is called the gray matter (other subcortical regions also receive this classification). The physical fact list indicates that the gray matter consumes much of the oxygen that the brain employs in its tasks, although it is much smaller in volume than the white matter (age 20).

The qEEG measures the activity in the gray matter just below the skull, which places it at a critical location to measure cortical cognitive activity. Coherence values reflect white matter activity.

Sex Differences

Differences between the sexes always provide some interesting data. While it may be tempting to make broader statements about sex differences and intelligence, the reader is cautioned to not conclude beyond what the data is telling us.

Using MRI data, research has shown that "Men have approximately 6.5 times the amount of gray matter related to general intelligence than women, and women have nearly 10 times the amount of white matter related to intelligence than men. Gray matter represents information processing centers in the brain and white matter represents the networking of – or connections between – these processing centers. The study also identified regional differences with intelligence. For example, 84% of gray-matter regions and 86% of white-matter regions involved with intellectual performance in women were found in the brain's frontal lobes, compared to 45% and 0% for males, respectively.

The gray matter driving male intellectual performance is distributed

throughout more of the brain. According to the researchers, this more cen-
tralized intelligence processing in women is consistent with clinical findings
that frontal brain injuries can be more detrimental to cognitive performance
in women than men." Compared to men, women show more white matter
and fewer gray matter areas related to intelligence. In men IQ/gray matter
correlations are strongest in frontal and parietal lobes whereas the strongest
correlations in women are in the frontal lobe along with Broca's area (left
frontal area – F7 in the 10-20 system). Men and women apparently achieve
similar IQ results with different brain regions, suggesting that there is no
singular underlying neuroanatomical structure to general intelligence and
that different types of brain designs may manifest equivalent intellectual
performance. (Haiera et al., 2005)

Brain Developmental Issues – Gray and White Matter

Research had shown that the brain overproduces gray matter for a
brief period in early development—in the womb and for about the first 18
months of life—and then undergoes just one bout of pruning. The teen's
gray matter waxes and wanes in different functional brain areas at different times in development. For example, the gray matter growth spurt just
prior to puberty predominates in the frontal lobe, the seat of "executive
functions"—planning, impulse control and reasoning. In teens affected by a
rare, childhood onset form of schizophrenia that impairs these functions, the
MRI scans revealed four times as much gray matter loss in the frontal lobe
as normally occurs. Unlike gray matter, the brain's white matter—wire-like
fibers that establish neurons' long-distance connections between brain regions—thickens progressively from birth in humans.

Another series of MRI studies is shedding light on how teens may
process emotions differently than adults. Using functional MRI (fMRI),
a team led by Dr. Deborah Yurgelun-Todd at Harvard's McLean Hospital
scanned subjects' brain activity while they identified emotions on pictures
of faces displayed on a computer screen. Young teens, who characteristically perform poorly on the task, activated the amygdala, a brain center that
mediates fear and other "gut" reactions, more than the frontal lobe. As teens
grow older, their brain activity during this task tends to shift to the frontal lobe, leading to more reasoned perceptions and improved performance.
Similarly, the researchers saw a shift in activation from the temporal lobe to
the frontal lobe during a language skills task as teens got older. These functional changes paralleled structural changes in temporal lobe white matter."
(NIH Publication No. 01-4929)

These references are only the tip of the scientific iceberg on what has been occurring in this field for the past several decades. They are provided to give the reader an appreciation of the recent developments in neuroscience.

Many complex brain functions cannot be understood / explained by reference to a single location, but involve interactions between locations. The functional descriptors to be provided are inaccurate in many ways, as the assumption behind localizing a function is that the location operates independent of other locations, which is an error in understanding how the brain functions. What follows are the simplified functional descriptors of locations.

What the Lobes do.

Frontal lobe:

Functions: Personality functioning, judgment, planning and organizational ability, memory functioning, problem solving, expressive language, attentional abilities, flexibility of thought, sequencing actions, social behaviors.

Parietal Lobe:

Functions: Location for visual attention, location for touch perception, goal directed voluntary movements, manipulation of objects, integration of different senses that allows for understanding a single concept, naming objects, writing, reading, drawing, distinguishing left from right, mathematics, awareness of body parts and space, eye-hand coordination.

Occipital Lobes:

Functions: Vision, identifying colors, movement, reading, writing, locating objects in space.

Temporal Lobes:

Functions: Hearing ability, memory acquisition, some visual perceptions, catagorization of objects, recognizing faces, understanding words, short term memory, sexual behavior and interest, control of aggressive, verbalizing.

There are other areas of the brain which we will not be discussing as they are not directly amenable to Neurocognitive interventions. These areas include the brainstem and cerebellum.

Neuroscience Discoveries in Learning Disabilities, ADHD and TBI

Galaburda et al. (1985) was the first researcher to look at the physical properties of a dyslexic brain. He conducted post-mortem examinations of four dyslexic subjects and showed abnormal neuronal development (dysplasias – extra large neurons) along the left hemisphere superior temporal lobes (T3 - Peri-Sylvian regions) and frontal lobes. Most of these were located in the cortical regions.

A distinction between cortical and subcortical would be helpful in the discussion which is to follow. Cortical locations refer to the gray matter just below the skull. These are the locations that are addressable with the qEEG technology. Subcortical structures refer to everything else below these cortical locations. They can consist of gray matter or white matter. We will avoid detailed references to subcortical anatomical locations. When discussing cortical locations, the nearest corresponding location in the 10-20 system will be immediately provided to render it easier for the reader to understand and follow the discussion.

Since the advent of new neuroimaging techniques, studies using Positron Emission Tomography (PET), Magnetic Electroencephalography (MEG), functional Magnetic Resonance Imaging (fMRI), and Diffusion Tensor Imaging (DTI) have identified differences in the functional and structural organization between dyslexic and typical readers. (Temple et al. 2003). McCandliss and Noble (2003) reviewed the literature on functional neuroimaging of dyslexia in adult and pediatric samples. A summary of the two reviews will serve to identify the brain regions associated with dyslexia.

Dyslexic adults show dysfunction in the left temporoparietal cortex (T3-T5-P3) during phonological processing of visual stimuli as evidenced by PET studies (Paulesu et al, 1996).

Figure 13 shows roughly where this location is on a brain figure. The labeling (T3, T5, P3) indicates how the 10-20 system would label these locations. We will insert the closest 10-20 label when discussing the anatomical references made in these studies to avoid complexity in the discussion. Modern neuroscience research has attempted to fine-tune these localization issues. For the purposes of this book, it is not useful for the reader to be provided with a series of complex Latin names of cortical and subcortical structures. We will keep the discussion simplified to the 10-20 system of cortical locations (Figure 12) and reference all structures below the cortical surface merely as subcortical locations. The reader should keep in mind that we are simplifying the locations for readability reasons and some loss of specificity will result.

Figure 13 – locations of dyslexic problem

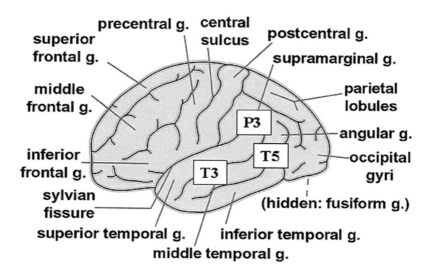

For the dyslexic subject, the physical dysfunction is located in the superior temporal gyrus (T3) and inferior parietal cortex (P3-T5), particularly in the left hemisphere (Rumsey et al., 1997a; Rumsey et al, 1997b). Studies involving the fMRI have confirmed this finding in adults who showed decreased activity in the T5-P3 locations (temporoparietal regions), including T3 (superior temporal gyrus) and P3 (angular gyrus), during phonological processing of letters and pseudoword rhyme (Shaywitz et al, 1998). Dyslexic children ages 8 to 12 years undergoing fMRI showed reduced activity at T3, T5, & P3 during phonological tasks, suggesting that the disruption is fundamental to the disorder and not a compensation effect that occurs with maturation.

In addition to identifying the areas of activation, MEG provides data about the temporal course of activation. A regular progression of activation was found for both normal and dyslexic readers from O1-O2 (occipital) to the T3 & T5 (basal temporal) region, P3 and above P3 (supramarginal gyri) (Simos et al, 2000).

Dyslexic readers responded as quickly as normal readers in the activation of all areas except the left temporal (T3 – T5) and left parietal (P3), areas which are known to be involved in word recognition and phonological analysis. These findings indicate that the T3-T5-P3 area (left temporoparietal) is slow to respond and responds with less activation in dyslexic readers than in nonimpaired readers. A MEG study was conducted on a sample of 45 children (5 to 7 years old) at the beginning of their reading experience. The children were either at risk for reading difficulties or not at risk (Simos et al, 2002). The imaging scans showed that children at risk had greater right hemisphere activity, while children not at risk had greater activity in left posterior superior temporal gyrus (T3-T5). These findings suggest that the dysfunction occurs early in development.

A number of fMRI neuroimaging studies have compared cortical activation patterns under reading related tasks in readers with dyslexia (DYS) and control groups of nonimpaired readers (NI) (Shaywitz et al, 1998; Shaywitz et al, 2002; Shaywitz et al, 2003). This series of studies showed that non-impaired (NI) adults increased their activation at T5 (posterior superior temporal gyrus), P3 (angular gyrus), and above P3 (supramarginal gyrus) as the task demands increased from orthographic comparisons to phonological comparisons (Shaywitz et al, 1998)

In contrast, dyslexic adults showed over-activation in response to increasing task demands in anterior regions including the F7 location (inferior frontal gyrus). While the nonimpaired readers showed activation of a widely distributed system for reading, the dyslexic readers had disrupted activity in the posterior cortex that involves traditional attentional, visual and language areas. The pattern of moving from a left frontal activation pattern to a left posterior activation pattern was evidenced in developmental data (Thornton, 2001). Thus the dyslexic reader may not be progressing in the normal developmental manner.

The anatomic correlates of the reduced dysfunction in left temporoparietal regions can also be visualized by diffusion tensor imaging (DTI), which identifies the white matter tracts. (Watts et al, 2003) Using DTI, Klingberg et al. (2000) showed that reading ability is directly related to the degree of connection activity between T3, T5, & P3 (water diffusion of the long myelinated neurons connecting different regions of the brain) for both dyslexic and nonimpaired readers. For example, in a PET study of adults, the nonimpaired readers, but not the dyslexic readers, showed positively correlated activation between the P3 location (angular gyrus) and subcortical locations (lingual and fusiform gyri) and between the T3 location (left superior temporal gyrus - STG) and the F7 location (left inferior frontal area) (Horwitz et al., 1998).

In summary, the T3-T5-P3 (left temporoparietal) region is disrupted in developmental dyslexia. The magnitude of activation is low, and there is decreased coordination of activity between the T3-T5-P3 locations and between the T3 (left superior temporal gyrus) and F7 (left frontal) areas. The evidence indicates that the disruption is in place before children learn to read, is related to difficulties with phonological processing and is related to underdevelopment of white matter fibers in the region.

Evans & Park (1996) identified significant deviations from a normative database in a group of 8 dyslexic children and 2 adults. These deviations were evident in the left posterior region (in particular the P3 position) and revealed reduced coherence values, usually involving the theta bandwidth (4-8 Hertz). As coherence values reflect white matter activity, these results correspond with the DTI study. Nagy et al. (2004) used the DTI technology in studying reading development (ages 8-18) and found that myelination at the T3 location (left temporal lobe) was positively related to reading.

In conclusion, from a number of scientific viewpoints the problem for the dyslexic reader is in the T3-T5-P3 (left temporal / parietal) areas and the F7 location (frontal region) and is reflected in underactivation and poor connection activity patterns.

ADHD Neuroscience

The physical problem for the ADHD child resides in a different pattern, predominantly showing a frontal cortical and subcortical dysfunction concomitant with a slowing (increased theta activity) of the qEEG parameters in frontal and central locations. A number of magnetic resonance imaging (MRI) and functional MRI studies (Hynd et al., 1990; Hynd et al. 1993; Castellanos et al., 1994; Giedd et al., 1994; Aylward et al. 1996; Castellanos et al., 1996; Castellanos, 1997; Mostofsky et al., 1998) have found differences between the ADHD and normal child in size and symmetry of specific brain areas. These areas include both cortical and subcortical structures: (basal ganglia, cerebellum, anterior cingulate gyrus, right frontal, anterior and posterior corpus callosum, caudate). These areas have been implicated in ability to inhibit responses and attentional abilities.

Giedd et al. (2001) summarized the volumetric studies in their statement that the research studies consistently point to involvement of cortical (frontal lobes) and subcortical locations (basal ganglia, corpus callosum) as well as the cerebellum in ADHD. SPECT and PET studies have also indicated a F8-F4 cortical (right frontal) to subcortical (basal ganglia) circuit problem as well as the cerebellum in ADHD (Lou et al., 1984; Lou et al.,

1990; Sieg et al., 1995; Kim et al., 2002). Zametkin et al. (199) and Ernst et al. (1994) had originally demonstrated decreased glucose metabolism (PET) in the ADHD subject in their response to cognitive tasks. Figure 14 provides an approximate location to these structures.

Figure 14 – A location of ADHD problem

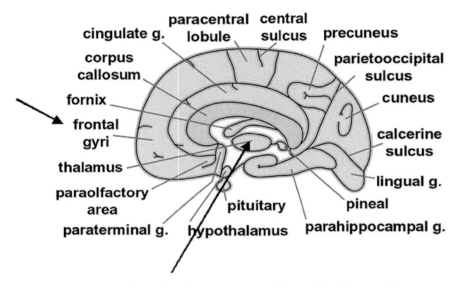

Basal Ganglia (putamen, caudate nucleus, globus pallidus, claustrum, amygdaloid complex)
Cerebellum not presented

Courtesy of Prof. Mark Wm. Dubin, University of Colorado-Boulder. Standard Location Nomenclature of brain structures g.=gyri

QEEG studies of the ADHD population have shown two distinct types of patterns. The first is slowing over frontal and central, midline cortical regions in approximately 80-90% of patients with ADHD (Mann et al., 1992; Chabot et al. 1996; Clarke et al., 2001a). Slowing in qEEG terms refers to elevated (compared to a normative reference group) values of relative power of theta, reduced relative power values of alpha and beta, and elevated theta/alpha and theta/beta ratios, primarily over frontal, frontal-midline (Fz), and central-midline (Cz) cortical regions. Visual representation of these frequencies is provided in Figure 16. This is a hypoarousal condition and occurs in about 80% of the subjects (Chabot et al., 2001); Barry et al.,

64

2003).

The other subtype is hyperarousal of the frontal lobes. This pattern also meets the criteria for ADHD but are more likely to exhibit conduct, mood or anxiety disorders (Clarke et al., 2001b) and may have ADHD symptoms that are secondary to these other DSM-IV diagnoses.

Chabot et al. (1996) used the qEEG measure as a test for ADHD and reported a test sensitivity of 94% and test specificity of 88%. Similar sensitivity and specificity levels have been subsequently reported (Monastra et al., 1999; Monastra et al., 2001). Sensitivity refers to the ability of a test to identify any of a broad number of conditions. Specificity refers to the ability of a test to identify a specific condition versus other possible conditions.

As researchers continue to look into these variables there is more that is found. Barry et al. (2005) found qualitative differences in EEG coherence values in girls with ADHD compared to normals and quantitative differences between girls with different subtypes of ADHD.

Medication Effectiveness with different qEEG patterns

The ADHD patients who have demonstrated such cortical slowing (elevated theta levels) have been shown to respond positively to stimulants, whereas, ADHD patients who do not demonstrate cortical slowing on qEEG examination are typically stimulant non-responders (Clarke et al., 2002; Chabot et al., 1999).

Methylphenidate (Ritalin) has been shown to increase blood flow in cortical and subcortical locations (prefrontal-striatal areas) (Kim et al. 2002; Matochek et al., 1993; Krause et al., 2000). However, Greenhill et al. (1999) reviewed 161 random controlled trials (RCTs) and found that 25% to 35% of the ADHD sample did not show any reduction in symptoms of hyperactivity or impulsivity. Other researchers (DePaul et al., 1998) estimate that the percentage of patients who do not demonstrate significant improvements in attention may be somewhat higher (40-50%).

Dr. Amen has employed the SPECT scan to delineate 6 ADHD subtypes. He describes the subtypes as follows. (Amen, 2004) The SPECT scans show the focus of the problem in cortical and subcortical locations (frontal, temporal and basal ganglia) and medication intervention differ according to subtype.

Type 1. Classic ADD -- inattentive, distractible, disorganized, hyperactive, restless, and impulsive.

Type 2. Inattentive ADD -- inattentive, sluggish, slow moving, low motivation, and often described as space cadets, daydreamers, and couch potatoes.

Type 3. Overfocused ADD -- trouble shifting attention, frequently get stuck in loops of negative thoughts or behaviors, obsessive, excessive worrying, inflexible, frequent oppositional and argumentative behavior.

Type 4. Temporal Lobe ADD - inattentive, irritability, aggressive, dark thoughts, mood instability, and severe impulsivity.

Type 5. Limbic ADD - inattentive, chronic low-grade depression, negativity, "glass half empty syndrome," low energy, and frequent feelings of hopelessness and worthlessness.

Type 6. Ring of Fire ADD - inattentive, extreme distractibility, angry, irritable, overly sensitive, cyclic moodiness, hyperverbal, and extreme opposition.

While intriguing, the author is not aware of any published research to date that supports this classification or the differential effects of the different medications on the different subtypes.

Traumatic Brain Injury Neuroscience

The majority of studies on the biomechanical effects of closed head injury have concluded that there are three force vectors that contribute to the injury, a rotational vector, a sheer vector, and a centripetal force vector; which is maximal at the outer cortex with a gradient to the subcortex and brain stem. In other words, the brain twists around, stretches the neurons between layers, and most of the damage is done on the cortical surface.

The geometrical summation of these forces results in maximum injury in that part of the brain that is in contact with the skull, e.g., the gray matter of the frontal and temporal lobes, which largely occurs independent of the direction of impact to the skull. Two other invariant consequences of blunt force injuries to the skull are: 1- sheer forces that are maximal at the boundaries between different densities of tissue (e.g., gray vs. white matter), and 2- a percussion shock wave that travels from the point of impact making contact with the opposite side of the skull in <100 msec., resulting in a "coup-contra-coup" injury. All these forces are capable of seriously disrupting the molecular integrity and function of cortical neurons and glia." (Thatcher, 2000)

A brief introduction to the quantitative EEG concepts are relevant at this point in the discussion. The cortical gray matter is constantly producing electrical energy which can be measured on the scalp and presents itself as wave forms. These wave forms can be divided according to how many sine waves per second can be measured. The traditional breakdown and nomenclature of the EEG follows the following definitions: delta (0-4 Hertz or sine waves per second), theta (4-8 Hertz), alpha (8-13 Hertz), and beta (13+

Hertz). Chapter 10 will provide a much more thorough discussion of the qEEG and its measures.

Dr. Hudspeth (2006) has been able to measure the coup-contra-coup effects on the qEEG. Figure 15 presents the statistical analysis of the coup-contra-coup effect reflected in a visual format. What the figures indicate is that there is an electrophysiological breakdown in the brain.

Figure 15 - See insert at end of book - page 315

The theoretical interpretations of biomechanical effects of TBI have found support in the interaction between qEEG frequency analysis, fMRI data (relaxation times of the signals) and correlates with cognitive function. The relaxation concept refers to the release (relaxation) of energy from an excited state to a lower energy. The MRI "excites" a magnetic field and then measures the time it takes to return to normal. The longer the recovery the slower the time. For example, TBI patients have increased delta (0-4 Hertz) amplitudes and increased white matter signal on T2 MRI indicating dysfunction, and there are associations of decreased alpha (8 - 13 Hertz) and beta (13+ Hertz) amplitudes with increased gray matter T2 MRI relaxation times (Thatcher, 1998). While increases in both relaxation times were associated with cognitive dysfunction, decreased amplitudes (alpha and beta) were also associated with decreased cognitive function.

Experimental studies have demonstrated that diffuse white matter injuries may occur with traumatic brain injury irrespective of skull deformation. The mechanism for diffuse axonal injury (DAI) is a shear-strain deformation, a change in shape of the brain without a change in volume. The three areas most commonly involved in DAI are in subcortical structures (white matter, corpus callosum, and the upper brain stem (dorsolateral)).

With the advent of diffusion tensor imaging (DTI), we have a new way of viewing the effects of a TBI on an individual's physical brain. Arfanakis et al. (2002) looked at TBI subjects shortly after the injury (within 24 hours) and found significant loss of tissue structure (reduction of anisotropy) in subcortical structures of the patients with mild traumatic brain injury. A follow-up study in two patients with mild traumatic brain injury revealed that in some regions the damage was partially or completely corrected 30 days after injury. In some subjects, several affected white-matter regions did not improve after 30 days. In these cases, a disconnection might have happened, and Wallerian degeneration of the injured neurons might have occurred. Wallerian degeneration refers to degeneration of the distal segment of a peripheral nerve fibre (axon) that has been severed from its nutritive centres (cell body). In other words, it dies backward starting from the end section and moving to the main body.

Inglese et al. (2005) were also able to demonstrate DTI differences between normals and TBI patients. The main finding was a significant reduction of tissue structures (fractional anisotropy) in the TBI patient's subcortical structures. The authors noted that these are frequent sites of diffuse axonal injuries (DAI), a relatively common effect of a brain injury. The subject's time since accident varied from 4 days to 5.7 years, reflecting both an immediate and long-term effect.

Intervention Effects on Neuroscience Measures
Magnetic Electroencephalography (MEG) studies on Phonic Interventions

Neuroimaging studies have shown changes in the functioning of the brain that accompany the improvements in reading abilities. For example, Magnetic Electroencephalography (MEG) images showed that dyslexic children increased their activations in important cortical locations T5 (left posterior superior temporal gyrus), above P3 (left supramarginal gyrus) and P3 (angular gyrus), after an intervention of 80 hours of one-on-one instruction in phonological structure. (Simos & Breier, 2001).

fMRI Effects of FastForWord Educational Interventions

FastForWord interventions have been shown to appropriately increase activations in the T5 and P3 locations (as well as T3 and F4) with resultant improvements on language measures. The T5 and P3 (left posterior) locations are known to be problem locations for dyslexic students.

Temple et al. (2003) treated a group of 20 children with dyslexia (age range 8 to 12 years) with the Fast ForWord Language program. A control group, matched to the experimental group on age, gender, handedness, and nonverbal IQ, was examined twice by behavioral testing and fMRI with 8 weeks between examinations. The children in the dyslexia group trained on the program for 100 minutes each day, 5 days a week, for an average of 27.9 training days or 46.5 hours. The control group received no intervention. Behavioral testing consisted of Woodcock-Johnson Reading Mastery Test- Revised, Clinical Evaluation of Language - Fundamentals-3 (cELF-3), and the Rapid Naming subtest of the Comprehensive Test of Phonological Processing.

There were three visual tasks for subjects to perform while fMRI data were collected. In the first task (phonological processing), the child judged whether two single letters rhymed with each other (rhyme letters). In the nonphonological task, the child judged whether two letters were identical (match letters). A third task served as a baseline and required the child to judge if two lines were in the same orientation (match lines). A comparison of brain activation between rhyme letters and match letters yielded brain regions involved in phonological processing, not areas involved in orthographic processing (matching visual shapes of the letters). The treatment group improved significantly (ranging from +.70 SD to +1.02 SD) in word identification, pseudo-word decoding, and passage comprehension. Language measures (Celf-3: Receptive, Expressive, Rapid Naming) improvements ranged from +.53 SD to +.73 SD. Whole brain analyses of the fMRI data showed increased activity in brain regions for the treatment group.

Normal reading children and adults show activation of relevant cortical structures T3-T5-P3 (left temporoparietal cortex) in phonological processing, and children with dyslexia show underactivation of these areas during the task. These two regions of interest showed increased activity in the dyslexic children after treatment. Many additional areas showed increased activation after the remediation program, including the cortical locations of F4 (right frontal) and T3 (middle temporal gyrus), two areas that are not typically recruited by normal reading children. Increased activation of a subcortical structure (bilateral anterior cingulate) was interpreted to be due to increased attention to task. A correlation was found (r = +.41, p < .05) between increased MR signal in cortical locations T5-P3 (left temporo-parietal region) and change in total language score. The authors indicated that there were limitations in the study. First, the control group helped to rule out changes due to maturation over the 8-week period of the study, practice and familiarity effects of repeated fMRI studies, and practice effects on the behavioral tests. However, the authors recommended repeating the study with an untreated control group of children with dyslexia, perhaps using a delayed entry into the treatment program. Another recommendation was to treat a second group of dyslexic children with another program or a placebo.

EEG Biofeedback effects on fMRI structures

Structural magnetic resonance imaging (MRI) studies have found significantly smaller sizes of the prefrontal cortices in children with ADHD (Castellanos et al., 1996; Durston et al, 2004; Mostofsky et al. 2002). Single photon emission computed tomography (SPECT) studies have shown decreased blood flow (perfusion) in prefrontal areas, which have been implicated in the control of attentional processes in ADHD individuals (Amen and Carmichael, 1997; Kim et al. 2002). A functional MRI (fMRI) study has demonstrated a dysfunction of a subcortical structure (anterior cingulate cortex (ACC)) in adults with ADHD while they performed a Counting Stroop task (Bush et al, 1999), a variant of the Stroop (Stroop, 1935). The Stroop test asks the subject to read words of colors that are presented in different colors, i.e. the word red printed in blue. It is considered a test of the ability to inhibit as the subject must resist the temptation to read the printed color of the word rather than the word itself.

Converging lines of evidence from positron emission tomography (PET) and fMRI indicate that this subcortical structure (dorsal division of the Anterior Cingulate Cortex) plays a pivotal role in the various cognitive processes implicated in the Stroop task (Bush et al., 1998; Bush et al., 2000).

An experiment was conducted to determine if there were physical changes in the subcortical structures implicated in the fMRI studies of ADHD with EEG biofeedback treatment. Lévesqu et al. (2005) conducted 40 1-hour EEG biofeedback sessions focused on increasing 12-15 Hz at Cz and decreasing 4-7 Hertz. The experimental group's (N=15) brain response pattern during a selective attention task (Stroop) was different as there was a significant activation of the right ACC (BA 32), which did not occur with the no treatment group following the treatment. There were also significant activations in other subcortical structures (left caudate nucleus and left substantia nigra). In addition, as previous research has continuously documented, there were improvements on tests of attention (Digit Span, Integrated Visual Attention- IVA) and decreases on inattention and hyperactivity measures. The digit span test (of the standard IQ test) asks the subject to repeat a list of numbers (of varying length) that the examiner reads. The IVA test requires the subject to click the mouse only when he sees the number 1 and to inhibit clicking when he sees the number 2. It is commonly employed to assess for ADHD. Thus it has been shown that the EEG biofeedback can change relevant subcortical response patterns, a truly remarkable finding.

Neurocognitive Interventions on qEEG variables

The effects of EEG biofeedback upon cortical electrophysiological measures have been documented in previous EEG research which will be discussed more thoroughly in chapter 11. A much more thorough analysis of individual response patterns will be presented in the examples chapters 14 and 15. The conclusion from these case studies is that we are pretty much able to change any qEEG variable that we wish to change; it is just a question of how responsive that particular brain is to the interventions and how long it takes. Some variables respond relatively quickly, others take longer. The possible reasons underlying these differential response patterns will be discussed. The effect of the intervention on subcortical structures is largely unknown at this point. Subcortical structures, however, present a critical component of mental functioning. For most cases, however, it appears that the Neurocognitive cortical interventions are sufficient to obtain significant and impressive results.

Qualifications

There are other physical issues in the dyslexic condition which have been reported on in the literature, such as the role of cerebellar dysfunction. As this aspect of the dyslexic problem is not amenable to the Neurocognitive approach, it was not addressed. In addition, alternative therapies have also been reported that we have not covered due to the problem of finding adequate research studies which report the means and standard deviations pre and post treatment.

CHAPTER 6 – Behavioral manifestations of Brain Functioning Problems
DSM IV Diagnostic criteria

The previous neuroscience discussion lays the basis for the physical problems in brain functioning in our reading and learning disabled population. However, there are more consequences to these brain functioning problems than just a reading or learning problem. Behavioral manifestations are often the most difficult for a family and society to deal with and can extract considerable financial resources out of a family's budget as well as societal resources.

The economic costs of brain functioning problems (LD, ADHD, TBI) have been more researched on the attention deficit/hyperactivity (ADHD) population than the "pure" learning disabled (LD) or reading disabled (RD) population. Therefore, we will analyze what the research has reported for the ADHD child. However, due to the large overlap of these conditions, a brief discussion of comorbidity issues is relevant. The term comorbidity refers to an overlap of diagnoses. A subject can often receive one or several additional diagnoses to their central diagnosis.

The following diagnoses have been involved in the research regarding comorbidity issues in the ADHD child and adult. The Diagnostic and Statistical Manual IV (DSM IV) criteria are summarized here to allow the reader an understanding of how these disorders manifest themselves behaviorally. The DSM IV is the psychiatric guide to defining certain psychological/behavioral conditions.

DSM IV Diagnostic Criteria

314.00 ADHD or ADD is manifested by symptoms of inattention, hyperactivity or impulsivity. According to the DSM the symptoms should be inappropriate for the particular age of the child (i.e. the child is more impulsive than other members of his age group) and should be present for more than 6 months.

Examples of inattentiveness include: 1) careless errors in homework or schoolwork, failure to pay close attention to detail; 2) doesn't appear to listen; 3) doesn't follow through on chores; 4) has problems holding attention while playing or working on tasks; 5) problems in organizing; 6) avoids tasks that require cognitive activity; 7) forgetful; 8) distractible; 9) loses material required for homework. The child must have at least 6 of these behaviors to qualify.

Examples of hyperactivity-impulsivity include: 1) leaves seat when he shouldn't; 2) always "on the go"; 3) physically squirms or fidgets in his chair; 4) runs around or climbs on things when he shouldn't; 5) talks incessantly; 6) has a hard time playing quietly. The child must have 6 of these symptoms.

Examples of impulsivity include: 1) interrupts or intrudes upon others; 2) answers questions before the speaker has finished question; 3) has trouble waiting in line.

The symptoms should appear before age 7 and appear in two situations (home, work, school), and should not be able to be explained by other problems such as depression or anxiety.

Dyslexia - DSM IV 315.00

Dyslexia is called developmental reading disorder (DRD) in the DSM IV and is defined as a deficit in the brain's ability to process symbols. The DSM also notes that these children have trouble rhyming and separating sounds in spoken words. Part of the definition resides in the child's reading ability to be substantially less than what is expected based upon the child's age, IQ and education.

Some of the additional symptoms noted in the preschool child include: 1) tendency to jumble words and phrases; 2) dressing difficulty, tying shoe laces; 3) clumsiness or coordination problems; 4) loss of concentration when stories are read; 4) left handedness/ambidextrous; 5) difficulty in associating sounds with words; 6) appreciating rhymes; 7) family history of reading problems.

The DSM IV breaks down the symptoms according to age group. For the 5-7 year old it includes: 1) inability to learn alphabet; 2) problems reading more than simple words; 3) can't put sounds together to make words; 4) can't use a pencil to write correctly; 5) can't recall sequences; 6) dressing problems; 7) coordination problems; 8) concentration and attention problems.

For the 7-11 year old more symptoms are added which include: 1) problems learning multiplication tables; 2) memory problems; 3) low frustration leading to behavior problems such as becoming withdrawn. For the 11-16 year old the following symptoms appear: 1) difficulty in organizing tasks; 2) copying problems with dictation and oral instructions; 3) low self-confidence; 4) studying problems; 5) school work takes longer; 6) problems with spelling and writing; 7) severe problems with foreign languages; 8) reads inaccurately with poor comprehension.

DSM IV 315.10
Mathematics Disorder

The defining characteristic is performance in math below what would be expected for the child's age, IQ and education.

DSM IV 299.80; Pervasive Developmental Disorder

This diagnosis is intended for those children who have severe and global problems in social interaction skills and communication skills as well as stereotypical behavior, interests and activities. These children have some degree of mental retardation.

Behavior Disorders
DSM IV 312.8
Conduct Disorder

This diagnosis is defined as the child's repetitive violation of the rights of others and social norms with 3 of the following behaviors in the previous 6 months: 1) aggression to people and animals in the form of bullying or intimidation; 2) initiates physical confrontations; 3) has used a weapon which can cause physical damage; 4) has been physically cruel to people or animals; 5) has stolen; 6) has forced someone into sexual activity; 7) engaged in destruction of property; 8) has engaged in fire setting with the intention of destroying; 9) has destroyed property; 10) has lied to obtain goods ("cons" others); 11) has broken into someone's house, etc.; 12) has stolen objects from others; 13) stays out late at night past parental rules (before age 13); 14) has run away from home at least twice; 15) is truant from school (before age 13). The DSM IV distinguishes severity type according to how many of the behaviors are evident.

DSM IV 312.81
Oppositional Defiant Disorder

This diagnosis is defined in terms of a persistent pattern of lack of cooperation, defiance and hostile behavior towards authority figures, which does not involve antisocial behavior. The behaviors should be present for at least 6 months and 4 of the following are required: 1) loss of temper; 2) arguing with adults; 3) refusing to follow rules of adults; 4) blaming others for their mistakes; 5) easily annoyed by others; 6) angry and resentful; 7) doing things which annoy other people; 8) spiteful or vindictive

There are many diagnoses in the DSM IV. This brief summary is focused on the diagnoses which have been the focus of research studies in this area and have been associated with the ADHD diagnosis.

In the academic / cognitive arena, the probability of an underlying brain functioning problem would appear to be intuitively correct. What is less clear is why behavior problems would be tied to brain functioning issues. Most individuals would expect that these behaviors are due to "poor parenting" and explanations of such ilk. However, as this discussion continues it will become clear that these behavior problems can often be linked to brain functioning issues.

Chapter 7 - Comorbidity relationships in the ADHD condition

The DSM IV provides the diagnostic categories from which we can start to examine the interrelationships and overlap between the diagnoses. These relationships can become a bit muddy due to different research criteria. The real problem, however, resides with the problem of relating brain functions and structures to behavior, apart from environmental and cultural issues. We haven't solved all of these problems and it will probably be decades before we begin to have a thorough understanding of how this works. What is important in this chapter is that there are significant overlaps that we can report. The exact numbers will vary by research report and in the final analysis the particular number is not as important as the fact that there is a considerable overlap or no overlap. The problem for this scientific research area is not to spend research dollars pinpointing the exact number but to provide the broad strokes of the overlap. This will enable different research approaches to look for where the problem may reside (DNA research, genetic research, etc.)

The following diagnoses have been linked to ADHD with varying degrees of comorbidity, some of which we will examine in detail.

1)   Behavior relationships:

Oppositional Defiant Disorder and Conduct Disorder, Obsessive-Compulsive Disorder, Enuresis, accidental injury, sleep problems, Tourette's Disorder, social skill deficits, and drug abuse. Emotional issues: Anxiety, Depression, Bipolar Disorder

Table 9 presents the ADHD comorbidity figures estimated by different organizations for some of the behavior and emotional issues. The comorbidity issues reported by these organizations address the overlap between the ADHD diagnosis and a single other disorder. Other studies have examined the overlap with multiple simultaneous diagnoses.

Table 9 - Comorbidity Figures of ADHD & other DSM IV Diagnoses

	The American Academy of Pediatrics, 2000	Oregon Health & Science University (OSHU), 2005
Oppositional Defiant Behavior	35.2%	42.8%
Conduct Disorder	25.7%	23.7%
Anxiety Disorder	25.8%	21.7%
Depressive Disorder	11.1%	3.6%

a) Oppositional Defiant/Conduct Disorders

A number of other studies have shown co-morbidity of ADHD with Oppositional Defiant Disorder (Hinshaw, 1992; Biederman et al., 1991; Biederman et al., 1987; Werry et al., 1987) and Conduct Disorder in both clinic (Biederman et al., 1991; Barkley 1990; Lahey et al., 1987; Yule and Rutter, 1985; Stewart, Cummings, Seiger et al., 1981) and community samples (San Miguel et al., 1996; Szatmari, Boyle and Gifford, 1989).

Schachar and Tannock (1995) tested patterns of cognitive, developmental risk and psychological factors characterizing the pure forms of ADHD and Conduct Disorder. They found that the ADHD group was significantly impaired on cognitive measures, while the Conduct Disorder group was exposed to significantly greater environmental adversity.

Thapar et al. (2001) concluded in a twin study that conduct disorder (CD) and ADHD share a common genetic etiology; ADHD+CD appears to be a more severe subtype in terms of genetic loading as well as clinical severity.

Behavioral problems, such as Conduct Disorder and Oppositional Defiant Disorder are particularly common among children with ADHD, with comorbid rates of roughly 50%. (Guevara, 2001)

The Center for Disease Control report (CDC, 1997-8) concluded "Individuals affected by ADHD rarely have ADHD alone. Nearly 70% of those with ADHD simultaneously cope with other conditions such as learning disabilities, mood disorders, anxiety and more."

In conclusion the comorbid rate of ADHD with behavior problems can run as high as 70% and there is a genetic component to the comorbid relationship.

b) Antisocial Behavior

The developmental overlapping Conduct Disorder and Oppositional Defiant Disorder can manifest itself in criminal behavior during childhood, as well as when the child reaches adolescence and adulthood. These antisocial behaviors cost the individual and society considerable time, resources and money.

Several longitudinal studies have shown that childhood ADHD is associated with criminality in adolescence and adulthood. For example, a study conducted in Los Angeles found that children diagnosed with ADHD between the ages of 6 and 12 years old had significantly higher juvenile (46% versus 11%) and adult (21% versus 1%) arrest rates compared to normal control subjects (Satterfield et al., 1997).

A similar study conducted in New York found that children with ADHD were more likely than controls to later be arrested (39% versus 20%), convicted (28% versus 11%), and incarcerated (9% versus 1%) (Mannuzza et al., 1989). Another study, conducted with 17–18 year old adolescents in San Francisco, found that the ADHD group was more likely than the control group to be on probation, in jail, or assigned to a social worker by the court (Lambert, 1988).

One study has estimated the economic impact of criminality associated with ADHD (Swensen et al., 2001). Data from a sample of children (149 children, 4–12 years old) identified in 1979 and 1980 was obtained. Follow-up interviews were conducted between 1991 and 1996 with 149 children diagnosed with ADHD and 76 control children when the sample ranged in age from 19 to 25 years. Criminal history was assessed through self-report, including crimes (e.g., stealing, assault), juvenile detention, probation, and jail. Compared with the control group, the ADHD patients were more than twice as likely to have been arrested (48% versus 20%).

The costs of crimes incurred by victims and costs to the criminal justice system were estimated based on information from the Bureau of Justice Statistics, the Federal Bureau of Investigation, and the Criminal Justice Institute (Klaus, 1994). The mean total criminal costs were dramatically greater for ADHD patients than for the controls ($12,868 versus $498) between 1991 and 1996. All differences were statistically significant. The phrasing of the results would appear to indicate that each ADHD child ran up $12,868 in criminal costs over the 6-year period or $2,144 per year. If this interpretation is correct; then an estimate of the yearly criminal cost to society of the ADHD population (3 million) is **$6.4 BILLION dollars.** Although this study should be considered a rough estimate, findings strongly suggest that criminality associated with ADHD results in a significant cost to society. (Stephan, 1996)

c) Substance Abuse

Researchers have found that children with more severe attention problems were more likely to become substance abusers than children with hyperactivity and impulse control as their defining symptoms. The severity of symptoms and the persistence of ADHD into adolescence are the most important predictors of future smoking and alcohol and drug abuse. In one study nearly twice as many of the ADHD group (compared to a normal group) reported having been drunk more than once in the past six months. (Molina, 2003) Another study (Kollins et al., 2005) reported that self-reported ADHD symptoms were positively associated with adult smoking outcome. Over 60% of the adults with ADHD surveyed had been addicted to tobacco while 52% had used drugs recreationally. (Biederman, 2004c)

In conclusion, ADHD predisposes (particularly for those subjects with conduct disorder and parental substance abuse) the subject to substance abuse.

d) Enuresis

An article in the Southern Medical Journal published in 1997 compared a group of 6-year-old children with ADHD to a non-ADHD control group selected from a pediatric clinic population. They found that the 6-year-olds with ADHD had 2.7 times higher incidence of enuresis and a 4.5 times higher incidence of diurnal (daytime) enuresis as compared to a control group. (Watkins, 2005)

f) Emotional Comorbidities with ADHD
Depression

The high rate of learning disabilities found among children who commit suicide is reflected in a study that found that in a three-year period, 50% of the children who had committed suicide in Los Angeles County had been identified as learning disabled (Peck, 1985).

Kashani et al (1982) studied the co-occurence of major depressive disorder and learning disabilities in 100 children ages 9-12 and found that 62% of children with major depressive disorder had a learning disability, whereas only 22% of non-depressed children had LD.

In another study, conducted in Ontario, Canada, Hazel et al. (1997) analyzed all the available suicide notes (n = 27) from 267 consecutive adolescent suicides for spelling and handwriting errors. The results showed that 89% of the 27 adolescents who committed suicide had significant deficits in spelling and handwriting that were similar to those of the adolescents with LD.

In conclusion, depression is a major additional concern in the LD group, as one would expect.

Anxiety

Prior et al., (1999) found that in children with math difficulties, phobic disorder of anxiety was the most common co-morbidity (30%). Of the children with both spelling and math problems, 24% had phobic disorder or anxiety compared to about 10% of the general population.

In conclusion, anxiety is also a major concern in the LD group.

g) Social Skill Deficits

A meta-analysis suggested that social skill deficits are not invariably characteristic of children with learning disabilities. This meta-analysis made it clear that most studies on social skills deficits of children with learning disabilities do not provide sufficient data to determine the prevalence of social skills deficits within this population. Instead, most studies present mean differences on social skills ratings between samples with and samples without learning disabilities. (San Miguel et al., 1996) With that qualification it appears that social skill deficits are not necessarily related to learning disabilities.

2) Academic problems: Learning and communication differences, Pervasive Developmental Disorder.

a) Learning Problems

Probably the most researched overlapping diagnosis is learning disability. The reported association between learning disability and ADHD varies from 10 per cent to 92 per cent, depending on how the research is conducted (tests used, subjects selected, selection criteria, etc.). (Biederman et al., 1991)

About one-half of the 1.6 million elementary school-aged children diagnosed with attention-deficit/hyperactivity disorder (ADHD) have also been identified as having a learning disability (LD), according to a study (1997-8) by the Centers for Disease Control and Prevention (CDC). (CDC report, 2003) Within 5 years (2003) the CDC estimate of the prevalence of ADHD had risen to 4.4 million, an increase of 275%.

The CDC concluded "Individuals affected by ADHD rarely have ADHD alone. Nearly 70% of those with ADHD simultaneously cope with other conditions such as learning disabilities, mood disorders, anxiety and more." The report found that among children with the LD diagnosis, 54% were in special education. This was nearly five times greater than the percent observed for children with ADD and no LD and over 23 times the percent reported for children with neither ADD nor LD. Among children with LD and no ADD, 46% attended special education, and among those with both ADD and LD, 65% were in special education. Among children with LD, the percent of boys and girls in special education was similar. According to the report, the percent of boys with only ADD was almost three times greater than the percent of girls with ADD, and the percent of boys with both diagnoses was over two times greater than the percent of girls with both diagnoses. (CDC, 2001)

In a review of the school performance of children with ADHD, Biederman et al. (1991) highlighted the following findings:

(a) Children with ADHD perform more poorly than controls in school in terms of grade repetitions, grades in academic subjects, placement in special classes and need for tutoring.

(b) The ADHD child performed more poorly than controls on standard measures of intelligence and achievement (Campbell & Werry, 1986).

(c) The academic and learning problems of children with ADHD continue into adolescence and are related to chronic underachievement and school failure (Gittelman et al., 1985; Weiss. Milroy, & Perlman, 1985).

McGee et al. (1989) found up to 80 per cent of 11 year-old boys with ADHD (DSM-III criteria) were at least two years delayed with learning disabilities.

In conclusion there is a very large overlap in these conditions.

b) Reading Problems

Gerhardstein et al. (2001) reported an overlap of 50% between reading disabilities and ADHD. They failed to confirm a relationship between early symptoms of ADHD and future phonological processing skills. They did not find that the ADHD symptoms predicted future phonological skills, but rather that both measures remained constant over time. (Gerhardstein et al, 2001) Therefore, ADHD symptoms are not predictive of future phonological abilities.

August & Garfinkel (1990) evaluated a consecutive series of 115 boys diagnosed in a university outpatient clinic as ADHD and found that 39% also demonstrated a specific reading disability. Pure ADHD patients were compared with mixed ADHD + RD and normal controls on a battery of cognitive and attentional measures. The aim was to determine whether a distinct pattern of deficits would distinguish the groups. Both ADHD subgroups performed significantly worse than controls on measures of sequential memory and attentional tasks involving impulse control and planful organization. Only ADHD + RD boys differed from controls on measures of rapid word naming and vocabulary. Thus, the RD problem is a separate problem from ADHD although there is an overlap.

McGee et al. (1986), in a New Zealand study, found that reading-disabled boys were about 3 times as likely to have an externalizing disorder - ADHD, Conduct Disorder (CD) or Oppositional Defiant Disorder (ODD). Thus, reading disability may be tied to behavior problems more than the ADHD diagnosis.

The Dunedin study shows that hyperactivity is more significant in

81

ADHD children with or without reading disability than in children with only a reading disability, or in a comparison group (Pisecco, Baker, Silva et al., 1996; San Miguel et al., 1996). Thus, hyperactivity is a separate issue from reading disability.

In conclusion, the overlap of ADHD and reading disabilities is high (39% to 50%), and if a comorbid diagnosis exists, it is likely a behavior problem.

3) Physical Illness:

Additional concerns for the ADHD child are impaired vision and hearing, allergies, chronic health conditions, and asthma.

The CDC report (1997-8) found that health problems, including impaired vision and hearing, allergies, and chronic health conditions other than asthma, were reported more frequently for children with LD than for children with neither ADD nor LD.

The percent of children with four or more health care visits during the previous 12 months was 34% for children with only LD, 45% for children with only ADD, and 51% for children with both diagnoses. Among children with neither ADD nor LD, 23% had four or more health care visits during the past 12 months. The study noted that the regular use of prescription medication was highest among children with ADD: 54% for children with only ADD and 61% for children with both ADD and LD. Prescription medication use for children without ADD was lower: 14% for children with only LD and 6% for children with neither ADD nor LD.

Epilepsy

It has been estimated that 13–24% of people with a learning disability have epilepsy (Jenkins & Brown, 1992; Deb, 2000). Tan & Appelton (2005) have also documented a relationship between ADHD and epilepsy.

4) Related Problems

a) Accidents

Research indicates that children with ADHD are significantly more likely to be injured as pedestrians or while riding a bicycle, to receive head injuries, injure more than one part of the body, and be hospitalized for accidental poisoning. Children with ADHD may be admitted to intensive care units or have an injury resulting in disability more frequently than other children. (US Surgeon General report, 2001-3)

Children with ADHD have been shown to be more accident prone than other children (Gayton et al., 1986) because of their tendencies toward impulsive, overactive behavior. They are also more likely than other children to experience injuries due to accidents, such as broken bones, lacerations, head injuries, bruises, lost teeth, or accidental poisonings (Barkley, 1998)

Furthermore, it has been documented that adults with ADHD tend to have poor driving records and relatively high rates of traffic accidents (Barkely, 2002) (Mannuzza and Klein, 2000) (Murphy and Barkely, 1996).

b) Family problems

Conversely, the symptoms of ADHD have profound effects not only on the child, but also on the child's parents. For example, children's ADHD is frequently linked with strain in the parent-child relationship, disturbance in parents' marital functioning (e.g., less marital satisfaction and more conflict than parents of children without ADHD), and extremely high parental stress. (Anastopoulos et al., 1992; Johnston and Mash, 2001)

In this study (Anastopoulos et al., 1992) parents were asked whether they perceive their child's hyperactivity as a serious problem. The strongest predictor of whether parents considered ADHD to be a serious problem was the financial impact related to work, defined as the impact of the child's behavior on either parent's employment patterns or chances of a career (e.g., leaving work to pick up the child). Compared with parents who did not think ADHD was a serious problem, parents who perceived their child's ADHD to be a serious problem were 17.6 times more likely to say that there child's ADHD had a financial impact related to their work.

Need for psychotherapy

Adult ADHD – Poor self image and less stable relationships

Adults with ADHD are less likely to express a positive self-image. One study reported that only 40% of the adults with ADHD "strongly agree" that they have a bright outlook on their future, versus 67% of the adults surveyed without ADHD. Additionally, only half (50%) of the adults with ADHD surveyed like being themselves and accept themselves for who they are compared to 76% of the adults without ADHD. Adults with ADHD have less stable relationships than those adults without ADHD. The survey found that people with ADHD are twice as likely to be divorced and/or separated. Less than half of those surveyed who are currently in a relationship say they are "completely satisfied" with their relationship partners or loved ones, compared to 58% of those people surveyed without ADHD. (Biederman, 2004c)

In summary, approximately 70% of ADHD children will have other problems, such as learning (reading), behavior (oppositional, conduct disorder, substance abuse, enuresis, accident prone, family problems), emotional (anxiety, depression), and physical problems (epilepsy, vision and hearing problems) and will be more likely than a normal child to be on medication, be classified in need of special education services by the school system, be involved in the mental health and criminal justice system, have a poor self image, be less satisfied in relationships and earn less money over his/her lifetime. This is clearly a disastrous diagnosis to have.

CHAPTER 8 – Cost Issues

Cost issues can be divided between direct (medical, career, interventions) and indirect (quality of life) costs to the subject and the subject's family. The cost to society can be measured in terms of the educational, criminal justice and insurance industry.

General Costs

The ADHD Child/Adult

Prevalence Issues

It should not be surprising that wide differences in prevalence have been noted. Prevalence figures refer to how many (of a condition) exist in a population at a given time period. Across cultures, prevalence rates ranging from 1 to 20% have been reported (Bird et al., 1999). Within the United States, prevalence rates of 4-5% are generally accepted. Evidence to date indicates a 6:1 to 9:1 ratio of males to females in clinical settings. However, in epidemiology studies, ratios drop to 3:1. (Jensen et al., 2005) Epidemiology refers to the study of the relationships-of various factors determining the frequency and distribution of diseases in the human community.

The recent OHSU (2005) report indicated prevalence rates of 1.7% to 16% based on some community studies, which is a larger range than the NIH Consensus Development Conference on Diagnosis and Treatment of ADHD in 1998 of 3% to 5% or the DSM IV (1997) estimate of 3-7%. Limited prevalence data on adult ADHD are available, but estimates generally indicate that 30% to 70% of children with ADHD continue to have symptoms in adulthood (Silver, 2000) (Wender et al, 2001).

Costs - General

Over eight million adult Americans suffer from ADHD. ADHD costs sufferers approximately $77 billion in lost income every year or $9,625 per person. By comparison, the direct and indirect costs of drug abuse are estimated at $58.3 billion a year, depression about $43.7 billion, and alcohol abuse about $85.8 billion (Biederman, 2004a). Estimated costs can vary according to what organization is making the estimate and what they are estimating. For example, the CDC (2005) very conservatively estimated that health-care costs associated with currently diagnosed ADHD (4.4 million children, ages 4-17) are $3.3 billion annually, or $1,875 per child per year. High school graduates with ADHD had household incomes about $18,900 (10,800 English pounds in 2004) lower than those without the disorder. For college graduates, household incomes were about $4,300 lower (Biederman, 2004a).

Thus, from these reports, the ADHD population could include 8 million adults and 4.4 million children or 12.4 million individuals. This would be about 4% of the US population (298 million). It is conceptually difficult to imagine how 4.4 million ADHD children could turn into 8 million ADHD adults. This type of discrepancy is inherent in different organizations rendering different numbers with different criteria and instruments.

Educational Intervention Costs
State/Federal

If we employ the estimated $55 billion dollars that was spent on special education in 2004 and divide that number by the estimated 6.5 million students requiring services, the obtained estimated cost is $8,462 per student. These figures, of course, vary according to what organization is providing the numbers and thus should be considered rough estimates. This estimate is about $1,000 less than what the National Education Association (NEA) estimates for Special Education. The NEA estimates that the average yearly cost for a regular student is $7,552 and the special education student is an additional $9,369 per student, or $16,921 (NEA, 2005).

The cost is similar to the most expensive programs that a parent will spend in the private sector for a tutoring program (Huntington, Sylvan) for a year. The federal government has increased its spending on special education programs from $1.6 billion in 1980 to $8.5 billion in 2003, a 400% increase. (NCES, 2004)

Private Interventions

The cost structure for the most popular programs is provided in Table 10. The table employs, when appropriate, a $50 an hour cost per session and the reported number of sessions employed. The Sylvan and Hunterdon Learning Centers (Hunterdon & Sylvan) have advertised costs available. The estimated costs left out the costs of evaluations and related costs to simplify the comparison. As the table indicates, the Neurocognitive program is presently one of the least expensive and 3-10 times more effective than all the other programs, given the estimated cost structures and standard deviation effects presented in Figure 3. However, if a parent wants to enroll their LD child in a special school, the costs can run up to $30,000 a year or more.

Evaluation and other costs omitted, Figures are estimates and will vary by state and provider

The cost of educational intervention, however, is only one of the potential costs to the parents of these children or the children. Cost issues can be analyzed into direct costs, such as medication, therapies, and hospital visits, and indirect costs such as employee productivity, work loss, accident proneness, criminal activity, and quality of life.

Table 10

Program	# Sessions	Total Cost	SD	Est. $/Hr.
qEEG Activation	40	$4,000	3.50	$100
Tutoring	75	$3,750	.50	$50
qEEG Standard	40	$4,000	1.00	$100
Phonics	80	$4,450	1.02	$50
Lindamood-Bell	89	$4,450	.95	$50
FastForWord	100	$5,000	.60	$50
Sylvan Learning Ctr.	1 Yr. Program	$9,152	.50	Minnesota Advertised Program
Huntington Tutoring	1 Yr. Program	$9,984	.50	Minnesota Advertised Program
Orton-Gillingham	350	$17,500	.34	$50

Direct

The ADHD child is more likely to see their family doctors for mental health issues than the normal child and this utilization has been on the rise.

For example, 60% of all office visits for mental health problems by youth in 1996 were associated with a diagnosis of ADHD (Liebsen & Long, 2003). Kelleher et al. (2000) reported that there was an increase in clinician identified attentional problems, resulting in increased medical office visits from 1.4% in 1979 to 9.2% in 1996.

ADHD patients were treated for other mental disorders (e.g. depression, conduct disorder, and oppositional defiant disorder) 5 times more frequently than their matched controls - i.e., 28.7% vs. 5.9%. (Swenson et al., 2003)

ADHD children were 9.02 and 8.75 times more likely than other children (matched on age and sex) to have outpatient mental health visits and pharmacy fills, respectively. (Guevara et al., 2001)

The child with ADHD experiences a number of social problems, which are probably caused by their behavior. Children with ADHD are frequently rejected by their peers as early as the first day of contact, likely as a result of their tendency toward disruptive and aggressive behavior. (Mrug et al., 2001) Children with ADHD tend to have elevated rates of other psychiatric conditions, which could be contributing to their social rejection. (Swenson et al., 2003; Pliszka, 2000; Spencer et al., 1999)

Analyses were conducted using 1996 and 1997 data from the North Dakota Department of Health's Claims Database. Generally, comorbid psychiatric disorders substantially increased the costs of treating children with ADHD. Table 11 presents the results of the Burd et al. (2003) two year study.

Table 11 CoMorbid Cost Estimates - (Burd et al, 2003)

Emotional	Cost / Year
Bipolar Disorder	$541
Depression	$358
Anxiety	$449
Personality Disorders	$247
Behavior	
Nondependent Drug Use	$868
Conduct Disorder	$448
Oppositional Defiant Disorder	$258
Tics	$198
Medical Disorders	
General Injuries	$972
Acute Sinusitis	$670
Respiratory Illness	$630
Allergies	$507

Another study has estimated the incremental increase in costs of treatment for ADHD with comorbid conditions, compared with treatment of ADHD alone. (Guevara, 2001) and reported additional cost of $583 a year. Health-care costs associated with ADHD are conservatively estimated at $3.3 billion annually (CDC, 2005) or $1,875 per child per year.

Medication

There are no firm figures on how many children are taking stimulants. In the 1980s it was estimated that between 200,000 and 500,000 children were receiving stimulants.

In 1987, 750,000 children were believed to be on stimulations. Both of these figures were the result of extrapolation from regional studies.

A study done (1993) by the University of California, Irvine, Child Development Center estimated that 3 million children were diagnosed with ADHD (Gray, 1998). Ninety percent of these children were on medication or 2.7 million, up some 2 million between 1987 and 1993.

Four years later (1997), 5 million people, most of them school-aged children, were reported being prescribed psychotropic drugs in the US, mostly Ritalin for ADHD.

The 1990s had witnessed a startling increase in the number of children diagnosed with ADHD and a corresponding increase in the use of Ritalin and similar drugs for its treatment. (Gray, 1998)

The Center for Disease Control estimated (2005) that in 2003 there were approximately 4.4 million children (ages 4 - 17) reported to have received a diagnosis of ADHD in their life; of these, 2.5 million (56%) were reported to be taking medication for the disorder. (CDC, 2003)

Sales of ADHD drugs rose to $3.1 billion in 2004 from $759 million in 2000, according to IMS Health, a pharmaceutical information and consulting firm. Adult prescriptions alone jumped 90% from March 2002 to June 2005, according to the FDA. (Shin, 2006)

The problem with these different numbers is that different organizations are doing different estimates with different procedures. The CDC estimate was based upon parental report of diagnosis and medication treatment via telephone survey, and excluded institutionalized persons and non-caucasian individuals, and thus is probably an under-representation of the numbers.

Medical Costs: Family members: medicine
Medical Costs- General

The studies in this area can be divided between those that compare the ADHD subject to another condition (usually normal) and calculate the differences. Table 12 presents the studies that employed this result and the resulting data.

The table reflects an average incremental cost of an ADHD child of some $1,089 greater than a normal child. For an adult, the corresponding figure is $3,048. The overall average yearly incremental cost is $1,578. Thus, from the age of 7 to 21, the total cost would be some $15,246. For an adult (ages 21-50), the cost would be $91,440.

Liebson et al. (2001) had calculated direct medical costs and determined that the ADHD child mean costs for a 9 year period was more than double that of other individuals ($4,306 vs. $1,944). The study did not include outpatient pharmacy costs or mental health visits. Table 12 averaged that value over the 9-year period to obtain a yearly cost for the Liebson value.

Table 12 – Costs of ADHD child

Study	Year	Subjects	ADHD	Normals	Difference
Birnbaum, 2005	1996-8	ages 7-14	$3,525	$1,398	$2,127
Burd, 2003a	1996-7	age 0-21	$870	$663	$207
Swensen, 2003	1996-8	age 0-18	$2,046	$703	$1,343
Mandell, 2003	1993-6	ages 3-15	$1,630	$74	$1,566
Leibson, 2001	1987-95	ages 5-19	$684	$309	$375
Matza, 2005		children			$923
Average	**Child**	**across 6 studies**	**$1,751**	**$629**	**$1,089**
Secnik, 2005b	1999-2001	ages 18-64			
		outpatient costs	$3,009	$1,491	$1,518
		inpatient costs	$1,259	$514	$745
		prescription drug costs	$1,673	$1,008	$665
	Adults	**Total**	**$5,941**	**$3,013**	**$2,928**
Matza, 2005		Adults	$5,290	$2,122	$3,168
	Averaged	**across 8 studies**	**$2,449**	**$1,027**	**$1,578**

From a national perspective, the excess ADHD-related treatment costs were $0.13 billion for women and $0.40 billion for men, and the excess overall healthcare costs were $4.79 billion for women and $8.51 billion for men. (Birnbaum et al. 2005)

Medical Costs of ADHD Family Members

Family members of individuals affected with ADHD had 1.6 times as many medical claims as matched control individuals without a family member diagnosed with ADHD (matching based on age, gender, geographical location, and employment status). This greater healthcare utilization resulted in increased costs. Annual direct per-capita medical costs were twice as much for family members of ADHD patients ($2,740) than for family members of control patients ($1,365). Indirect costs related to disability and absenteeism followed a similar pattern (family members of ADHD patients, $888; family members of controls, $551). (Swenson, 2003)

Indirect Costs on Families

For example, the indirect costs (employee productivity and work loss) and direct costs (therapies and medication) to a family with an ADHD child are 90% more than those for families with unaffected children (Business Week, 2004)

Medicine

No other nation comes close to the US in the production and use of Ritalin. Ninety percent of all Ritalin is produced and used in the United States. Only Australia is close to the US in per capita use. Canada has seen a comparable rise, although it is still at about one-fourth of per capita use as compared to the United States. Britain has had a policy of intervening with social support for children with ADHD and using Ritalin only as a last resort, although these measures are being attacked because of budget cuts. Sweden prohibits use of the drug. (Gray, 1998)

Medication Choices

Marchetti et al. (2001) examined the costs of six different ADHD drug therapies: generic and branded (Ritalin) MPH immediate release (IR) therapies, two branded MPH extended release (ER) therapies (Concerta and Metadate CD), generic MPH IR/ER, and a combination therapy of amphetamine salts (Adderall). The annual expected cost of treatment with each drug therapy, including costs incurred with physician visits and lab exams, was highest for Adderall at $2,567 (2004 US $) and lowest for Metadate CD at $1,710. The cost for the other therapies ranged from $2,061 (Concerta) to $2,392 (Ritalin).

When per-patient costs are multiplied by ADHD prevalence rates (4.4 million – CDC, 2003), the total expected cost for treating all the ADHD children with medications would range between $7.5 and $11.3 Billion dollars.

Indirect

Adults

Employment

Perhaps the largest consequence of the ADHD diagnosis on the adult is the effect on their careers and income which manifests itself in terms of lower income, loss time from work, less promotion at work and higher job turnover.

Lower Income

The researchers found that ADHD sufferers who had graduated from high school had an annual income $18,900 (10,800 English pounds in 2004) lower than non-sufferers. ADHD sufferers who had a college degree earned $4300 less. (Biederman, 2004a)

"The symptoms of ADHD are very visible to employers. Many of these adults report, for example, that they are the last ones to be considered for promotions." Many adults with ADHD suffer from low incomes, higher risk of divorce, a higher risk of being involved in car crashes and a higher chance of losing their jobs." (Biederman, 2004b)

Adults with ADHD are three times more likely to suffer from stress, depression or other problems with emotion. These emotional and physical effects can cause people with ADHD to "lose" days of their lives. "Lost days" may manifest as a day absent from work or several times throughout the month when the person is not fully engaged both physically and emotionally. About one in four (24%) adults with ADHD said that 11 days per month, on average, they were prevented from normal activities, such as work, due to poor mental or physical health, compared to only 9% of the adults without ADHD. (Biederman, 2004c)

Higher job turnover

Adults with ADHD generally had a higher number of jobs over the course of the past ten years than adults without ADHD. On average, those with ADHD had 5.4 jobs compared to adults without ADHD who had 3.4 jobs. Of those surveyed, only 52% of the adults with ADHD are currently employed, compared to 72% of the adults surveyed without ADHD. (Biederman, 2004c)

ADHD is associated with work-related problems in adulthood such as poor job performance, lower occupational status, less job stability, and increased absence days in comparison to adults without ADHD (Barkley,

2002; Murphy and Barkley, 1996; Secnik et al., 2005a; Bronfenbrenner, 1979).

This poor performance and work loss is likely to have profound economic implications. One study quantified this impact by estimating the excess costs (i.e., the difference between adult ADHD patients and matched controls) related to work loss (Birnbaum et al., 2005). Indirect work loss costs were calculated based on employer payments for disability claims and imputed wages for medically related work absence days (e.g., days in the hospital, physician visits). The excess costs were $1.20 billion for women with ADHD and $2.26 billion for men with ADHD.

Educational

ADHD adults are less likely to be high school or college graduates. Approximately 17% of the adults surveyed with ADHD did not graduate high school, while only 7% of those without ADHD did not graduate from high school. Only 18% of the adults with ADHD graduated from college, compared to 26% of the adults without ADHD. (Biederman, 2004c)

Accident Rates

One study estimated the incidence and cost of accidents among individuals with ADHD using an administrative database of medical, pharmaceutical, and disability claims for national manufacturers' employees, spouses, dependents, and retirees. (Swensen et al, 2004) (Birnbaum, 2004) Analyses were conducted for the whole population, adults alone, children under age 12, and adolescents aged 12 to 18 years. ADHD patients in all age groups were more likely than a matched control group to have at least one accident claim: children - 28% versus 18%; adolescents - 32% versus 23%; and adults - 38% versus 18%. Among adults, the accident-specific direct medical costs were significantly higher among ADHD patients than among the control group ($642 versus $194). Among children and adolescents, there were no significant differences in accident-specific costs between the ADHD groups and the control groups.

Societal Costs

Criminal Behavior

The mean total criminal costs (Swensen et al., 2001) were dramatically greater for ADHD patients than for controls ($12,868 versus $498). All differences were statistically significant. Although this study should be considered a rough estimate, findings strongly suggest that criminality associated with ADHD results in a significant cost to society.

Foster et al., 2005 estimated that the additional public costs per child related to conduct disorder exceeded $70,000 (Foster et al., 2005) during a

7-year period.

Child ADHD Costs
Summarized Costs for Parent and Insurance Company

Direct parental costs are 3 fold: medication (Ritalin - $2,392 (Marchetti et al, 2001)), medical treatment (Leibson et al. 2001) was $375 (Table 11), and therapy (1.35 outpatient trips - $169 (Guevara et al, 2001) or $3,039 per year. The Leibson study did not include medication and therapy costs. The second, more conservative way to calculate the yearly cost is to employ the averaged figure from Table 12, which is $1,089. All these figures are, of course, just estimates and each individual family will have their own particular expense issues.

However, these values assume medication over an entire year period. In one study involving patients who were carefully diagnosed and highly motivated (MTA Cooperative Group, 1999, 2004, 2005), only two-thirds of the patients were treated with any medication during the fourteen-month study.

Indirect annual direct per-capita medical costs were twice as much for family members of ADHD patients ($2,740) than for family members of control patients ($1,365). Indirect costs related to disability and absenteeism followed a similar pattern (family members of ADHD patients, $888; family members of controls, $551). (Birnbaum et al., 2005) The total combined difference is $1089+$337+$1375 or $2801 per year. This cost does not include educational costs if the ADHD student has a comorbid learning disability diagnosis.

If a diagnosis is made at age 5 and treatment is continued until age 18, the total estimated costs would amount to $39,214. Employing an 80% insurance payment and 20% co-payment ratio, the estimated costs to the parents would be $7,842 and to the insurance company $31,371. Although these figures are rough estimates, it would certainly be advantageous to all concerned to have an intervention approach that would substantially reduce these costs, particularly the insurance companies. Neurocognitive intervention is that alternative.

Adult ADHD Costs to the patient and the insurance company

For an adult ADHD, the costs of addressing the condition are somewhat different. Medication costs would remain (Ritalin $2,392). High school graduates with ADHD had household incomes about $18,900 lower than those without the disorder. For college graduates, household incomes were about $4,300 lower (Biderman, 2004b). The average loss of income would be $11,600. Thus over a 40 year career period (age 18-58) an estimated total loss of income would be $464,000.

Using the figures from Table 12 the annual medical costs for an ADHD adult is $3,048. Over a 40-year period, the total costs would be $121,920.

The insurance company (at 80%) would be responsible for $97,536 and the ADHD adult $24,384. Thus overall the diagnoses of ADHD on an adult would result in a loss of ($464,000+$24,384) $488,384 over his/her lifetime.

In conclusion, the overall life-time cost of being an ADHD patient is $496,226 ($488,384 + $7,842) to the patient and his family, and some $128,907 ($97,536+$31,371) to insurance companies. The total cost to all concerned is $625,133.

A Neurocognitive program cost structure is considerably less than $625,000 and should look very appealing to both the parents and the insurance companies if the program can successfully and permanently remediate the ADHD condition. The author of this book believes it can be done.

These figures do not take into account accidents (estimated at $17,920), criminal justice legal costs, etc., and are just rough estimates. However one adjusts these values according to different perspectives, it is clear that the ADHD condition is a very expensive one for all concerned (family, patient, society, and insurance companies).

Chapter 9 – Drugs and the Quality of Life

The other way our society has attempted to address brain functioning problems is with medications. Billions of dollars have been spent on research by the major drug companies to see how it is possible to change the brain's functioning with drugs. Due to the complexity and variability of the human biological system, these attempts yield undesirable side effect problems. Even a relatively safe drug such as aspirin can have severe detrimental effects if entered into the wrong body. The issue for the drug companies then becomes one of risk control and minimization of side effects. This chapter will focus on some of the problems with specific drugs and the research supporting or not supporting their value and effectiveness. Overall, the conclusion is that little benefit is actually gained from the use of medications and the side effect problems can range from minimal to dangerous and life threatening with no certain way to predict the range of responses.

The concept of quality of life has been employed by some reviewers to address the positive effects of medications. A brief discussion will address these arguments.

The Concept of Cost Effectiveness and Quality of Life
Quality of Life of an ADHD child

The concept of quality-adjusted life years (QALYs) is a recent measure of the benefit of a medical intervention. It is based on the number of years of life that would be added by the intervention. Each year in perfect health is assigned the value of 1.0 down to a value of 0 for death. If the extra years would not be lived in full health, for example if the patient would lose a limb, or be blind or be confined to a wheelchair, then the extra life-years are given a value between 0 and 1 to account for this. QALYs are controversial as the measurement is used to calculate the allocation of healthcare resources based upon a ratio of cost per QALY. As a result some people will not receive treatment as it is calculated that the benefit to their quality of life is not warranted by the cost.

Two published studies have utilized decision analytic modeling techniques to assess the cost-effectiveness of drug therapy (i.e. methylphenidate – MPH - Ritalin) for ADHD (Gilmore and Milne, 2001; Lord and Paisley, 2000). These quality-of-life benefits are quantified using utility scores, which have been shown to be feasible and valid for assessment of children with ADHD in the opinion of some authors (Matza et al., 2005; Matza et al. (in press); Secnik et al., 2005b).

Overall, results of the modeling analyses indicate that Ritalin (MPH) is a cost-effective treatment option for children with ADHD. The cost per QALY gained in the Gilmore and Milne (2001) study ranged from $15,509 to $19,281 when considering the short-and medium-term benefits of MPH. The authors note that evidence of cost-effectiveness beyond 6 months is poor. In a Novartis study (manufacturers of Ritalin), the cost per QALY gained was $27,766 (Lord & Paisley, 2000). Each of these studies represented "complete" economic evaluations (i.e. estimated both the incremental costs and incremental effects associated with treatment).

Thus, the mean cost across the two studies was about $22,000 to improve the quality of life of an ADHD child for one year.

Questionnaire Approaches

Other studies have studied the problem with a questionnaire approach. In the Zupancic et al. (1998) study, treatment effectiveness was based on gains in the Conners Teacher Rating Scale, a commonly used teacher-report questionnaire for assessing children's classroom behavior. The medication (MPH) cost of improvement of one standard deviation (6 points on this measure) was $560.

Non-drug related research addressing quality of life issues has also been conducted. Klassen et al. (2005) employed a parental questionnaire approach to the assessment of the quality of life in children and adolescents who are diagnosed ADHD. The questionnaire assessed physical health with the following constructs: physical functioning (PF), role/social limitations as a result of physical health (RP), bodily pain/discomfort (BP), and general health perception (GH). There was no difference between the ADHD and normal group on these measures and the physical measures did not significantly correlate with the psychosocial measures.

The following constructs and effect sizes (in standard deviation units) in the psychosocial domain are displayed in Table 13. The negative values indicate that ADHD families were lower (in SD units) than the normal families. Parental report of increase in comorbid conditions and greater ADHD symptomatology were related to decreased overall quality of life measures (PsS). No financial figure was calculated.

Table 13- Klassen et al. (2005)

Psychosocial Measures	SD Differences between ADHD & Normal Families - sign indicates negative ADHD family effects
Emotional / Behavioral	-1.60
Self-Esteem	-.90
Mental Health	-.97
General Behavior	-1.73
Emotional Impact on Parent	-1.87
Time Impact on Parent	-1.07
Family Activities	-1.95
Family Cohesion	-.66

Drug Types

We will go through the medications currently employed in this area, examine their side effect problems, their current status in research, and current controversies. Some of the material is a symptom list and not a discussion. The reader familiar with this material may prefer to just skip over these sections.

Stimulants

Medicines like Concerta, Metadate, and Ritalin all work by blocking the "reuptake" of the neurotransmitter, dopamine, which allows increased availability of this chemical in the brain, thus promoting improved attention, concentration, behavioral control and mood. Adderall-XR stimulates increased release of dopamine, as well as that of the neurotransmitter, norepinephrine, and blocks the "reuptake" of both neurotransmitters. Strattera is relatively specific to norephinephrine and blocks its reabsorption. The goal of each of these medications is to treat the cortical underarousal that is commonly found in patients with ADHD.

Positron Emission Tomography (PET – blood flow) studies have indicated that dopaminergic brain cells in patients with ADHD tend to "reabsorb" 70% more dopamine (interfering with neural transmission) and receptors appear to "take in" dopamine approximately 16% slower. These two factors may be responsible for the "cortical slowing" demonstrated on the QEEG studies, which we will discuss in a later chapter. (Monastra, web site)

The most commonly used drugs for ADHD are the stimulants. Stimulants are generally considered effective in treating inattentiveness, impulsivity, and hyperactivity. Specific agents include: Concerta (methylphenidate); Ritalin - immediate and extended release (methylphenidate); Adderall - immediate and extended release (amphetamine); Metadate - CD or ER (methylphenidate); Dexadrine (dextroamphetamine); Dextrostat (dextroamphetamine); and Cylert (pemoline).

Common side effects of the stimulant class are: loss of appetite - occurs in 41% of children; trouble sleeping - 28% occurrence; irritability - 26% occurrence; nausea - 23% occurrence; headache - 10% occurrence; weight loss; stuffy nose; and nervousness. Table 14 presents the common side effects of these different medications in terms of the cardiovascular, central nervous system (CNS), gastrointestinal, and endocrine / metabolic systems of the body.

On Feb. 10, 2006, a federal advisory panel reported to the FDA that a "Black Box" warning for all stimulant (Ritalin, Concerta, Methylin and Metadate) drugs due to the reported death of 25 patients should be applied. The "Black Box" label is considered the most serious type of warning. Strattera, a non stimulant, had received the "Black Box" label from the FDA in Sept., 2005. About 3.4 million adults and children have been prescribed Strattera.

Dr. Sax, in his book "Ritalin: Better Living Through Chemistry" (2000), estimated an increase in increase in the number of children taking Ritalin from 150,000 in 1975 to 6 million in 2000 (1 out of 8 children). He also reported that the United States, which is composed of 5% of the world's population, consumes 85% of the world's production of Ritalin and that Ritalin is in the same class of drug as cocaine. The Drug Enforcement Administration (DEA) has always assigned Ritalin to "Schedule II," the same schedule as amphetamine. In other words, the DEA considers Ritalin to have about the same potential for abuse as amphetamine. Laboratory animals given the choice to self-administer cocaine or Ritalin make no distinction between the two.

Table 14- – Potential Adverse Effects of Psychostimulant Medications

Organ System	Adverse Effect	Dextroam-phetamine: Dexedrine Adderall	Ritalin; Concerta	Pemoline Cylert
Cardiovas-cular	Palpitations, Tachycardia, increased blood pressure	yes	yes	not at recommend-ed doses
Central Nervous sys-tem (CNS)	CNS stimu-lation: psychosis, dizziness, insomnia, headache, nervousness, irritability, tics & other involuntary movements	yes, psychosis with prolonged use	yes	yes, all but dizziness, headache
Gastrointes-tinal	Anorexia, nausea, vom-iting, stom-achaches, stomach cramps or pain, dry mouth	yes, all but stomach-aches	yes, all but stomaches	yes, all but vomiting, stomach cramps or pain, dry mouth
Endocrine / metabolic	Weight loss Growth sup-pression	yes -weight loss with prolonged use growth: rebound occurs after cessation	yes -weight loss with pro-longed use growth: re-bound occurs after cessa-tion	yes -weight loss with prolonged use growth: only in doses > 4 mg/kg/day

Other less common side effects not listed.

101

Ritalin
Common Side Effects

Nervousness and insomnia are the most common adverse reactions but are usually controlled by reducing dosage and omitting the drug in the afternoon or evening. Other reactions include hypersensitivity (including skin rash, urticaria, fever, arthralgia, exfoliative dermatitis, erythema multiforme with histopathological findings of necrotizing vasculitis, and thrombocytopenic purpura); anorexia; nausea; dizziness; palpitations; headache; dyskinesia; drowsiness; blood pressure and pulse changes, both up and down; tachycardia; angina; cardiac arrhythmia; abdominal pain; and weight loss during prolonged therapy. (Rxlist.com)

Additional Research Effects
Depression
Preteen Ritalin May Increase Depression
Early Use of ADHD Drug Alters Brain, Rat Studies Show

William A. Carlezon Jr., PhD is the director of the behavioral genetics laboratory at McLean Hospital and associate professor at Harvard Medical School. He reported "Rats exposed to Ritalin as juveniles showed large increases in learned-helplessness behavior during adulthood, suggesting a tendency toward depression." These experiments suggest that preadolescent exposure to Ritalin in rats causes numerous complex behavioral adaptations, each of which endures into adulthood," Carlezon and colleagues conclude: "This work highlights the importance of a more thorough understanding of the enduring neurobiological effects of juvenile exposure to psychotropic drugs." (Carlezon et al., 2003)

The Physician's Desk Reference (PDR), however, fails to mention other possible adverse side effects. According to the American Psychiatric Association, SUICIDE is the major adverse consequence of withdrawal from Ritalin and similar drugs. Suicides and attempted suicides by children on Ritalin have occurred when the drug was withdrawn or the dosage reduced. Suicides and attempted suicides have also occurred at normal dose levels without warning.

Clarke (1997), in his book, "How Psychiatry is making drug addicts out the America's school children" provides additional information in this area.

Cancer
Does Ritalin Increase Cancer Risk in Children?
Small Study Suggests Possible Chromosome Damage,

but Some Experts Skeptical

All 12 of the children included in the study experienced a 3 fold increase in chromosome abnormalities three months after starting Ritalin. (El-Zein et al., 2005) Chromosome damage has been linked to heightened cancer risk and to other health problems. "We all have chromosomal breaks," he says. "That is part of the normal behavior of a cell. But fortunately, we have repair mechanisms which keep us from getting into trouble." (Kattlove, 2005)

Ritalin is a stimulant widely prescribed for the treatment of attention deficit hyperactivity disorder (ADHD), with roughly 10 million prescriptions filled each year in the United States. The amphetamine-like drug has been approved for more than five decades. But sales of Ritalin and chemically similar drugs increased by more than 500% in the 1990s.

Death

Between 1990 and 2000 there were 186 deaths from methylphenidate reported to the FDA. (MedWatch) In June 2005, the FDA announced it would be investigating all attention deficit hyperactivity disorder drugs including Strattera, Ritalin, Concerta, and Adderall in response to reports of serious psychiatric side effects in patients taking Concerta and Ritalin.

Adderall

The medication was approved by the Federal Drug Administration for ADHD in 1996. Adderall is the new variation on one of the first stimulants, dexedrine, which is designed to produce a more even effect over about six hours per dose

Side effects

Accidental injury, changes in sex drive, constipation, depression, diarrhea, dizziness, dry mouth, emotional instability, exaggerated feelings of well-being, fatigue, fever, headache, high blood pressure, hives, impotence, indigestion, infections, insomnia, loss of appetite, mental disturbances, nausea, nervousness, overstimulation, rapid or pounding heartbeat, restlessness, stomach and intestinal disturbances, tremor, twitches, unpleasant taste, vomiting, weakened heart, weight loss, and worsening of tics (including Tourette's syndrome).

Health Canada suspended Adderall XR

Health Canada has suspended marketing of Adderall XR products from the Canadian market due to concern about reports of sudden unexplained death (SUD) in children taking Adderall and Adderall XR. Sudden unexplained death (SUD) has been associated with amphetamine abuse and reported in children with underlying cardiac abnormalities taking recommended doses of amphetamines, including Adderall and Adderall XR. In addition, a very small number of cases of SUD have been reported in children without structural cardiac abnormalities taking Adderall. (Health Canada, 2005) The FDA has concluded that **recommended doses** of Adderall can cause SUD and is continuing to carefully evaluate these data.

Cylert (Pemoline)
Side Effects
The following CNS effects have been reported with the use of Cylert: convulsive seizures; literature reports indicate that Cylert may precipitate attacks of Gilles de la Tourette syndrome; hallucinations; dyskinetic movements of the tongue, lips, face and extremities: abnormal oculomotor function including nystagmus and oculogyric crisis; mild depression; dizziness; increased irritability; headache; and drowsiness. Insomnia is the most frequently reported side effect of Cylert. It usually occurs early in therapy prior to an optimum therapeutic response. In the majority of cases, it is transient in nature or responds to a reduction in dosage.

Gastrointestinal:
Anorexia and weight loss may occur during the first weeks of therapy. In the majority of cases it is transient in nature; weight gain usually resumes within three to six months. Nausea and stomachache have also been reported. There have been isolated reports of transient psychotic symptoms occurring in adults following the long- term misuse of excessive oral doses of pemoline.

Concerta
Concerta was FDA approved for treatment of ADHD on 8/2000. It is a reformulation of Ritalin for sustained delivery.

Side Effects
The most common side effects reported were headache (14%), upper respiratory tract infection (8%), stomach ache (7%), vomiting (4%), loss of appetite (4%), sleeplessness (4%), increased cough (4%), sore throat (4%), sinusitis (3%), and dizziness (2%). Other side effects are reduced stature, ticks, "zombie" demeanor, stomachaches, moodiness, and death. (ADHDHelp.org)

Antidepressant Drugs
Antidepressants are considered second line agents for ADHD, and are used in individuals who did not respond to stimulants, experienced intolerable side effects from stimulants, or developed or worsened tics. Tri-

cyclic antidepressants (TCA's) are useful in treating hyperactivity and inattentiveness, but lack efficacy for impulsiveness. (Calis et al., 1990)

The most commonly used tricyclic antidepressants for ADHD include Imipramine, Desipramine, Nortriptyline, and Amitriptyline. TCA's may cause a variety of side effects, including fatigue and sedation, constipation, dry mouth, and blurred vision.

Strattera
Adverse Effects

Straterra side effects include dizziness, dry mouth, nausea or vomiting, tiredness, mood swings, decreased appetite, weight loss, and sleepiness. Depression, tics, mood swings and irritability are also side effects shared by Straterra and other ADHD drug medication. Straterra can increase heart rate and blood pressure like other ADHD drug medications. Though rare, some patients have reported hives and allergic reactions to Straterra.

Strattera is the only non-stimulant medication approved by the FDA for the treatment of attention-deficit/hyperactivity disorder (ADHD) in children, adolescents, and adults. Strattera is a norepinephrine reuptake inhibitor, a class of ADHD treatment that works differently from the other ADHD medications available. Strattera has been prescribed to over 2 million patients since it was approved in 2002.

Eli Lilly warned doctors to stop prescribing Strattera for patients with jaundice or for those patients who show signs of liver damage and warned that Strattera can cause severe drug related liver injury that can progress to acute liver failure resulting in death or the need for a liver transplant. In December, 2004, the FDA updated Strattera's label to include the serious liver side effects.

Clonidine - Antihypertensives

Another medication that is used to treat ADHD is found in the antihypertensive class. The drug is Clonidine and is generally used in conjunction with stimulants. It is rarely used alone because it is effective for impulsivity and hyperactivity only. Clonidine's side effects include sedation, dry mouth, blurred vision, constipation, and heart effects. (Biederman and Spencer, 2000)

Research Effectiveness of the Medications
Ritalin

According to Dr. Diller in his book Running on Ritalin (1999), studies conducted in the 1960s show that drug treatment, isolated from behavioral modification and talk therapy, produces no long-term benefits for the child. In these studies, researchers found that children treated only with Ritalin were just as likely as the ADHD population as a whole to suffer problems of unfinished education, drug addiction, and criminal behavior.

Dr. Diller's statement was matched by the findings of the major research review released by the National Institutes of Health (NIH) (1998), which acknowledged that behavioral changes as a result of Ritalin use did not translate into significant "improvements in academic skills or social achievement." On the other hand, numerous studies indicate Ritalin is highly effective in keeping kids quiet. Since Dr. Diller's book was written, it has been documented that the future drug addiction problem has proven to be possibly inaccurate (Biederman et al., 1999), that psychotherapy does not improve the core symptoms of ADHD, and that medications can improve the core symptoms of ADHD, but that there is no evidence of long-term positive effects of medications.

Miller et al (1998) estimated that in 10-40% of treated cases stimulant medication for ADHD may have been prescribed inappropriately.

Investigators reported in Pediatrics (Biederman et al., 1999) that ADHD adolescent subjects receiving medication have an 85% risk reduction for substance abuse disorder (SUD). However, boys who had not received treatment for ADHD were at a significantly increased risk for any SUD when compared with the treated ADHD and control groups; 75% of the untreated ADHD subjects developed SUD in adolescence, versus 25% of the treated group and 18% of the control group. Conduct disorder and parental SUD were associated with an increased risk for SUD in all groups.

The OHSU (2005) review of the literature reported on 2 studies, each of which found no difference for the stimulant-treated group compared to controls on subsequent use of tobacco, marijuana or alcohol. (Noble, 1972; Nolan et al., 1997)

In conclusion, ADHD predisposes (particularly for those subjects with conduct disorder and parental substance abuse) the subject to substance abuse. Medication may reduce the risk.

Comprehensive Overview of Effectiveness of Drugs for ADHD – OHSU review

The Oregon Health and Science University (OHSU) published, in Sept. 2005, the Drug Class Review and Pharmacologic Treatments for ADHD. The report looked at the comparative effectiveness and safety of the various medications for ADHD. The medications reviewed were: Stimulants (amphetamine mixture, methylphenidate HCL, Dexmethylphe-

nidate HCL, Pemoline, Modafinil)
Non-stimulants (atomoxetine HCL)
Antidepressants (Bupropion HCL),
antihypertensives (Clonidine HCL, Guanfacine HCL))
Atypical antipsychotic medications (Aripiprazole, Clozapine, Olanzapine, Quetiapine, Risperidone, Ziprasidone).

They noted that the antihypertensives, Bupropion and the atypical antipsychotic medications are not currently approved for use in ADHD.

The review looked at 2,287 articles addressing use of the drug in children and adults and narrowed the selection to 180 after applying their eligibility and exclusion criteria for research studies. They noted that three previous reviews in this area in Canada, the UK, and the US had failed to find evidence for difference in efficacy or side effects when comparing MPH IR & SR, Dex, atomoxetine (Strattera), pemoline (cylert), and bupripon & clonidine.

The summary of the review indicated that the quality of research varied between poor to good but the overall conclusion was that "no conclusions about comparative effectiveness of different pharmacotherapies for ADHD can be made." (page 56) In other words, they all obtain about the same result.

There were some additional points of interest from the report that included such summary statements as:

In one study (NIH, 2004) families were contacted after the end of a 14-month study (N=579). Medication alone resulted in better scores on ADHD and ODD symptoms than behavioral therapy and community care. However, effect size changes for the combined medication and therapy groups were +.60 SD while the therapy group alone obtained effect size changes of +.30 SD. For ADHD symptoms and for ODD symptoms the comparative numbers were +.39 SD (medication plus therapy) and +.21 (therapy alone). Previous studies had reported a dissipation of the effect over time.

OSHU Report: Medication Adverse Effects

Ritalin (MPH IR (immediate release)) (age 3-5) was clearly associated with higher rates of increased sadness, decreased appetite and sociability impairments than placebo after 7-10 days in 31 preschoolers. This result provides some support for the Carlezon et al., 2003 rat study. In elementary school children (age 6-12), adverse effects were noted in 18 (of 39) head-to-head trials. (OHSU report, pg 38)

Clonidine was found to have significantly higher rates and greater severity of sedation among children with both ADHD and Tourette's disorder.

In adolescents, MPH IR was associated with significant appetite and sleep disturbances across some, but not in all placebo-controlled trials. Adolescents frequently reported increases in dulled affect, social withdrawal, irritability, and stomachache in two placebo-controlled trials. Adolescents taking pemoline in two trials also reported insomnia at a greater frequency than those taking placebo. Other adverse events included loss of appetite, stomachaches, and "picking" at skin.

"In summary, randomized controlled trials do not provide evidence that any one stimulant is more tolerable than another or that nonstimulants are more tolerable than stimulants." Ritalin (MPH IR) studies showed inconclusive effects on children's height and weight and no significant effect on worsening or causing onset of tic behavior (pg 45). No evidence was found for efficacy of the atypical anti-psychotic medications. Atomoxetine (Strattera) showed higher rates of insomnia, appetite loss, and withdrawal due to adverse effects. (Oshu Review, 2005) (pg. 58)

In conclusion, although the stimulant approach appears to be grounded in neuroscience research regarding dopamine, there is evidence supporting the following conclusions:

1)	No evidence that one stimulant medication works better than another.
2)	No evidence that stimulants have any positive effect on academic performance or do much more than calm the child.
3)	Considerable risk of side effect problems.
4)	SD effect sizes of +.18 to +.30 on behavioral questionnaires.
5)	Considerable prevalence of over prescribing.
6)	Conflicting evidence whether medication use decreases future drug use.
7)	No long-term assessment effect after medication is stopped (Monastra & Monastra, 2002, 2004, 2005)
8)	Is costly over time.

Now let's examine biofeedback's benefits that have been reported to date. These details will be elaborated on in later chapters.

1)	No published, researched side effect problem. Sporadic, anecdotal clinical reports of negative effects lack scientific confirmation and thus could be present due to multiple causes. However, it has been noted (Lubar, 2003; Monastra, 2003), clinically, that when EEG biofeedback is employed in conjunction with stimulation medication there can be increased irritability, moodiness, and hyperactivity. These responses typically occur in the mid to late phase of the treatment process with patients who are improving their EEG patterns. Reduction of the medication generally eliminates the problem. Additional side effects noted (Monastra, 2005) were headaches and dizziness (1-3%) which typically respond positively to a brief resting period or consumption of food.

However, it is clear from the literature that use of inappropriate protocols (such as increasing theta, increasing beta in obsessive compulsive cases) can have negative effects. The use of a database and an awareness of this potential can mitigate against these potential problems. This issue is an additional argument for expertise and the use of a database in pursuing this type of treatment. One size does not fit all.

2)   Decreased use or cessation of medication from 50% to 80% (Lubar et al., 1995; Thompson and Thompson, 1998; Monastra, 2005) in treated subjects.

3)   Maintenance of gains after cessation of program up to ten years. (Lubar et al., 2003; Tansey, 1993)

4)   SD effect sizes range from +.50 SD to +3.50 SD on objective cognitive measures.

5)   Significant improvement in academic performance and self-esteem.

6)   Considerably less expensive to obtain a QALY ($5-$10 thousand) compared to $22 thousand for the medication approach.

7)   Considerably less expensive when long-term costs of ADHD are examined.

It has been argued in the literature that 20 hours of treatment is sufficient for the ADHD problem (Steinberg and Othmer, 2004). While this may be true in certain cases, it is advisable to expand the option of more treatments to address other problems not assessed in the typical situation or perceived without a thorough Neurocognitive evaluation. The effect of the treatment, however, is much greater than one year, as ten-year follow up studies have demonstrated (Lubar et al., 1995; Lubar et al., 2003; Tansey, 1993).

Chapter 10 - What is the EEG?
What is traditional EEG?
The signal

The original analog EEG recording involved the direct, continuous printing of the brain's electrical signal onto paper. The sensors record the electrical activity generated by a thin strip (1.5 - 4.5 millimeters) of cortical gray matter that resides just below the scalp. The signal recorded does not directly pick up the electrical activity in subcortical parts of the brain. With the advent of the digital age, the electrical signal of the brain could be translated into numbers and the information stored on a hard disk. This development allowed for:

1)   development of concepts with precise mathematical definitions which referred to the different aspects of the signal and

2)   comparing an individual's value on a measure to a normative reference group.

This approach also minimized the use of human judgment in the analysis of the EEG data. The only human judgment that was involved was in the artifacting of the data. Artifacting of the EEG data refers to the deletion of the data which does not represent the electrical activity of the brain but rather extraneous signals generated mostly either by eye movement or muscle activity. Other sources of artifact are also possible. Once artifacting is accomplished, the analysis becomes a number crunching exercise conducted solely by software. Once the statistical analysis is completed, an examination of the data based upon neuropsychological and neuroanatomical knowledge becomes particularly relevant.

The locations

The traditional 10-20 EEG system is employed in the location of the sensors (Figure 12). The 10-20 system localizes the sensors in a consistent manner across different head sizes to ensure that the locations of the sensors reside on similar anatomical locations, despite differences in head size. The consistent locations are obtained with different sized nylon caps that can stretch to adjust to different head circumferences.

The information recorded by the sensors is sent to a computer that digitally analyzes the signal. The analysis employs what is called a sine wave or Hertz approach. This nomenclature refers to how many waves of a given frequency are evident during a certain time period, which is called an epoch (usually one second). There are certain common definitions or labels for certain waveforms, which occur within a certain frequency during an epoch.

The standard frequency ranges are delta (0-4 Hertz), theta (4-8 Hertz), alpha (8-13 Hertz) and beta (13+ Hertz). Figure 16 visually presents these frequency ranges. However, not all investigators use the same frequency definitions, leading to difficulties in interpreting across studies. Most investigators don't analyze the data above 32 Hertz, due to the erroneous historical belief that signals above that frequency are dominated by muscle activity. The availability of data beyond the 32 Hertz range has proven to be a critical component in the analysis of cognitive function, especially in the traumatic brain injury case. (Thornton, 1999a, 1999b, 2000a, 2002a, 2002b; Thornton and Carmody, 2005a, 2005b, 2006)

Figure 16 - Standard Frequencies

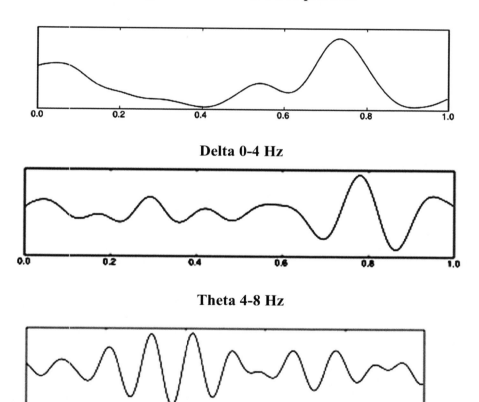

Delta 0-4 Hz

Theta 4-8 Hz

Alpha 8-13 Hz

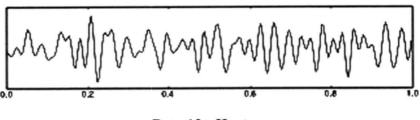

Beta 13+ Hertz

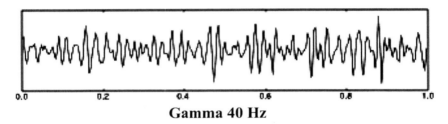

Gamma 40 Hz

There are two general classes of qEEG measures. The first class examines the type of activity at each of the 19 locations in reference to a specific frequency. The value is usually collected over a period of time or epoch. This period of time can vary according to how the evaluator collects the data. Examples of such quantitative measurements include the following:

Type of Activity at a location

The measures that we will be examining in the examples section include the following.

Magnitude: The average strength in absolute magnivolts of the signal of a band during an epoch. This measure merely reflects how strong the signal is in terms of magnivolts. The measure is affected by the skull thickness. If an individual has a very thick skull, the magnitudes will be lower than for a person with a thin skull. This is purely a reflection of the problem of measuring signals through a thick substance (the skull).

Relative Power: The magnivolts of the particular band divided by the total magnivolts generated by all bands at a location, averaged over the epoch time period. This measure is insensitive to skull thickness as it measures the total magnivolts at a location and determines the percentage of the total magnivolts that are within a particular frequency range.

Peak Frequency: The highest frequency obtained during an epoch within a frequency range. For example, if we are looking at the alpha frequency (8-13 Hertz) during an epoch, and during a particular part of the

112

epoch the alpha frequency "hits" its highest frequency (between the 8 and 13 Hertz range) of 11, then the peak frequency is 11.

Additional measures that are available are as follows. However, these variables did not prove useful in the original research (Thornton, 2001)

Peak Amplitude: The peak value in magnivolts of a frequency band during an epoch.

Symmetry: The peak amplitude symmetry between two locations (A & B) in a particular bandwidth – i.e. defined as (A-B)/(A+B). This measure analyzes the amplitude relationships that are not necessarily dependent upon connection activity, but reflect differences in activity levels between different locations.

Spectral Power: The square of the magnivolts of a frequency during an epoch.

Connection patterns

The second major class of variables addresses the issue of the connectivity patterns between locations. These variables are assumed to reflect the activity occurring in the long myelinated fibers connecting the different regions and are known as the white matter of the brain. Both are important contributors to effective cognitive function. The coherence variable proved to be the more powerful predictor in the original research, especially with adults. These variables are:

Coherence: The average amplitude similarity between the waveforms of a particular band in two locations over an epoch. This variable is defined within a particular frequency range.

Phase: The time lag between two locations of a particular band as defined by how soon after the beginning of an epoch a particular waveform at location #1 is matched in amplitude at location #2. The measurement time period for this variable is considerably less than for the coherence variable and can occur over a period of milliseconds.

Figure 17 presents a graphic display of the visual meaning of the coherence concept.

Figure 17 Coherence : Locations A and B have high coherence values, while B and C have low coherence values

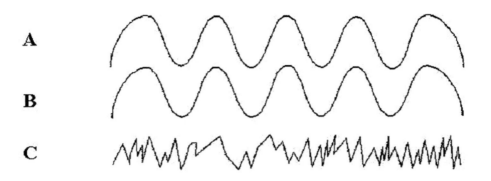

A

B

C

The "meaning" of the frequencies.

When we are asleep the EEG pattern is predominantly one of delta waves, although during dreaming (REM stage – rapid eye movement) the brain will generate beta activity. The awake brain is producing different frequencies at the same time and thus an epoch can contain multiple frequency ranges simultaneously. The "meaning" of a frequency could be understood as the mental state that the dominant frequency is associated with. For example, the theta frequency has been associated with a "dreamy" state, the alpha frequency with a relaxed state of mind and the beta frequency with a cognitive working brain. Coherence and phase have been interpreted as representing the strength of the connections between different locations or reflecting the amount of white matter connecting the brain's locations.

A useful way to understand these values is to view them as representing communication abilities. As coherence is represented by a value obtained for an entire epoch, it is a more useful variable than the phase figure that represents activity during a very short, arbitrarily selected time period. Labels can be useful but they can also blind us to alternate meanings. For example, theta can be viewed as a negative "dreamy" state, yet creativity could involve the theta frequency. When we try to recall information during a test, excessive amounts of high frequency beta (associated with anxiety) would inhibit our ability to recall facts resulting in the well-known test anxiety situation. In the testing situation, it can be more productive for the mind to "go into" a theta state to recall the information. There is also the issue of the ability of the mind to shift between different frequencies and to employ different locations for different tasks. Although there has been substantial growth in our understanding during the past several decades, we still don't have satisfactory answers to many questions or even know if we are asking the right questions. The next chapter will address some of the basic questions that have been addressed successfully.

Chapter 11 - The quantitative EEG (qEEG)

There are several critical questions regarding the qEEG technology.

1- Does the qEEG technology provide reliable data?

The question of the reliability of the qEEG signal was the focus of initial investigations.

Hughes & John. (1999) concluded:

"The independence of the normative QEEG descriptors from cultural and ethnic factors enables objective assessment of brain integrity in persons of any age, origin, or background. This independence and specificity, as well as high replicability, has been established in studies from Barbados, China, Cuba, Germany, Holland, Japan, Korea, Mexico, Netherlands, Sweden, the United States, and Venezuela."....." Numerous studies have confirmed the high specificity of normative distributions of power in the delta, theta, alpha, and beta bands. Positive findings different from the normative database in healthy, normally functioning individuals have repeatedly been shown to be within the chance levels, with very high test-retest reliability. (Niedermeyer, 1987; Oken, 1988)

This statement indicates that the values obtained for the different frequencies during a qEEG session are the same no matter what country the individual is from.

There is, in addition, a large genetic component to the qEEG parameters (vanBeijsterveldt et al., 2000). Studies indicate that the effect size of the genetic component varies between 76% and 89% (vanBeijsterveldt et al., 1996) and that around 60% of the variance in theta, alpha, and beta coherence was explained by genetic factors. Environmental factors did not seem to affect the coherence values (vanBeijsterveldt et al., 1998) Swets (1987) asserted that the qEEG is more reliable than other modern medical testing such as mammograms, cervical screenings, or CT brain scans.

The average test – retest reliability of 50-second samples of artifact free qEEG in the hands of a competent person is >.90. (Thatcher et al., 2003) McEvoy et al. (2000) demonstrated that the test-retest reliability of the qEEG signal is greatly enhanced under task or activation conditions, as it requires the subject to focus on a specific tasks, while the subject's state during the eyes closed condition may be expected to differ (due to vigilance, anxiety, cognitive processing variations). Seven-day test-retest reliabilities were higher for the activation condition (mean of .93) versus the eyes closed condition (mean of .84) and even within a single EEG ac-

116

quisition session, reliability varied more during the resting condition (.74 to .97) than the activation condition (.92 to .99) when analyzing particular frequency bands (theta, alpha).

These mathematical values simply indicate that cognitive activation tasks elicit more similar electrical response patterns than an eyes closed, resting condition when comparing two different time periods. This similarity of response pattern for a particular cognitive task across time makes intuitive sense. Why would the brain generate a completely different response pattern for the same task just because the same task occurred two days later? Human behavior is composed of a number of habit response patterns. We get up every morning, we got to work, etc. Very specific situations will often elicit the exact same verbal or emotional response. If such a complex human behavior such as going to work can easily become a routinized habit, then it would appear to be self-evident that the smaller units would also function as habits.

The logic of the habit response system can be easily carried down to the basic electrophysiological level of certain neurons in certain brain locations. In addition, it would be illogical to assume that a complex behavior can be a habit, yet the individual elements of the complex behavior do not function in that manner, but randomly.

2- Can the technology differentiate between clinical conditions?
a) Psychiatric conditions

During the last decade, more than 500 EEG and qEEG papers have reported well-designed studies, concurring that consistent EEG and qEEG abnormalities are found in a high proportion of psychiatric patients with the same diagnosis. The research findings have satisfied the criteria of statistical significance and have shown different patterns between different diagnostic categories. The integration of the qEEG findings with other modern neurodiagnostic testing such as MEG, fMRI, DTI, SPECT, and PET continues to be a fruitful scientific area and will remain so for decades to come as our measurement abilities continue to evolve. This book, however, will not focus on these conditions in terms of specific finding

b) ADHD/LD conditions

In reference to the subject population we are concerned with, the authors note, "In QEEG studies, a high incidence of excess theta or decreased alpha and/or beta activity has been reported in specific developmental learning disabled (SDLD) children (John et al., 1983; Ahn et al., 1980; Matsuura et al., 1993; Dykman et al., 1982; John et al., 1977; Kaye et al., 1997; Dykman et al., 1982; Gasser et al., 1983; Lubar et al., 1985; Lubar et al., 1991;

Marosi et al., 1992), with theta or alpha excess often seen in children with ADD or ADHD. The types of QEEG abnormalities found in SDLD children are related to academic performance. (Harmony et al., 1990) A large percentage of children with attention deficit problems (more than 90%) show QEEG signs of cortical dysfunction, the majority displaying frontal theta or alpha excess, hypercoherence, and a high incidence of abnormal interhemispheric asymmetry. (Marosi et al., 1992; Mann et al., 1992; Evans, 1996)

Using QEEG measures, it has been possible to discriminate reliably ADD/ADHD versus normal children, with a specificity of 88% and a sensitivity of 94%, (Chabot et al., 1996) and ADD versus SDLD children, with a sensitivity of 97% and a specificity of 84.2% (Chabot et al., 1996). " Children with ADHD or ADD could be distinguished from LD children with a sensitivity of 97% and a specificity of 84.2% (Chabot, 2005). A Thatcher et al. (2002) study employed theta/beta ratios, amplitude asymmetries and coherence values to obtain an ability to discriminate between normal and LD children with a 99.43% overall classification accuracy. The variables were validated on a second group of LD and ADD children and obtained an overall cross-validation classification accuracy of 96.95%.

The concept of sensitivity refers to the ability of a test to indicate that an individual could have condition A, B, C, etc. The specificity concept refers to the ability of a test to indicate that the person has condition A and not B or C.

In contrast, "The conventional EEG has been reported to be abnormal in 30% to 60% of children with ADHD or with specific learning disability (SLD or LD), as reviewed by several authors. (Small et al., 1993; Fein et al., 1983; Hughes & John, 1999; Fein et al., 1986; Byring et al., 1991; Flynn et al., 1989; Hughes, 1971) Reported abnormalities have often included diffuse slowing and decreased alpha activity." This direct comparison underscores the superiority of the qEEG in the detection of the LD child. The position paper of the Electrodiagnostic and Clinical Neuroscience Society (Hughes and John, 1999) concluded that qEEG assessment was recommended in the **ADHD and Learning disability situation.**

Figure 18 reflects the qEEG patterns that have been discovered for the ADHD and LD diagnostic situations. (Chabot et al, 2005) The ADHD group (95%) has two patterns. The first is a pattern of high alpha and low delta values combined with high frontal coherence values. The second pattern is characterized by high levels of theta activity, low levels of peak frequency of alpha and high frontal coherence patterns. The learning disabled patterns can include the ADHD patterns as well as a patterns characterized by high theta and delta (with low alpha) or high alpha and delta (with low beta and theta). Both of these additional groups evidence low frontal coherence patterns. The research results in discriminating ADHD from normals has sufficiently advanced to be considered a diagnostic test in the psychiatric field (Boutros et al., 2005). Although children have been the primary subject population of the research, the elevated theta levels have also been reported in adult samples (Bresnahan & Barry, 2002). Of some interest to note is that theta values are "resistant" to aging, while the beta values can improve with age (Lazzaro et al., 1998).

It is of some value to address a technical issue regarding the discriminate nature of the theta variable. Initial research and interventions in this area focused on the magnivolt measure of a particular frequency as the critical value (see Chapter 10) and calculated ratio measures between the theta and beta magnivolt values. The ratio approach has some inherent limitations as the ratio value could change as a result of either variable changing. The Boutros et al. (2005) study reported that the theta relative power (see Chapter 10) value had greater mean effect size than the theta magnivolt measure (.91 vs .59) across all studies reviewed. For the nine studies in which both values were available the mean effect size was 1.07 (relative power) and .70 (absolute power).

These are broad electrophysiological patterns. It should be kept in mind that individual patterns will fall into these categories to different degrees. One of the tenets of this book is that although these research findings are definitely useful and move the science ahead, from a clinical point of view it must always be the individual case that determines the intervention protocols. For example, elevations in theta activity was reported evident in the occipital regions (O1-O2) in a group of ADHD children (Ucles & Lorente, 1996). We cannot intervene based upon group data. This will become very clear when we discuss the examples.

Figure 18 - See insert at end of book - page 316

c) Traumatic Brain Injury

Relation between qEEG variables and Cognition in TBI

Much of the original work on the relationship between the qEEG signal and cognition collected the qEEG data under eyes closed conditions and then correlated those values with well-known cognitive measures, such as the IQ test. Different investigators reported the results with terms such as level or activity. These references can refer to magnitudes, relative power, etc. These different measures are empirically highly intercorrelated.

Do the qEEG variables let us know if someone had a TBI?

Yes - Discriminate functions

Thatcher et al. (1991) sought to discriminate between normal and TBI subjects under the eyes closed condition and obtained discriminate values at or above .90 across three independent samples. The predominant finding was decreased posterior alpha and increased posterior beta activity, frontal connection abnormalities, and some long cortico-cortico connection deviations in the TBI group compared to the controls. What this means is that he developed a formula based on one group of TBI patients and was able to use that equation to determine whether an individual had a TBI with a very high degree of accuracy. The subjects were all within one year of accident.

Trudeau et al. (1998) demonstrated high discriminant accuracy of qEEG for the evaluation of combat veterans with a history of blast injury. Summarizing this body of research, he concluded, "EEG coherence has been shown to be the most sensitive EEG measure of TBI." He also concluded, "the standard or "routine EEG" and "conventional MRI" are essentially useless for the detection of TBI because of their low sensitivity and low reliability in detecting mild to moderate TBI (e.g. <20% accuracy in routine visual EEG and visual MRI)."

All the above-cited studies have focused on frequency ranges below the 32-Hertz range and have not investigated EEG activity under task conditions. Collectively, the studies have indicated elevated beta levels following the trauma, as well as decreased alpha in posterior locations, connection abnormalities, decreased alpha and beta amplitudes in frontal location, increased variance, and nonspecific generalized slowing. Some of the studies appear to have conflicting results (i.e. increased posterior beta, reduction in fast beta), possibly due to differing definitions of the frequency ranges studied or to differences in length of time since injury. Hughes and John (1999) concluded "there is a broad consensus that increased focal or diffuse theta, decreased alpha, decreased coherence and increased asymmetry are common EEG indicators of the post concussion syndrome." This position paper of the Electrodiagnostic and Clinical Neuroscience Society concluded that qEEG assessment was recommended in the traumatic brain injury situation.

The important frequency that was overlooked (32-64 Hertz) - gamma.
High frequency EEG activity in the TBI and LD subject

The 40-Hertz rhythm (gamma band) in animals has been found to be associated with the acquisition of learning. Basar et al. (1996) indicated that the 40 Hz rhythm exists spontaneously and can be evoked in the human brain, and suggested that it may have multiple functions in sensory and cognitive processing. Forty-Hertz activity has also been found during problem solving in children (Sheer, 1974) and adults (DeFrance and Sheer, 1988). Miltner et al. (1999) found increases in gamma-band activity and gamma coherence between areas of the brain that undergo an associative learning procedure. Although more research is needed to clarify the role of 40 Hz activity in brain function, these early findings suggest the possibility that this frequency may be an important missing element in the understanding of the TBI and LD patient.

The important condition that was not examined – The Activation condition.

Activation Conditions and the TBI patient

We know that we can obtain better reliabilities across different time periods if we examine the brain during a task versus just waiting with their eyes closed. The reliability concept refers to the consistency of the response pattern.

McEvoy et al. (2000) demonstrated that the test-retest reliability of the qEEG signal is greatly enhanced under task or activation conditions, as it requires the subject to focus on a specific tasks, while the subject's state during the eyes-closed condition may be expected to differ (due to vigilance, anxiety, cognitive processing variations). Seven-day test-retest reliabilities were higher for the activation condition (mean of .93) versus the eyes-closed condition (mean of .84) and even within a single EEG acquisition session, reliability varied more during the resting condition (.74 to .97) than the activation condition (.92 to .99) when analyzing particular frequency bands (theta, alpha).

The activation condition has proved to be useful in determining whether a subject had experienced a TBI. In two studies, Thornton (1999a, 1999b) compared TBI subjects (n=32) and normal controls (n=52) under eyes closed resting and activation conditions. The activation conditions were tasks involving auditory attention, visual attention and listening to paragraphs. In addition to measuring the traditional brain frequencies (1 to 32 Hz), this study measured higher frequencies in the 32 to 64 Hz range. An analysis of the EEG data collected in the eyes closed condition led to correct classification of 100% correct of subjects as belonging to the TBI or normal control group (for accidents occurring within 1 year of evaluation) and 93% (for all subjects regardless of time since accident). Separate analysis based upon each of the activation measures yielded respective percent cor-

121

rect hit rates of 95% (auditory attention task – 79 of 84 subjects completing the tasks), 91% (visual attention task – 79 of 84 subjects completing the task) and 88% (listening to paragraphs – N=84). The important point of this research is that it demonstrated that, despite the brain's adaptations to the injury over years, there was still a pattern that could be discerned.

The listening to paragraphs task analysis required the least number of variables to discriminate. The variables that were most often involved in successful discrimination were: high frequency (32-64 Hz) connectivity variables emanating from the frontal lobes, supporting Thatcher's emphasis (as well as the general thinking in the field) on the effect on the frontal lobes in TBI cases. A separate analysis indicated that the length of time that had elapsed since the accident did not positively correlate with these connectivity values, indicating that time does not result in improvement in these values (time does not heal). The lack of ability of the brain to actually self-heal is a critical point in the understanding of the brain's response. The brain reorganizes its response pattern, which is generally less effective (poorer memory) than the original "wiring" provided by nature. However, the self-healing can occur relatively easily if the information regarding the "bad wiring" is provided to the subject thru the Neurocognitive process, as one of the case examples will demonstrate.

The "bad wiring" effect of a TBI is mostly seen in the relationships between locations and reflects injuries to the long myelinated neurons. We will need to explain how we look at these relationships. The coherence and phase relationships between locations can be conceptualized in terms of a generator emanating from a particular location. This generator can be visualized as a "flashlight" effect, where the origin of the beam is one location and its destination all other 18 locations in a particular frequency. Figure 19 expresses this relationship.

Figure 19 The "Flashlight" generator

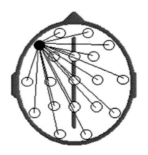

The important relationship which had not been examined in previous research - the relationship between success at the task and the qEEG variables during the task.

With a combined group of TBI and normal subjects, a correlational analysis was conducted to determine the qEEG parameters that correlate with successful auditory recall. (Thornton, 2002a) This type of analysis allows us to see what has happened to the TBI patient's electrophysiological function that could explain why their memory abilities have been affected. We know that memory is probably the most problematic cognitive consequence for this group.

The TBI group had significantly lower values than the control group for the beta2 frequency (32-64 Hz) coherence and phase values involving frontal lobe locations. These values were significantly negatively related to the total memory score (Figure 20). Figure 20 shows the connection patterns that are in the deficit range for the TBI group, but negatively correlate with the memory score when the TBI group is combined with the normal group. Thus, the figure tells us why the TBI patient can't recall information. This pattern was not observed when analyzing the reading task and reading memory scores (Thornton, unpublished data). Thus, the data gives us an understanding of the problems which we did not have before. These results indicate that the TBI injury is predominantly affecting the long myelinated fibers from the frontal lobes (although the effect is actually seen all over the head) particularly in the higher frequency (32-64 Hz). There is no clear explanation of why this would be the case. Nonetheless, that is the research result. There are TBI patients, however, in whom the problem in coherence and phase relationships will extend into the lower frequencies, as well.

123

Figure 20
Normal Vs TBI (Traumatic Brain Injury):
Listening To Paragraphs TBI: N=80 Normal: N=49
Flashlights that are positively correlated with total memory but significantly lower in TBI Subjects: Alpha set at .02

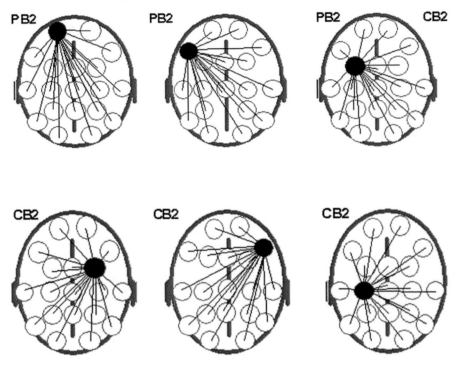

PB2: Phase beta2 CB2: Coherence Beta2
Negatively Correlated with total memory and higher in TBI subjects:
Alpha set at .05

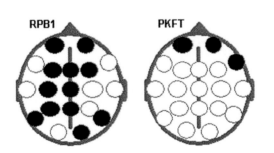

RPB1=Relative Power
Beta1
PKFT=Peak Frequency
Theta

3 - Is the electrophysiology of the brain responsive to operant conditioning? -- EEG biofeedback or Neurotherapy

Operant conditioning (the rewarding and inhibiting of spontaneous behavior) has existed as one of the classic psychological conditioning paradigms for over 50 years. The other conditioning paradigm is exemplified by Pavlov's dogs – called classical conditioning. If an individual spontaneously puts out his hand and $10,000 is placed in the hand, it is highly likely that the individual will repeat the behavior. In this situation, a complex behavior (hand going forward) is being rewarded with money. Many complex human behaviors are very amenable to operant conditioning.

The next question to be asked was whether the simple firing of a group of neurons of the human brain is equally responsive to operant conditioning. The important development in this particular area is that individual groups of neurons and their connection patterns are very amenable to operant conditioning. The most commonly employed terms for this intervention are EEG biofeedback or Neurotherapy.

Over 25 years ago, B. Sterman, Ph.D. (Sterman, 1973a, 1973b, 1977, 1986, 2000; Sterman & Friar, 1972; Sterman et al., 1974, 1978) demonstrated that seizure activity (in cats) could be reduced some 70%-80% by the rewarding of a certain frequency (beta SMR .. 13-15 Hz) and inhibiting another frequency (theta....4-8 Hz). As seizure activity is an easily measurable activity and cats are not prone to placebo effects, it seems a sound scientific conclusion that the operant conditioning of the cat brain's electrophysiology resulted in the decrease in seizure activity. Additional studies (Whitsett et al.,1982; Wyler et al., 1979, Seifert et al., 1975; Lubar & Bahler, 1976; Lubar, 1977; Lubar et al., 1981, Lubar, 2003) have confirmed the effect. Ayers (1995) has confirmed the long-term stability of the effect.

Walker & Kozlowski (2005) was able to obtain 100% reduction in seizure frequency by conducting an eyes-closed qEEG study and intervening on the deviant values.

These results would appear to not be subject to any of the following common research problems.

1. The Placebo Effect: This is based on the expectation of change, so that even a sugar pill will produce the effects that have been described.
2. The Pygmalion effect: This is found when teachers were simply told to expect great things from certain children. Their re-evaluation of the potential of the children does in fact lead to improvements.
3. The Hawthorne Effect: The belief that anything new is effective. The existence of this effect makes evaluation difficult. It needs objective long-

term monitoring.

While Sterman was able to train a particular frequency to effectively reduce seizure activity, it became important to demonstrate that other frequencies and other behaviors, such as cognition, could also be affected by the approach. Sheer (1974, 1977, 1984), Bird et al. (1978), and DeFrance & Sheer (1978) were able to document a particular deficiency (hi gamma frequency – 40 Hz) in the learning disabled child which was amenable to change with EEG biofeedback.

The effect on cognition was demonstrated by Lubar and Lubar (1984) some 20 years ago and has been replicated some 18 times (with control groups) in the following studies: Fine and Goldman, 1994; Cartozzo et al., 1995; Rossiter & LaVaque, 1995; Linden et al., 1996; Lubar, 1995, Thornton and Carmody, 2005a; Rossiter, 2002; Monastra, 2005, Xiong et al., 2005, Orlando & Rivera, 2004; Schoenberg et al., 2001; Tinius & Tinius, 2000; Keller, 2001; DeBeus et al., 2006, Fernandez et al., 2003 Heywood & Beale, 2003, Fuchs et al., 2003, Carmody et al., 2001), and some 9 times (without control groups) by: Othmer and Othmer, 1992, 1999; Kaiser & Othmer, 2000; Tansey, 1991; Thompson and Thompson, 1998; Walker et al., 2002; Bird et al., 1978; Boyd, 2005; Joyce, 1997; Vernon et al., 1983.

The Heywood & Beale (2003) study employed a sham, placebo control group which received a series of randomized bandwidths that were reinforced or inhibited as well as an ABAB reversal design to control for maturation and treatment sequence effects. The authors noted significant effects on attention and behavior measures on the subjects who completed the treatment.

The deBeus et al. (2006) study is a double-blind, "sham" treatment control group study which documented positive effects. This study will be discussed in greater detail later in this chapter.

Implementation into the school system has been reported by Boyd (2005), Orlando & Rivera (2004) and Joyce (1997).

The sheer number of replicated studies (27) (with and without control groups) would argue for mass application at this point in time. All the traditional scientific criteria have been met with these studies and stand well above the alternate approaches in terms of scientific criteria, longevity of effects, effect sizes and logic of approach.

The subject examples provided in Chapter 15 will further document the plasticity of these signals and reflect how relatively easy they can be changed.

4- What is the EEG biofeedback/Neurotherapy procedure?

126

The EEG biofeedback procedure involves placing non-invasive sensors (electrodes) on the scalp. During an intervention the software will display the activity recorded by the sensors on the screen. What activity is displayed will depend upon specific hardware specifications and what the therapist deems to be the important variable to address. The software is programmed to provide the subject with both an auditory signal and a visual display indicating when the subject's electrophysiological pattern is obtaining the values desired for the variable(s). In classical psychology terms the paradigm is called operant conditioning (e.g. rewarding/inhibiting) of spontaneous behavior and is well established as a powerful determinant of behavior.

The realization that individual groups of neurons were responsive to the operant conditioning paradigm was the major advance that has allowed this field to develop. The brain is in a constant state of fluctuation. The software doesn't respond until a programmed value is obtained, whereupon it provides auditory and visual feedback. Gradually, the brain learns to produce or exceed the value that the therapist has selected as the goal. The conditioning of the EEG signal is largely an unconscious phenomenon. Intuitively, appropriate levels of motivation and attention would be necessary psychological components. Artifact issues of EMG (muscle activity) and eye movements have been a manageable problematic contaminant to the evaluation and treatments. The goal of the training is to condition the brain's electrophysiology to new response patterns, which hopefully can then be generalized to different cognitive tasks.

5- Do changes in the electrophysiology of the brain result in changes in cognition?

Historically, these "standard" interventions have involved the placement of the electrodes at the top central portion (sensori-motor strip) of the head (C3, Cz, C4), the protocols employed attempted to decrease the magnivolts of the theta frequency (4-8 Hertz) and increase the magnivolts of certain frequency ranges within the beta frequency (13-32 Hertz). The sensori-motor strip receives sensory information from the body and is involved in the motor control of the body. This approach (Sq - standard qEEG) did not employ the use of a database to determine whether a subject's values were within the normal range. The subject's task was to observe the computer screen (which graphically displays the variable's value) and listen to the audio feedback. The major area of improvement has been in software graphic displays, which have employed a more video game interaction format. The interventions generally have not asked the subject to engage in an academic cognitive task (reading, homework, etc.) during the session, but engage the subject in a video game type interaction. Four studies (Linden et al., 1996; Othmer & Othmer, 1992; Tansey, 1991; Thompson & Thompson, 1998) have documented changes on IQ measures averaging 15 points (1 standard deviation) with this approach. Other studies (Rossiter, 2002; Byers, 1995; Keller, 2001; Kaiser & Othmer, 2000; Lubar et al., 1984; Lubar & Lubar, 1995; Thornton, 2000c, 2002b; Thornton & Carmody, 2005a, 2005b, 2006) have reported positive results with this approach for the TBI and LD/ADHD group.

With the development of eyes-closed resting condition databases (Ecq), the field advanced to the next level of being able to determine if a subject's qEEG values were deviant from a normative database. These deviations then became the focus of the intervention. One of the limitations of these initial databases was the limitation of the frequency range employed in the development of the database. The databases generally stopped at the 32-Hertz range or below. The database-guided published research (Tinius & Tinius, 2000; Walker, 2002; Orlando & Rivera, 2004) have reported positive results in the traumatic brain injured patient and the LD/ADHD subject on attention, problem solving, and IQ measures, thus confirming the hypothesis that changes in electrophysiology will result in changes in cognitive abilities.

Position Statements on the qEEG and EEG Biofeedback

Frank H. Duffy, M.D., a Professor and Pediatric Neurologist at Harvard Medical School, stated in an editorial in the January, 2000 issue of the "Journal of Clinical Electroencephalography" that the scholarly literature suggests that neurofeedback "should play a major therapeutic role in many difficult areas. In my opinion, if any medication had demonstrated such a wide spectrum of efficacy it would be universally accepted and widely used" (p. v). "It is a field to be taken seriously by all" (p. vii).

During the past several decades, there have been 5 professional organizations which have rendered supportive position statements with respect to the use of EEG biofeedback for a number of clinical conditions. These include the Electrodiagnostic and Clinical Neuroscience Society (ECNS), American Academy of Child and Adolescent Psychiatry (AACAP), The National Institute of Health Consensus Statement on the Diagnosis and Treatment of ADHD, the International Society for Neuronal Regulation (ISNR), and the Association for Applied Psychophysiology and Biofeedback (AAPB).

The Electrodiagnostic and Clinical Neuroscience Society's (ECNS) position paper concluded that "Numerous EEG as well as QEEG reports agree that a high proportion of children with developmental disorders— among which learning disabilities and attention-deficit hyperactivity have received the most attention—display abnormal brain electrical activity. There is a wide consensus that delta or theta excess and alpha and beta deficits are commonly encountered in children with learning disorders and that theta or alpha excesses are often seen in children with ADD/ADHD. "

Hughes and John (1999) concluded (in the ADHD/LD situation), "On the basis of multiple Class II studies and abundant Class II evidence, Type B recommendation." The qEEG is recommended in the ADHD and Learning disability situation. ECNS also recommended the qEEG in the traumatic brain injured situation "on the basis of several class II studies and multiple concordant class III studies, type C recommendation."

Class II studies consists of "Evidence provided by one or more well-designed clinical studies, such as case control or cohort studies." Class III evidence is provided by expert opinion, non-randomized historical control, such as case control or cohort studies." The type B recommendation is a "Positive recommendation, based on Class II evidence. The type C recommendation is a positive recommendation based upon strong consensus of class III evidence."

More recently these findings have been further reported and reviewed in neuropsychology and psychiatric journals (Monastra et al., 2001; Monastra, 2005; Chabot et al., 2005), one of which (2005 articles) were published by Brown University, contributed to by medical professionals and edited by L. Hirshberg, PHD (Neurodevelopmental Center), S. Chiu, MD (Department of Psychiatry, University of California – Davis), and J. Frazier, MD (Department of Psychiatry, Harvard Medical School, Cambridge Hospital).

The author also reviewed the American Academy of Child and Adolescent Psychiatry (AACAP) guidelines for recommending evidence-based treatments and concluded that "EEG biofeedback meets the AACAP criteria for "Clinical Guidelines" for treatment of ADHD, seizure disorders, anxiety (e.g. Obsessive-compulsive disorder, GAD, posttraumatic stress disorder, phobias), depression, reading disabilities and addictive disorders. This finding suggests that EEG biofeedback should be considered as an intervention for these disorders by the clinician. Clearly, there is stronger evidence of efficacy – the strongest….is for the use of EEG biofeedback for ADHD in children and adolescents. Because of this high level of empirical support, the use of EEG biofeedback for ADHD will (with the publication of the second RCT (randomized control trial) meet the most stringent American Psychological Associations criterion of efficacious and specific, which requires two independent RCTs, among other factors." The authors added, "there are few risks or contraindications for EEG biofeedback."

The criteria for "Clinical Guidelines" are "recommendations that are based on limited empirical evidence and/or strong clinical consensus. "Clinical Guidelines" apply approximately 75% of the time. These practices should always be considered by the clinician, but there are exceptions to their applications."

In addition, the National Institute of Health Consensus Statement on the Diagnosis and Treatment of ADHD concluded "EEG biofeedback is a nonpharmacological treatment associated with clinical and functional improvements in patients with ADHD in case and controlled group studies." (Monastra, 2005)

These recommendations have been rendered as a result of over 20 years of research, starting with individual case studies and moving through the control group research design. We will not delve into all of the research that led to these recommendations. However, some recent research deserves particular attention due to the questions being asked.

Monastra & Monastra (2004, 2005) reported the follow up results of their 2002 control group study, which involved medication and EEG approaches to the ADHD subject. Their conclusions were as follows:

"1. There was no indication that the use of stimulant medication yielded any enduring benefits after three years (total) of pharmacological treatment. Although patients who had never been treated with EEG biofeedback continued to demonstrate positive response (behavioral ratings, the T.O.V.A., QEEG) when tested with medication, relapse occurred in each of these participants when tested without medication, 12, 18, 24 and 36 months after initial evaluation/treatment.

2. Patients whose treatment included EEG biofeedback continued to demonstrate significantly improved levels of cortical activation on the QEEG measure, as well as sustained gains on the T.O.V.A. and behavioral ratings throughout the three year period, even when medications were withdrawn.

3. Thirty-four (80%) of the patients whose treatment included EEG biofeedback were able to decrease daily dosage of stimulant by at least 50%. By contrast, none of the patients who did not receive EEG biofeedback were able to reduce dosage and 85% increased their dose.

4. Parents who rated themselves as "non-systematic" reinforcers of

130

appropriate behaviors at the conclusion of the first year of treatment varied in their eventual response to our parenting program. Those "non-systematic" parents whose children participated in EEG biofeedback tended to return for "booster" parenting sessions, and reported improved ability to "follow-through" on recommended strategies for addressing child behavioral problems. Examination of their behavioral ratings at two and three year follow-up assessments revealed significant improvement in their child's functioning at home.

Conversely, "non-systematic" parents, whose children did not participate in EEG biofeedback, rarely returned for "booster" classes. Their primary reasons for contacting the clinic was to assist in adjustment of medication or the revision of the child's IEP or behavioral program at school. Although their children continued to display improved attention and behavioral control at school (while taking medication), no indication of significant functional improvement at home was evident in these families." (Monastra, 2005)

The conclusions that can be rendered from this study are as follows:

1) The effects stopped upon cessation of the medication.
2) EEG interventions worked and held.
3) 80% of the EEG treated children reduced their medication amount by 50% or more vs. none of the medication treated children.
4) The parents of the children who were engaged in the EEG biofeedback treatment returned for parenting aid and improved in their ability to implement strategies, with resulting improvements in the child, while those parents whose children were not engaged in the EEG biofeedback did not return for parenting classes and their children did not improve at home.

A research study by deBeus et al. (2003), presently in the peer review process, will be the first randomized controlled trial (RCT) that employs the classic double-blind paradigm and incorporates a "sham" biofeedback treatment. There are 52 ADHD patients (ages 7-10) in this study. Half of the sample was diagnosed with the inattentive ADHD diagnosis and the other half with a comorbid diagnosis.

Participants were randomly assigned to either a bona fide EEG biofeedback treatment (40 sessions) (theta suppression; beta or SMR enhancement) or a "sham" biofeedback condition in which "rewards" (i.e. movement on a Sony PlayStation game) were provided randomly. Because a Sony PlayStation interface was used, neither the participants nor the therapist was aware of treatment condition (i.e. bona fide vs. sham biofeedback). Monitoring of EEG activity was conducted in both types of treatment.

131

Twenty-eight of the children (equally represented in the two groups) were being treated with stimulant medications during their participation in treatment.

The evaluation procedure involved a power spectral analysis of qEEG data, event-related potentials, intelligence measures, academic achievement, attention (via continuous performance tests and behavioral ratings), and an extensive behavioral assessment using the Behavioral Assessment System for Children (Reynolds & Kamphaus, 1994). This system provides a comparison of a child with age peers with respect to attention, hyperactivity, aggression, conduct problems, anxiety, depression, somatization, and adaptive skills (e.g. leadership, social skills, adaptability and study skills).

The participants who received bona fide EEG biofeedback were rated as demonstrating significantly less hyperactivity at home and school; improved attention at home; less anxiety, depression; and complaints of minor physical problems at home; better adaptability to change; improved ability to work with others, improved peer interactions, organizational skills, and study habits; and a better attitude towards school. In addition, on computerized tests of attention, the children who had received bona-fide EEG biofeedback demonstrated significantly better scores than age peers diagnosed with ADHD who received sham biofeedback.

On the physiological side, demonstration of improvements in cortical arousal (reduced theta, increased beta or SMR (12-15 Hz)) was evident only in the bona-fide biofeedback groups. Within this group, approximately one-third of the patients were able to reduce dosage of medication.

The deBeus study and Monastra studies demonstrate a research level of efficacy that has not been obtained in any of the current psychoeducational treatment models and argue convincingly for a radically different approach to the ADHD problem then that which we are currently using.

Chapter 12

The development of the activation database guided Neurocognitive interventions.

The logical extension in database development was the creation of an activation database. The activation approach engages the subject in ecologically relevant cognitive tasks (reading, auditory memory, problem solving, math problems, etc.) and examines the relationship between success at the task and the qEEG variables. The value of the database developed by one of the author (Thornton, 2001) resides in understanding the empirical relationships between electrophysiological variables and cognitive variables. The frequency range of the database was extended to 64 Hertz, thus doubling the amount of data available for understanding these empirical relationships. This high frequency range has proven to be particularly important in traumatic head injury cases (Thornton, 1999a, 1999b, 2000b, 2002a, 2002b, 2005a, 2005b).

Equally important, however, is that the higher frequency ranges are intimately tied to metabolism rates. Oakes et al., (2004) studied the relationship between the EEG frequency ranges and metabolic activity. The results **indicated negative relationships between metabolic activity and lower EEG frequencies (-.25 (6.5 – 8 Hz), -.38 (8.5 - 10 Hz), +.08 (10.5 - 12 Hz) and increasing positive relationships as the beta frequency increased: correlation of -.06 (12.5-18 Hz), +.19 (18.5 – 21 Hz), +.34 (21.5-30 Hz), and +.48 (36.5 – 44 Hz). Thus, the higher the bandwidth examined the greater the metabolism rate.**

In addition to the use of activation norms, empirically related variables and high frequency data analysis, the approach also differs in the conception of how the treatment should be conducted. The Neurocognitive approach addresses a particular intervention as just one of many in its goal to improve a system. The assumption behind historical methods has been that the improvements will generalize to other cognitive tasks. This assumption has been supported with the improvements on IQ tests, behavioral indices, etc. However, an approach, which addresses relevant variables during a particular cognitive task and addresses the whole system, would intuitively appear to be potentially more effective. The treatment sessions, under this conception, have the subject engage in reading, listening to audiotapes or problem solving while the feedback is being provided.

Results of Research – Relationships between qEEG variables and effective cognitive functioning

We will present the results of the initial research in this area for

133

auditory and reading memory for adults. The results have been previously published in the Journal of Neurotherapy. (Thornton, 2002c, 2000b). The auditory memory results have been reanalyzed in line with the flashlight concept and thus are somewhat different than the originally published results.

Auditory Memory

Figure 21 presents the coherence alpha predictors of effective auditory memory recall in the adult sample during the input stage (subject listening to stories). Notice that the predominant flashlight origin is in the left hemisphere (4 of the 5 flashlights) and all involve coherence alpha relationships. The fifth flashlights emanates from the right frontal position (F8). What is not presented in the figures are the negative effects of excessively high levels of theta/delta activity or low levels of beta activity in the posterior region. These variables become more important with children, while the coherence alpha values are less critical to success. Figure 21 also presents the predictors during the immediate recall of the auditorily presented paragraphs. Note that the predictors are exactly the same. The only additional predictor (not displayed due to graphic limitations of the page) is the F4 coherence alpha flashlight. The consistent overlap between PET study results and qEEG results argues for the validity of both sets of data. Figure 22 presents the correlates during the delayed recall (about 20 minutes later). Observe how the flashlights (F7, F8, & T3) are the same ones involved in the successful input and immediate recall processing tasks.

Figure 21
Coherence Alpha flashlight predictors of auditory memory during input stage and immediate recall stage

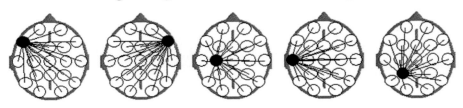

From Thornton (2002b) and unpublished

134

Figure 22
Coherence Alpha flashlight predictors of auditory memory during delayed recall stage

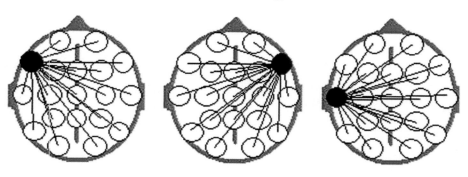

From Thornton (2002b) and unpublished

The role of the right frontal region in recall tasks has been previously documented in PET studies and theories regarding memory functioning. Tulving et al. (1996) discussed the Hemispheric Encoding/Retrieval Asymmetry (HERA) pattern model, which states, "(1) the left frontal lobes are differentially more involved than the right frontal lobes in the retrieval of general knowledge (semantic memory information); (2) left frontal lobes are more involved than the right in the encoding of novel aspects of incoming information into episodic memory, including information retrieved from semantic memory; and (3) right frontal lobes are more involved than left in episodic memory retrieval" (p. 71). The "novelty/encoding hypothesis" states that the left-frontal cortical regions are involved in the encoding of novel information for episodic memory storage. "Neuroimaging studies have shown that left frontal regions are differentially involved in encoding operations that determine the efficiency of subsequent retrieval." (Tulving et al., 1996) (pg. 76)

Figure 23 presents the results of a stepwise multiple regression equation employing the qEEG variables and memory scores. The R^2 value of +.94 represent an almost perfect correlation between the qEEG variables (posterior beta and coherence alpha variables) and the total memory score. This extremely high level of correlation between two measures is unheard of in the social sciences. However, the equation is exploratory at this point and requires further validation with a larger sample. The figure does, however, provide a basis to address issue 5 (Do changes in the electrophysiology of the brain result in changes in cognition?) in chapter 15 in very specific examples. If, as this figure demonstrates, there are specific relationships between successful specific cognitive functions and the qEEG variables, then it becomes a relatively easy procedure to intervene on the qEEG variables that relate to success at the task to improve that specific cognitive function.

The clinical examples that will be examined (Chapter 15) provide the data that support such a statement. Once this is established with the individual and group data, it will become clear to the reader that special education and cognitive rehabilitation programs require a complete restructuring with the neurocognitive approach as the cornerstone of the intervention approach. The preceding discussions have laid the logical and empirical neuroscience basis for what is to follow.

Figure 23
Stepwise Multiple Regression Equation for Total Memory Score
N=34, ages 7-14, R^2=.94
Memory predicted from qEEG values using
Beta and Coherence Values

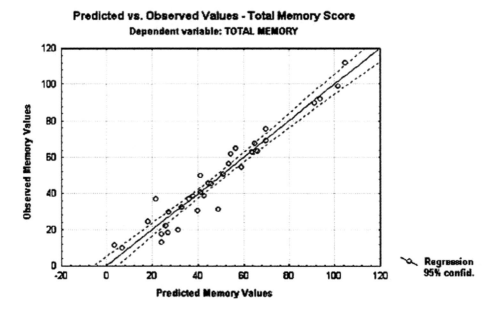

From Thornton, unpublished

Results of Interventions

The employment of the activation qEEG database in the rehabilitation / improvement of cognitive function in the traumatic brain injured, learning disabled, ADHD, and normal populations has been published in several reports (Thornton & Carmody, 2005a, 2005b; Thornton, 2000b, 2002b). The improvements noted were dramatic in their effect size. For both the TBI patient (N=15) (Thornton & Carmody, 2005b, in press) and the LD/ADHD subject (N=14) (Thornton & Carmody, 2005a) the improvements in auditory and reading memory averaged three standard deviations or more with additional evidence of generalization of improvement to a number of other cognitive abilities in several cases. The number of sessions (33 minute session) required to obtain the effect for the LD child was between 40-50 sessions (20-25 hours), while the TBI subject averaged about 108 sessions (54 hours) (Thornton & Carmody, 2005b, in press).

Of practical educational importance is the comparison of the effectiveness of the Neurocognitive approach to other modalities currently in existence (Orton-Gillingham, Lindamood-Bell, FastForWord, etc.). Figure 3 (Lloyd et al., 1998, Forness et al, 1997) presents the standard deviation effects of a number of interventions.

As different studies often employ different measures in their outcome research, the figure represents the stated standard deviation effect according to whatever measure the researchers were employing. Many of these alternative intervention models can range between 100 and 350 hours and generally obtain improvements averaging in the +.50 to +1.00 standard deviation (SD) range, as the figure indicates.

In the educational arena, the Neurocognitive interventions are approximately 3-6 times as effective and obtain the results between 6% and 25% of the time required by other interventions. In the cognitive rehabilitation area the neurocognitive interventions are, on average, about 3 times as effective as alternate methods (computer, strategies, medication) (Figure 4). Time comparisons are more difficult to estimate for the cognitive programs.

Thus, the clinical and practical utility of the activation database-guided EEG biofeedback approach is well established with these research results.

All of the 20 LD/ADHD subjects treated to date have improved an average of 296%, with the least improvement being 40% and the best 970%. The mean pretreatment total auditory recall of the 20 LD/ADHD students was 8.40 (SD=5.48), and the post-treatment mean was 21.77. The comparative values for a control group of normal adults (N=15) were a mean of 18 and a SD of 2.45. The 20 LD/ADHD group was, therefore, 3.92 SD units below the norm prior the treatment and 1.53 SD above the norm by the end of treatment (employing the SD of the control group). From this perspective the LD/ADHD group moved some 5.5 SD units. By any reasonable criteria these children could be considered cured of their memory problems.

Employing the Wechsler Logical memory norms for age 13 (the approximate average age of the children), the children were functioning below the 5% range (cut-off score of 11.4) and improved to the 50% range (approximate mean of 23.7 with SD of 3.5 for 13 year olds). Thus, from this additional perspective, it could be asserted that the children were cured of their memory problems. The only direct missing evidence to this statement would reside in long-term follow up assessment. However, the follow-up reports obtained from parents, as well as other research reports (Tansey, 1993; Lubar, 1995), provide a strong basis to the belief that the effects have held.

Reading memory values for 5 of these subjects were available and reflected a total score of 6.6 prior to treatment (SD=3.8) and a post treatment mean of 24.6 for a resultant SD improvement of 4.74. Adult norms for the reading material were not available.

Figure 24

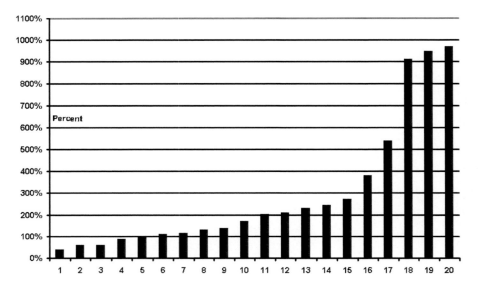

Distribution of % Auditory Memory Improvement

Figure 24 shows the distribution of the auditory memory percentage improvements. Figure 25 shows the distribution of the reading memory percentage improvements. For the five subjects for which reading memory scores were followed, there was a 273% average improvement.

Figure 25

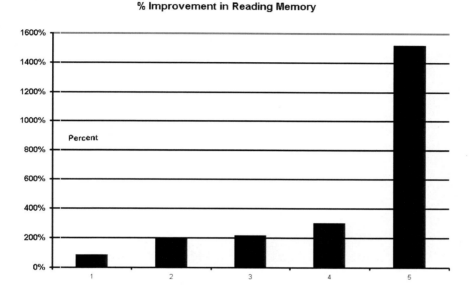

% Improvement in Reading Memory

The approach has also been useful in the normal population, as three normal subjects obtained improvements in auditory memory averaging 130% (Thornton, 2000b, 2002b). The consistency and magnitudes of the effect sizes in these populations argue strongly against a placebo effect. In addition, a control group (N=15) (Thornton, 2000c, 2002b) did not demonstrate any improvement in auditory memory functioning.

The purpose of this book is to examine in depth how the activation database is employed in the interventions in specific examples and provide, for the first time, the direct link between qEEG variables and specific cognitive changes.

Traumatic Brain Injury Improvements

Figure 4 (Chapter 3, page 46) documents the relative standard deviation effectiveness of the currently available cognitive rehabilitation intervention approaches in the area of cognitive rehabilitation of the TBI patient. The interventions for the 15 TBI patients were directed towards auditory memory (paragraph recall). Generalization effects were obtained on attention, problem solving and word list recall measures.

The Human Brain is a System

Two assumptions behind the activation approach are 1) the electrophysiology of the human brain functions as a total system, 2) particular locations / connection patterns / frequency can be involved in multiple cognitive operations, 3) interventions directed towards a particular location, connection pattern or frequency will not necessarily improve the specific cognitive skill. It is necessary to address all the variables which are involved in that specific cognitive activity. The treatment involves multiple interventions at and between different locations and frequencies to improve the functioning of the entire system. If a car is to operate correctly, all parts must be working. While appearing to be self-evident, this understanding has not been the major operating assumption of the field.

The data collected across the more than 20 cognitive tasks also indicates that the patterning of effective electrophysiological functioning can differ according to the task. For example, there is some indication in the data collected that mathematics abilities may reside in the higher gamma frequency. Much of the data collected by the author addresses cognitive functioning which is essential to academic and occupational success. The manifestations of emotional functioning on the brain's electrophysiology has also been the focus of some research across neuroscience fields.

Some results obtained in the original research (Thornton, unpublished) would seem to indicate that the right temporal lobe (T4) is intimately tied into the experience of love. Other research in the field has pointed to a left/right hemisphere difference in the experience of positive and negative emotions with the left frontal implicated in positive emotions. This line of research has already fostered some protocol constructions which have been useful in the depression situation and could prove, someday, to be the preferred (compared to medication) method of intervention in depression.

It is the author's firm belief that this method of intervention is the most viable approach to the problem of emotional dysregulation and much preferred over medication approaches. It requires federal funding for development.

CHAPTER 13 -The Activation qEEG Evaluation Procedure
The Mapping of the Brain's Electrical / Cognitive System

The human brain is the most complex organ on the planet. It has approximately 100 billion neurons localized in its 2-3 pound weight of tissue that has the consistency of gelatin. The membrane surface of the neurons would cover 4 soccer fields. It is about 2% of the body weight of an individual. In aggregate, there may be between 100 trillion and a quadrillion synapses in the brain.

The 1990's were declared the decade of the brain by President Bush. Since that time, there has been an exponential growth in scientific advancements regarding the brain in terms of its neurochemistry, and the visualization of its structure and function as well as a host of other scientific advancements. Many of the medical diagnostic advancements have focused on visualizations of the structures (MRI, fMRI, DTI), while some have attempted to understand its functioning (PET, qEEG, DTI). The integration of the structures with the functions (defined by cognitive measures) is the ultimate goal of the field of neuroscience. Implicit in that goal is the assumption that if we can understand how the system works, we will be better able to intervene to improve its functioning. Complex biochemical interventions are being sought after to improve the brain's functioning or cease its malfunctioning (schizophrenia, depression, mental retardation, etc.).

In the philosophy of science, a distinction is made between levels of analysis. Within a field of study (biochemistry, etc.), the data that is being studied is generally defined by the measures that are employed, the concepts developed concerning those measures, and how those measures relate to one another. When we move between fields (e.g. biochemistry to functional neuroimaging), the relationships often become less precise and relationships between the different planes or levels of analysis become the focus of the research. Yet the measures and concepts within one field cannot be directly assumed to be operational within another area. For example the question, What is the relationship between the neurotransmitter serotonin and a MRI image of the brain? has no direct answer, as serotonin can't be visualized on an MRI image.

The mapping of the human brain must eventually be able to integrate across all planes of analysis. Within each plane of analysis, the parameters will need to be clearly defined and interrelationships precisely specified.

The quantitative EEG technology has been able to mathematically define its parameters precisely. The value of this precision resides in its ability to apply standard mathematical analysis to the values, such as standard deviations.

The relationship between the analysis of the electrical parameters (qEEG variables) and psychological measures (memory, intensity of depression, etc.) can be easily investigated via a correlational analysis.

The methodology involves measuring the electrical activity while the subject is engaged in a task or experiencing subjective emotions. The interrelationships can then be studied directly. Most analyses of this type have correlated the qEEG variables obtained under an eyes closed condition and then obtain the psychological measure which occurred at a different time (e.g. scores on a depression inventory, educational testing scores, IQ scores, etc.). While this approach can be helpful and yield valid relationships, an inherently superior approach would be to obtain the relationships during the psychological or cognitive activity in question.

All of the original research in this area employed the eyes-closed database approach to analysis of the relationship between these two planes of analysis. A limitation of this approach was the confining of the frequency range to 32 Hertz and below and the lack of a direct relationship between cognition and the qEEG variables.

Evaluation procedures explained

The author of this book conducted research in this area to address the limitations of the previous eyes closed database approach. The qEEG data for some 100 normal subjects were collected while the subjects engage in over 20 cognitive tasks. Each individual epoch (one second) was labeled according to the task which was being administered at the time. The frequency range was extended to 64 Hertz to determine if cognitive activity was correlated with the qEEG measures in this high frequency range. The data was analyzed, via correlational analysis, for the relationships between effective cognitive activity and the qEEG variables. The relationship between a qEEG variable and cognitive effectiveness (recall score) was examined. Thus a correlational relationship between two planes of analysis was obtained.

This relatively simple procedure would provide the beginning of the mapping of the electrical brain. The implications, however, are quite profound. If it is possible to determine the specific relationships between cognition and the qEEG variables, then it becomes possible to change specific cognitive skills of an individual through the simple operant conditioning paradigm of EEG biofeedback.

142

Following years of research into this area, the number of cognitive tasks employed in the evaluation was reduced to 9 tasks due to the need to be more efficient with time and the redundancy of results across different tasks. The cognitive tasks which are currently being employed in the evaluation procedure include:

Auditory Attention:

The subject (with their eyes closed) listens for the tap of a pen on a table. When they hear the tap they are instructed to slightly raise their right index finger.

Visual Attention:

The subject looks at a sheet of paper with upside down Spanish text. A laser light is flashed onto the back of the sheet. When the subject sees the laser light, they are to slightly raise their index finger.

Both of these tasks can serve as a cognitive condition and as a comparison condition for other tasks. The auditory attention task serves as a comparison condition to the auditory memory task. Listening to auditorily presented paragraphs (auditory memory) requires auditory attention. To separate out the effects of auditory memory processing from simple auditory attention requires a subtraction of the brain's response during auditory attention from the brain's response during an auditory memory task. Although this type of analysis may prove fruitful with future interventions, it has not been necessary to employ this type of analysis to obtain the results presented.

Likewise, reading a page of text requires both visual attention and visual processing of the text. To map the visual processing response from simple visual attention requires both tasks and a subtraction of visual attention from visual processing.

As an analogy if we want to know the weight of an individual and he is fully dressed when he is weighed, we need to subtract the weight of his clothes and shoes to obtain his true weight.

This type of analysis is similar to what is currently being conducted in PET and fMRI research. A control condition is obtained, the cognitive activity is induced and the differences are reported. Generally, the relationship between success at the task and what gets activated in relationship to success at the task is not studied. The limitations of the approach are self evident, as the research does not let us know what really counts for success at the task. Although a beginning of understanding, the approach cannot answer the questions we really need answered.

An advantage of the qEEG approach (vs. PET) is that the measurements are obtained in terms of an absolute level and not just a degree of activation value. This allows us to know specifically where the subject is along the continuum of values available and also to know exactly where his values need to reside in order to be "normal".

Auditory Memory:

The qEEG variables are recorded while the subject listens to a paragraph read to them (input stage) and their eyes are closed. The subject is asked to recall the information silently to themselves (immediate recall stage) while his eyes are closed. The subject is asked about 30 minutes later to quietly recall the stories read to him (delayed recall) while his eyes are closed. This methodology provides three measures of auditory memory: input, immediate recall and delayed recall.

Reading Memory:

The qEEG variables are recorded while the subject reads a printed text quietly to himself (input stage). The subject is asked to recall the information silently to himself (immediate recall stage) while his eyes are closed. The subject is asked about 30 minutes later to quietly recall the stories he had read (delayed recall) while his eyes are closed. This methodology provides three measures of reading memory: input, immediate recall, and delayed recall.

Problem Solving:

The concept of intelligence is conceptualized in many different ways - speed of processing, concept formation, etc. The ability to solve problems is inherent in the concept of intelligence. To address the relationship between problem solving and the qEEG variables, the subject was asked to solve nonverbal problems. The Ravens Matrices were employed as the measure of problem solving. The Ravens Matrices are visual sequencing problems in which the subject is provided with a series of designs on a sheet of paper. The sequence of changing patterns reflects a logical change of patterns. The subject's task is to decipher the logical chain of events as it proceeds from both a vertical and horizontal direction. The subject's task is then to decide which of the provided 6-8 alternative designs completes the vertical and horizontal logic of the puzzle. The subject's qEEG patterns and verbal responses are recorded while he engages in the task and renders his guess.

The initial research, however, involved many more cognitive tasks, which will not be reviewed in this book. These tasks included spelling, math (spatial addition of two digit numbers, multiplication), visualization, recall of memories (earliest, normal important events from childhood, recalling a to do list, recalling where objects are placed, word lists) and the emotions of happiness, sadness, and love.

The value of this approach resides in its ability to precisely define what qEEG measures are not operating within the normal range.

The subject's qEEG response pattern is then analyzed by software that presents the deviations (standard deviation units and raw values) from the normative reference group on the variables that are correlated with successful recall in the normative sample. The reference group is divided between children (ages 10-14; N=30) and adults (greater than age 14; N=59), as the successful response pattern is different for these age groups (Thornton, 2001). These deviations, as well as other significant deviations not related to the normative successful response pattern, are analyzed in the context of a neuropsychological understanding of the brain's functioning. Treatment protocols are selected which reflect the treatment decisions.

There are two types of variables that can be the focus of the interventions. The first type is a frequency analysis of the nature of the activity that is occurring at a particular location. The standard 10-20 system (Figure 12) reflects these locations. As relative power figures have been determined to be a more powerful predictor (for adults) of success during the input stage of a cognitive task (Thornton, 2001), it is the treatment measure of choice. Previously, reduction in theta (4-8 Hz) microvolt activity and augmentation of beta1 microvolts (within the 13-32 Hz) have generally been the object of the interventions conducted in the research.

The Flashlight Generator

The second variable addresses the nature of the amplitude similarity between the waveforms at different locations, and thus is assumed to be a measure of the communication activity mediated by the long myelinated neurons connecting the locations. The concept of cortical generators assumes that the cortical structures are capable of generating a signal (within a particular frequency) and can transmit that signal to all the other cortical locations, like a "flashlight". When the signal reaches another cortical location, a normative value can be generated. If the subject's value is lower than the norm, it is assumed to be a deficit connection and a standard deviation value can be obtained. Figure 19 graphically presents the concept. The head figures provided operate under this concept, with the black circle representing the origin of the flashlight.

145

Chapter 14 – Evaluation examples

The next two chapters present the "meat" of the argument for why and how the Neurocognitive approach is more effective than all other currently available approaches. This chapter focuses on the evaluation results, which indicate where the problems reside. Chapter 15 shows how easy it is to change these values and the resulting changes in cognition and behavior.

The following examples provide some clinical examples of how these qEEG difficulties are manifested on the activation qEEG evaluation. The head figures report the standard deviation unit differences (from the normative database) of the subject for the variables that successfully relate to the task in a normal population. Occasionally, other variables require examination and integration into the treatment. The figures that will be presented in the case examples to follow will generally present the values that correlate with success for the task for the normal reference group for the subject (child vs. adult).

Figure 26 – Traumatic Brain Injury – Case #1
See insert at book end - page 317
Reading - Coherence and Phase Flashlight Effects from left frontal region (F7)

The subject presented in Figure 26 experienced a significant head trauma as a result of an auto accident. He was rendered unconscious as a result of the car's impact with a tree. He had no recall of the accident. He was in the hospital for 3 weeks and underwent a partial lobectomy in the left frontal region. There was also a hemorrhage about 3-4 cm in thickness located in the left frontal region. The activation qEEG study was conducted 27 years after the accident. Figures 26 and 27 reflect the consistency of deficits responding across different cognitive tasks.

Figure 27
Traumatic Brain Injured Subject – Case #1 – Problem Solving
See insert at book end - page 317
Coherence and Phase Flashlight Effects from left frontal region (F7)
Traumatic Brain Injury Case # 2

Case # 2 is a female who was the front passenger in a minivan. Her car was driving "fast" when her driver ran up a sidewalk, causing the air bags to open up. Everything went "black" and the air bag hit her face. She didn't recall if she hit her head on the windshield. Initially, she felt dizzy, had a headache, and was confused and in pain. Her car was totaled. The following morning she experienced headache and pain and stinging in her eyes. This is a case that appears to be a minor head trauma, yet the results of the qEEG study demonstrated significant problems across a number of connections from the frontal locations. Potentially confusing the issue is a history of a 6th grade education. Note in particular, however, the pattern of disconnection between the frontal regions and the T3, C3, and P3 flashlight origins. This pattern was evident during the input (top row) and immediate recall task (bottom row). Frontal lobe problems are characteristic in traumatic brain injury situations. Figure 28 presents the qEEG evaluation results for this subject.

Figure 28– TBI Case #2
See insert at end of book - page 318
Case 3 – Potential Asperger's Syndrome
Figure 29– Case #3 -Possible Asperger's syndrome
See insert at end of book - page 318

Some of the diagnostic criteria (provided by the DSM IV) for the Asperger's diagnosis are as follows. The criteria listed focuses on the emotional aspect of the disorder, as it is related to the findings in this case.

Diagnostic Criteria For 299.80 Asperger's Disorder

The DSM IV criteria for Asperger's disorder focus on the emotional and social interaction problems and the disorder is not characterized by poor academic achievement. Examples of problematic areas include: ability to use multiple nonverbal behaviors (eye-to-eye gaze, etc.), inappropriate peer relationships, lack of sharing with other individuals (enjoyment, interests, etc.), and lack of social and emotional reciprocity.

The subject is a 17-year old male who has a history of poor social relationships but generally good academic grades. The furthest left head figure in Figure 29 represents the relationships between the right temporal lobe and the other cortical locations in the beta frequency averaged across all cognitive tasks administered. Also displayed are the coherence alpha relationships averaged across all locations. Although this is a single case example, it does reflect the ability of the database to pick out a pattern, which may eventually reflect the Asperger pattern. The right temporal lobe is heavily involved in the emotional processing of information. It is possible that the emotional information is not being "communicated" to the left hemisphere allowing the subject to be unaware of the emotional meaning of what is occurring around him. Alternately, the disturbed coherence alpha relationships may present the underlying electrophysiological problem in

147

the Asperger syndrome. Only further research will be able to answer these questions.

Case #4 – Normal Individual with suspected ADD

The following individual is a successful businessman who believes that he has a history of ADD. The evaluation demonstrated that he did not have a traditional definition of ADD (i.e. increased levels of theta activity) but did demonstrate significant problems in coherence and phase relationships. Figure 30 indicates a consistent pattern of connection difficulty in the same connections whether he was engaged in listening or the immediate recall of the auditory information. His memory score was 8 ½ for the immediate recall and 2 for the delayed recall for a total of 10 ½. The approximate norm is 10 for the immediate and 10 for the delayed. By the time the 10th session was completed he was able to recall 8 ½ and 17 for a total score of 25 ½, more than 2 ½ times his initial score. By the 27th session, his score was 34 ½, up over 300% in 13 ½ hours.

Figure 30– Case #4 - Normal Individual – Auditory Memory
See insert at end of book - page 319

In Figure 31 (reading condition), he displays the same pattern of decreased posterior connection activity, this time in the beta 1 frequency from the posterior locations, while the connection activity to the frontal locations remains intact.

Figure 31 – Case #4 - Normal Individual - Reading
See insert at end of book - page 319

High Functioning Individual

Case #5 is an example (Figure 32) of a high-functioning individual. The value of these figures resides in their ability to show that differences in the qEEG values correspond to real-life achievements. Note the lower levels of theta in the left posterior versus the right posterior, as well as the corresponding higher levels of beta2 in the left posterior region. This data ties in nicely with the neuroscience results which focus on the left posterior region in the reading situation. This individual is clearly employing the left posterior more than the right posterior in the reading task. Current eyes-closed databases would not report this type of difference, as the frequency range stops at 32 Hertz and do not use activation approaches.

Figure 32
Case #5 - Example of High Functioning Subject
See insert at end of book - page 320

Theories of Brain Functioning

The figures present a different understanding of brain functioning than has been previously proposed in the scientific literature and challenges present clinical approaches. The pattern of electrophysiological activity which relates to effective cognitive functioning throughout the myriad of cognitive tasks evaluated (Thornton, 2001) is one of projection and activation (Thornton, 2002c) for adults. For subjects under the age of 14, the effective pattern is one of beta activations (Thornton, 2001). A qualitative change occurs around the age of 14 when the flashlight or projection patterns become the dominant effective method. The results indicate that a single location approach is insufficient to address cognition, despite its widespread clinical employment.

In addition, the concept that one location intervention can successfully address all issues is somewhat akin to Karl Lashley's equipotential theory of brain functioning (Lashley, 1950). Lashley trained rats in a maze, cut out parts of the rat's brain and then retested them. This theory "points to the conclusion that the memory trace is located in all parts of the functional area; that various parts are equipotential for its maintenance and activation." His second conclusion was called mass action and states: "The reduction of learning is roughly proportional to the amount of tissue destroyed." Thus Lashley concluded that memory is localized throughout the system, any part of the system can hold the memory and that the more of the brain you destroy the greater the memory loss. The results presented in this chapter support the notion that memory does involve the entire system. His misconception was that any part of the system could hold the memory. The research reported in this book, as well as other neuroscience research, indicates that memory involves the whole system and cannot be conceptualized as being localized in any particular location. Memory, as well as other cognitive functions, are not equipotential but diffusely distributed.

One well marketed approach assumes that one location can affect the whole system and it doesn't matter where that location is. The conception is a gross simplication of how the human mind works and is in stark contradiction to modern neuroscience discoveries. One of the unfortuneate consequences of this approach is that invariably there is a lack of a positive response or even possibly a negative response. The neutral or negative response then becomes part of the reputation of the field, without the concomitant knowledge that the particular approach was conceptually limited. Naysayers will proclaim "It doesn't work."

Chapter 15 - TREATMENT EXAMPLES

This chapter will present clinical case examples to demonstrate how the protocols are decided upon, as well as the results of the interventions. This chapter presents considerable detail regarding the approach. The data presented is the crux of the scientific argument. It is provided to give the reader a full appreciation of the technology and the plasticity of the brain's electrophysiological functioning. Figure 33 presents a visual display and explanation of the biofeedback procedure.

See Figure 33 - Insert at end of book - page 321

Many interventions "fix" the problem within one session. Other problems take longer. We don't know the reason for this. There is evidence in this data and other case examples seen by the author of generalization or improvement of a variable related to the location or connection pattern addressed, but not directly addressed in the intervention. This is an important finding as it demonstrates the responsivity of the system and can potentially reduce the number of sessions and cost structure required to bring a particular brain to normal levels. We are presenting clinical examples to demonstrate the consistency of the effect. Many other examples are available.

General Theoretical Orientation to Treatment

The treatment approach follows 3 main guiding principles.

1)   qEEG variables which are empirically related to a cognitive skill and are functioning below normal should be addressed and brought to normal levels or above.

2)   qEEG variables which do not correlate with success (in particular coherence and phase alpha and beta values) but which are significantly below the normative reference group value should be addressed until operating at least at normal levels, although above normative values are desirable. Values for these variables which are significantly above normal levels are not to be addressed, as they represent positive cortical functioning. It is desirable to have relative power of theta values (RPT) and relative power of delta (RPD) somewhat below normal values, and relative power of beta1 (RPB1) and relative power of beta2 (RPB2) above normal, depending upon the task. This principle is developed from clinical observation, research results and results published in the US patent (Thornton, 2001)

3)   The interventions should also be guided by research from other neuroscience areas (PET, fMRI and diffusion tensor imaging (DTI)).

We know that the left temporoparietal region is disrupted in developmental dyslexia. The magnitude of activation is low and there is decreased

150

coordination of activity between the left STG and left frontal areas. The evidence indicates that the disruption is related to underdevelopment of white matter fibers in the region. The left posterior deficit connection pattern has been documented with qEEG data (Evans, 1996) as a problem for dyslexic readers. From this type of evidence we can easily infer that proper levels of functioning in the left posterior quadrant are probably critical for a lot of academic areas (which require reading).

The treatment emphasis with subject #6 (and other examples) on the left posterior quadrant (T5-P3-O1) and left temporal (T3) locations is guided by these findings in related neuroscience research and research by the author (Thornton, 2001).

Case Example – # 6

The subject is a 10-year-old female with a history of learning problems, especially in mathematics. She was flown to the clinic by her mother for an intensive 10-day 52-session program. She was depressed and had a history of suicidal ideation and sexual abuse. Following the treatment, her depression and suicidal ideation disappeared and she was obtaining 90s on math tests and running for class president.

Evaluation results and results of treatment interventions

The activation qEEG evaluation revealed multiple deficit patterns. Almost all of the variables to be presented show positive and significant relationships to auditory memory scores for normal (free of neurological problems, learning problems, ADD, or brain injury) children (ages 10-14) (Thornton, 2001, 2000a, unpublished data). Some of the comparisons involved the predictors of adult memory (coherence alpha relationships other than from T3 and peak frequency beta1). Only the major deficit patterns which were addressed in the treatment are presented.

Figure 34 presents the coherence alpha deficits in standard deviation (SD) units resulting from the analysis of the evaluation data. The subject also showed significant problems in coherence alpha relationships under the immediate 30-second recall period (Figure 35), as well as theta and beta2 relative power values during the immediate recall period (not presented).

Figure 34– Case #6

Listening to Paragraphs – Coherence Alpha Flashlight Deficits in standard deviation (SD) units - page 322

Figure 35– Case #6 - Immediate Recall - page 323

See inserts at end of book

Figure 36 presents the coherence alpha values that improved as a result of the interventions. Clinical judgment was employed in the selection of the treatment protocols and the sequence of interventions. Due to time constraints, not all of the presented problems could be addressed.

Figure 36 Case # 6 - See insert at end of book - page 324

Figure 37 reflect the SD deficits on the theta and beta2 relative power values as well as peak frequency of beta1 in the left posterior locations.

Figure 37
Case #6 Listening to Paragraphs – See insert at end of book - page 325

Figure 38 presents the changes in the theta and beta values as a result of the treatment.

Figure 38
Case #6 - See insert at end of book - page 326

Progress of Treatment

To address the problem presented in figures 34 and 35 (coherence alpha deficits during the input and immediate recall stage) the subject was asked to pause the tape after about 30 seconds of listening and quietly recall the information she had just heard, while EEG biofeedback was still being provided. When she was unable to recall any more information, she was to play the tape again for an additional 30 seconds and repeat the procedure. The procedure was to be followed throughout the session.

Auditory Memory

Auditory memory assessment was conducted using stories developed by the author. Each assessment involved a different story and contained between 20 to 25 pieces of information. The stories were scored according to a "gist" method under which partial information is given a ½ point score. An example of a story is as follows. The forward slash divides the scoring segments.

The Apache were a proud nation./ Sitting Eagle/ had led the tribe for 11 years/. It was now the year of the Wolf/ and the big celebration was being planned/ for all the neighboring tribes/ at Big Fork ridge/. Little Brook/, a 6-foot beauty/ with long jet-black hair/, was to be the queen of the celebration/. She was to marry Long Knife./ For five days/, the tribe prepared the buffalo/ and other foods to be consumed/ over a three-day period./ The night of the celebration came./ It was a clear sky with a half moon./ From 30 miles around/, all the tribes came and ate/, laughed/ and drank/ for three days. When the party was over/, Little Brook and Sharp Knife/ went into the mountains/, as was the tradition/, where they lived for a week/ before coming home to the tribe/. N=29 Fleisch Grade Level: 4.8 The N value

152

represents the total number of segments that can be scored. The Fleisch grade level index is presented (4.8).

By the 20th session the following values were normalized: temporal & posterior (T3, T5, P3, O1, O2) and sensori-motor (C3, C4) strip theta and beta2 relative power values, left posterior (T5, P3) peak frequency beta1 values and coherence alpha values from T3 to Fp2, F4, C3, T5, and P3. Her auditory memory score had improved from 7 (initial evaluation) to 10.5 for the combined immediate and delayed memory score. The next 4 sessions continued to address coherence alpha relationships (T3-P3,T3-T5, T3-F7, F7-O1), with a resultant memory score of 15 and 14 (2 assessments during this period). Coherence alpha relationships from F7 continued to be the focus (F7-T3, F7-C3, F7-T4, F7-T5; 5 sessions). Her memory score dropped to 13. Coherence alpha (F7-P3, F7-O1) was then the focus of the next two sessions. Her memory jumped to 21.5.

The next 3 sessions addressed the coherence alpha relationships (F7-Pz, T5-P3, P3-O1). Her memory score was then 15. The F8 coherence alpha relationships were addressed next (F8-O1, F8-T3, F8-T4). Her memory score was then 17.5. Two more coherence alpha relationships were addressed (F8-T5, F8-O1) and her memory score dropped to 6.5 (session 38). Following a series of sessions devoted to reading memory, temporal and left posterior beta2 activity was addressed during auditory input and her memory scores jumped back up to 26 (session 52).

Figure 39– Case #6
Improvement in Auditory Memory of 205% or 3.57 SD units.

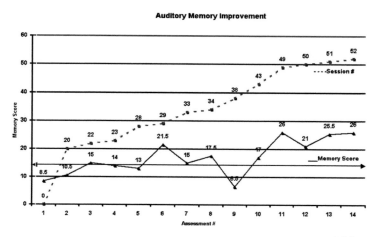

Dashed line: Session #
Solid Line: memory score
Double Arrow Line: mean memory score

Figure 39 presents her overall memory improvement during this period. Her percentage improvement was 205% and her SD improvement was 3.57. The SD and % improvement values were calculated by employing the subject's recall score (average for the 4 stories of 8.5) during the initial evaluation and comparing it to the last evaluation score of 26): (26-8.5)/8.5 for the % value and (26-8.5)/4.9 for the SD value. The software program, Excel, calculated a standard deviation value from the 4 stories during the evaluation.

Reading Memory

Her initial reading memory score was 8 for a text which she was allowed 100 seconds to read. The scoring for the reading material followed a similar approach to the auditory memory scoring. Figure 40 presents the deficit values evident on the initial evaluation. It wasn't until the 39th session that the reading problem was addressed.

Figure 40– Case #6 - page 327
Theta and Beta2 Z Score deficits during reading
Figure 41– Case #6 - page 327
Results of treatment on theta and beta2 relative power raw values
See inserts at end of book

Figure 41 presents the result of the 8 sessions directed towards the theta and beta2 values in the left posterior region. At session #43 her recall score was 15 and by session #44 her recall score was 30.5. Figure 42 presents the % improvement value. As there was only one story that the subject was required to read, it was not possible to generate a SD measure. The % improvement score employed the following formula: (final score-initial score/initial score) (30.5-8)/8. Her resulting percentage improvement was 281%.

Figure 42- Case #6
Improvement in Reading Memory of 281%

Reading Memory Improvement

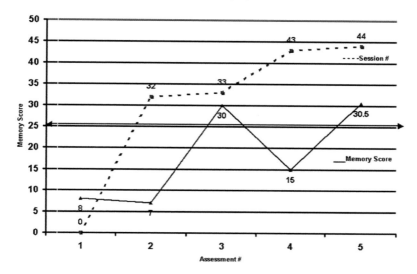

Dashed lines represent session #.
The 0 value represents initial evaluation session (assessment #1).
Solid line and Y-axis represents memory score.
X-axis indicates the assessment number during the treatment.
Solid double arrow end line represents norm value.

Case #7 - Auditory Processing Problem

Case # 7 is an 11 year-old male (4.5 grade level) with a history of learning problems, primarily manifesting as an auditory processing deficit due to low listening skills and oral direction scores on the tests listed below. An auditory processing problem is defined (by the author) in electrophysiological terms as lower levels than normal of beta activity and higher levels than normal of theta or delta activity, combined with deficit patterns in coherence alpha projection patterns, primarily from the left temporal location (T3) but also including other left hemisphere coherence alpha patterns (differing for children and adults). Table 15 reports the psychoeducational testing pattern

155

prior to the interventions, which were 46 sessions over a 10-day period. The father brought the subject back two months following the initial treatment for a "booster" treatment period. The improvements were generally maintained over the two-month break.

Table 15– Case example #7

Test	Percentile
Peabody Picture Vocab.	10
Detroit Test/Learning Ability-4	5
Word Opposites	<1
Oral Directions	
Stanford Achievement Test	
Total Reading	27
Total Math	30
Language	30
Spelling	31
Science	29
Social Science	34
Listening	17
Basic Battery	29
Complete Battery	30

Progress of Treatment

Figure 43 and 44 present the results of the initial evaluation and the post-treatment results on the qEEG variables for the auditory task and the coherence alpha issues.

Figure 45 presents the pre and post theta and beta values.

Figure 43– Case #7 – Auditory Processing Problem - page 328
Figure 44– Case #7 – Auditory Processing Problem - page 329
Figure 45– Case #7 – Auditory Processing Problem - page 330
See inserts at end of book

The calculation of the coherence and phase values were straight-forward, as the mean of the session was employed (only one connection addressed in each session) and compared to the value of the variable dur-

156

ing the original session. The Lexicor software can be programmed to address several locations for the relative power values. To maximize treatment effectiveness 2-3 locations were often addressed. To calculate the change value the averaged session values were compared to average evaluation values for the locations being addressed. For example, left posterior (T5-P3-O1) directed sessions would result in an averaged value (for theta or beta) for all 3 locations during a session. To calculate the change, the values for those 3 locations during the initial evaluation were averaged and compared to the session average.

The first 10 sessions were directed towards reducing RPT and increasing RPB1 in the left temporal (T3-T5: 2 sessions), left posterior (T5-P3-O1: 5 sessions), parietal (Pz-P4: 1 session), and right posterior regions (T6-O2: 2 sessions). His memory during this period increased to 15 (vs. 1 during the evaluation). During the next 7 sessions, coherence alpha relationships from T3 were addressed (T3-T5, T3-P3, T3-Pz, T3-Cz), followed by left posterior coherence alpha relationships (T5-C3, P3-Pz, P3-C3). During this period, his memory scores dropped to 8.5 and 2.5 respectively. The next 3 sessions were redirected towards left posterior (T5-P3-O1) relative power of beta1 (RPB1) and relative power of theta (RPT) values, which he continued to bring to normal levels.

This was followed by a coherence (CB2) beta2 (32-64 Hertz) relationship between F7 and T5 session (memory score 5 during this session) and 2 sessions directed towards T3T5 RPB1 and RPT (memory improved to 11.5). Relative power of theta values slipped back up some 4-5 points. Another session was directed at F7T5 CB2, followed by 3 sessions of left posterior (T5-P3-O1) and 1 session occipital (O1-O2), directed towards increasing RPB1 and decreasing RPT. Memory increased to 12 during this period. Three sessions directed towards relative power of beta2 (RPB2) and RPT were next, with memory scores of 12 and 2.2. A potential problem with sugar was discovered at session number 31, as his theta values jumped up another 4 points. It was undetermined how much sugar (ice cream) he had been consuming during lunch during the previous periods. Evaluation of his reading memory ability indicated no change (score of 1).

Six sessions were then directed towards coherence alpha relationships (F7-T5: 2 sessions, T5-P3: 2 sessions, T5-C3: 1 session, and T5-F3: 1 session) and his auditory memory jumped to 19, his best score yet, while reading memory remained low (.5). Figure 46 presents the auditory memory improvement results of 12.84 standard deviations or 1020%.

Figure 46– Case #7 – Auditory Processing Problem
12.84 SD Change or 1020% Improvement

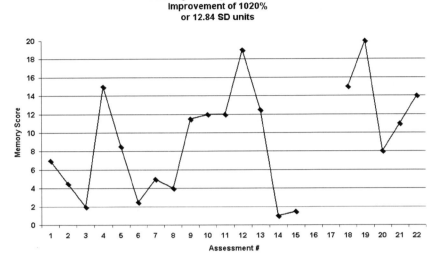

Auditory Memory Improvement
Improvement of 1020%
or 12.84 SD units

Solid Line: session # (axis on left) Dashed Line: memory score (axis on right)

The sessions (# 35 on) were then directed towards reading memory, while continuing to assess his auditory memory, which dropped precipitously during this period (1 and 1.5). His initial reading memory score during the evaluation was 5 points. As the F7 CA and CB2 relationships were addressed his reading memory score started to climb (3.5, 11, 5, 19). By sessions #53 his reading memory score had risen to 40 ½, but dropped back down to 13 at session # 68. Figure 47 presents the pre and post reading values for coherence beta activity. Figure 48 presents the pre and post values for the theta and beta values during reading.

Figure 47– Case #7 – Reading Deficits - page 331
Figure 48 – Case #7 Reading Deficits - page 332
See insert at end of book

Following a 2 month break the subject returned to treatment. The first object of reassessment were the RPB1 values in left posterior locations (T5-P3-O1). RPB1 had decreased 1 point and RPT had increased 1 point, reflecting a possible minor regression. The RPB1 values, however, were still several points above initial evaluation levels and the RPT values were 4 points below initial evaluation levels. The maintenance of the values argues for stability of the electrophysiological change induced by the treatment. His memory score had also returned to 15, reflecting maintenance of the cognitive improvement.

The RPB2 values (T5P3O1: 1 session, P3PzP4: 2 session) were also re-addressed (session # 49-51). The values had dropped about 1.5 points from the previous sessions (session # 29-31) but were still considerably (11 points) above evaluation levels, reflecting maintenance of electrophysiological gains. Sessions were then directed towards relationships from P3 (P3C3-CA; P3Pz-CB1, P3F8-CB1 & O1Pz-CB1) during reading task conditions.

Nine sessions were directed towards F7F3 CB2, with a resulting decrease in value (minus 2 points from evaluation level). Two sessions were directed towards F7Fp1CB2, with a resultant gain of 5 points. Although reading memory was the focus, auditory memory continued to be assessed and indicated scores of 8 and 11 during this period. The last 3 sessions were directed towards left posterior (T5-P3-O1) RPB1 and RPB2 with auditory memory score at 14. Figure 49 presents the reading memory improvement scores (435%). This figure was calculated by using the average of his last two memory scores: (40.5 + 13)/2=26.75. This value was then compared to the initial level with the formula: (26.75-5)/5, reflecting the last value minus the initial value divided by the initial value.

Figure 49– Case #8 17 year old male

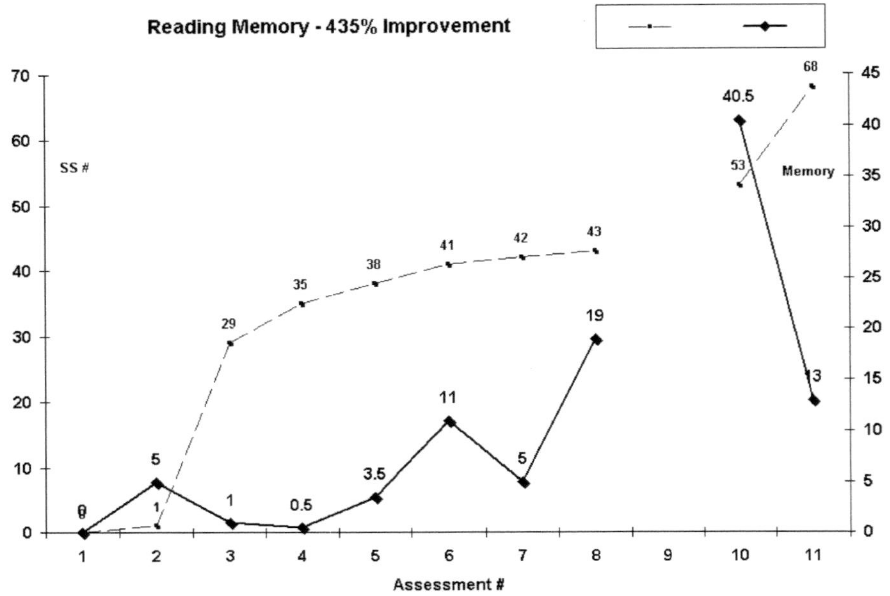

Reading Memory - 435% Improvement

Discussion

Of particular interest in this case is the effect of sugar on the relative power of theta values. The father would characteristically take the child out for lunch during the break midday to a local Friendly's restaurant. On occasion he would have ice cream for dessert. When he returned on those ice cream days, his theta levels would rise to evaluation levels and be recalcitrant to improvement during the session. The sugar effect occurred again during the return trip.

One of the problematic issues with this subject was the sugar issue. It was unclear exactly what sessions may have been affected by the lunch sugar intake. The sessions in which it was clear that sugar was an issue were not included in the analysis. The observation that sugar appeared to selectively affect the theta frequency is a subject for possible further research. However, of more immediate practical import is the necessity for clinicians to be aware of the potential confounding effect that sugar may have on their interventions.

The issue of generalization can be addressed with Figure 43 & 50.

160

The Lexicor software allows the therapist to follow four additional variables while one is being addressed. In Figure 43 we can see the large effect on the phase alpha values (10-30 points) even though they were not directly addressed. Figure 50 shows an effect on the F8 PB1 values, a generalization effect across a different frequency.

The subject showed maintenance of gains following the two-month interlude on both the qEEG measures and cognitive measures. The qEEG measures that were available for analysis were the left posterior RPB1 and RPT values. Neither the auditory nor reading memory scores showed deterioration of functioning during the second visit. It should be noted that the subject's initial memory scores would have been classified as severe by any method currently available.

As the EEG biofeedback field is a rapidly expanding new scientific field there are many questions which will require further addressing as the field develops. One such question is that regarding the higher responsivity of some variables compared to others. In case 7, the left posterior RPB2 values were very amenable to a rapid response (1 session - Figure 48), while left posterior RPB1 values (Figure 45) were responsive, but required considerably more sessions (11-15) to obtain and solidify the gains. Coherence and phase alpha values (Figure 43 & 44) were much more responsive to change than coherence beta2 values (Figure 47). There are no clear reasons for these different levels of responsivity.

Possible explanations would be as follows. 1) Individuals have different amounts of myelinated fibers connecting regions. 2) The treatment is resulting in growth of the myelinated neurons. Further research with DTI may elucidate the neuronal cause of this electrophysiological change.

Case #8

Case #8 is a 17-year old male whose parents reported considerable progress in social and academic functioning following the treatment. He was extremely nonverbal at the beginning of the treatment and was unable to maintain a conversation.

Figure 50 presents the coherence alpha problem evident in the evaluation, as well as the post treatment values. Figure 51 presents the theta and beta issues evident in the evaluation, as well as the post-treatment values.

**Figure 50– Case #8 17 year old male – Auditory Processing
page 333
Figure 51 - Case #8 17 year old male - page 334
See inserts at end of book**

Figure 52 presents the improvement in auditory memory scores obtained during the treatment.

Figure 52– Case #8 17 year old male

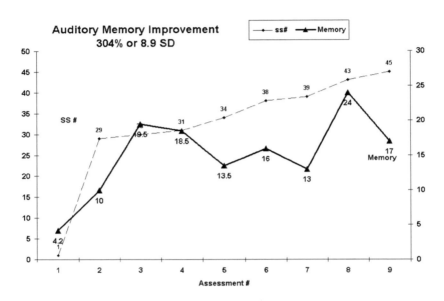

Figure 53 presents the coherence beta problems evident in the initial evaluation for reading.

**Insert Figure 53– Case #8 17 year old male - Reading
See insert at end of book - page 335**

Figure 54 presents the theta and beta issues which were present under the reading condition in the original evaluation and the post treatment scores.

**Figure 54-Case #8 17 year old male - Reading
See insert at end of book - page 336**

Figure 55 presents the reading memory improvement scores.

Figure 55

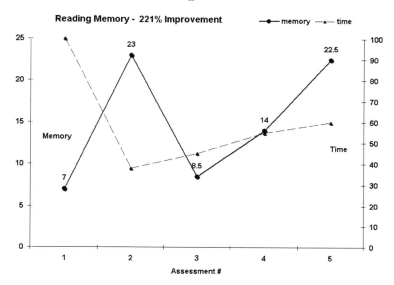

Solid Line: session # (axis on left)
Dashed Line: memory score (axis on right)

Case #9

Case #9 is a 13 year old who had been placed in a special school due to his inattention and difficulty in academic subjects.

Following over 100 sessions, he underwent a qEEG reevaluation more than a year after the original evaluation. There were over 100 sessions directed towards the F4 coherence beta2 relationship problem during reading recall. The Figures 56, 57, and 58 present the pre- vs post- evaluation effects on both the reading and problem-solving measures. Not all relationships between F4 and the other cortical locations were addressed, nor were the F8 coherence beta2 relationships addressed. The consistency of the effect to a different cognitive task documents the generalizability of the effect to different cognitive tasks as well as to different cortical relationships (F8).

Insert Figure 56 Case #9 – Reading - page 337
Insert Figure 57 Case #9 – Matrix Reasoning - page 338
Insert Figure 58 Case #9 – Matrix Reasoning - page 339
See inserts at end of book

Chapter 16 – The questions
Discussion

As in any new scientific area, numerous questions remain unresolved during the initial scientific development. Questions in this area concern the following:

1) Does EEG biofeedback work?
2) Assumption of one protocol fits all.
3) Individual cases versus group data.
4) Activation vs eyes-closed database norms.
   a. Relationship between qEEG variables and cognitive success.
5) Do we address the absolute level of a variable or its degree of activation from an appropriate comparison condition?
6) The nature of normative reference groups (sex and age considerations).
7) Assumptions regarding effect of improvement on single variables.
8) Lack of responsiveness of certain variables.
9) Standard deviation differences employed for reporting of significan differences.
10) What is physically happening as a result of the interventions?
11) Question of generalization to different cognitive tasks and variables within a frequency and across frequencies.
12) Issues of addressing variables which are not correlated with success at a task.
13) How many sessions are required?
14) Limitations of the approach.
15) Relationship to psychoeducational concepts.

1)   Does EEG biofeedback work?

If the research question being asked is, "Does EEG biofeedback work?" in the context of subjects undergoing a treatment which addresses one variable for all subjects, then the limitations of the approach will be shortly evident. This one variable fits all approach fails to consider issues of deviation from the norm and the variable's relationship to cognition. The original research in this area proceeded in such a manner (theta and beta magnitudes at C3 and C4) and was able to produce positive results on measures of attention, IQ, and behavioral scores. As most of the original subject population was comprised of children with attentional or learning problems, there are 3 possible interpretations.

a) **Deficit Hypothesis:** It is possible that the interventions were addressing a specific deficit (deviation from the norm) for this group of children. For this hypothesis to be true it would also be necessary that this deficit is related to the attention and behavior measures.

b) **Maturation Hypothesis:** The protocols were addressing a variable which is related to normal developmental trends for cognitive/behavioral maturation, and thus improvement would be expected to produce a maturational result. This explanation might account for the normal maturational improvement in attention and behavior, but not necessarily the IQ changes, which are relatively stable.

c) **Cognition/Behavior Hypothesis:** The variable is involved in successful cognition or appropriate behavior in all children, apart from maturational or deficit issues and thus if addressed in normal children one would expect improvement in cognition and behavior.

However, there were instances of lack of improvement in individual subjects who were being addressed with the protocols. Possible explanations include:

a) **Maturation Sufficient:** The qEEG variable was sufficiently matured in the particular subject so that further improvement would not result in cognitive or behavioral improvements. The assumption behind this argument is that once a variable reaches a certain level, further improvement will not result in further cognitive/behavioral improvement. A mathematical description would assert that the relationship is not a linear one, which just continues to rise, but a curvilinear one that reaches its peak at a certain point.

b) **Inappropriate Protocols:** The treatment did not address / was not related to the particular qEEG problem that the individual subject had.

c) **Subject Unresponsive**: The subject was unable to change the value of the qEEG variable.

d) **Adequate Response, but not Sufficient:** The positive change in one variable was not sufficient to address the cognitive or behav-

165

ioral problems because

    i.   **Subject's treatment response not large enough.**

    ii.   **Treatment response to one variable not sufficient to change cognition/behavior because cognition/behavior are con tributed to by multiple locations and connection patterns.**

All explanations may be applicable. Due to these confounding issues, the question "Does EEG biofeedback work?" is not the appropriate question to ask. The question which has been asked, "Does EEG biofeedback (sensori-motor location feedback on theta and beta microvolt variables) have a positive impact upon cognitive and behavioral functioning in general?" has been the research question and has received positive research support (Linden et al.,1996; Othmer & Othmer, 1992; Tansey, 1991;, Thompson & Thompson, 1998; Rossiter, 2002; Byers, 1961; Keller, 2001; Kaiser & Othmer, 2000; Lubar et al., 1984; Lubar & Lubar, 1995.

2)   **Assumption of one protocol fits all.**

Research studies generally approach the problem of treatment effectiveness by examining a particular fixed treatment on a group of subjects with a particular problem and comparing any change to a control group, sham treatment, etc. The implicit assumption is that one treatment can fit all. This is one of the inappropriate assumptions made by a federal agency in a recent response to a grant application. The assumption is still being employed in scientific and clinical arenas. However, in dealing with a complex system such as the human brain the assumption is inappropriate. It would be similar to assuming that you can fix all non-functioning cars with a new alternator, even though there may be hundreds of different reasons the car doesn't run.

The original research in the area proceeded to change variable(s) and study the effects upon cognition and behavior. The conclusion that the variable is related to the cognitive and behavioral effect seemed warranted. The assumption that the treated variable was the only variable that relate to the cognitive/behavioral measures, however, would be a clinical and logical error.

3) **Individual cases versus group data.**

It is the author's belief that specific protocols for an individual subject require a normative database comparison. The clinician is faced with over 2,900 variables (when sampling up to the 64 Hertz range) which could be addressed in a treatment. The problems with random selection are self evident and the problems with prior research results have been explicated (question 1).

a) If the clinician intervenes based upon group research studies, he is making a clinical error in his assumption that the particular patient he is treating has that particular deficit. Thus, there exists the requirement of at least an eyes-closed database comparison.

Therefore, it is minimally required that a clinical condition have substantive research backing its relationship and that the clinician obtain an eyes-closed database comparison to document that particular deficit in the patient.

In this situation the protocols are designed to return the subject's values to normal levels. The limitation here, however, is the lack of distinction regarding whether a high value is positive or negative. Although this is not generally a problem with respect to delta & theta values, there are considerable problems in reference to coherence and phase values. There is solid empirical evidence accumulated during the past 44 years that excessive amounts (above normal with respect to a database) of delta and theta are negatively related to successful cognition (Byers, 1961; Dykman et al., 1982; Lubar et al.,1984; Byring et al., 1991; Tansey, 1991; Galin et al., 1992; Harmony et al., 1990; Mann et al., 1992; Othmer & Othmer, 1992; Lubar & Lubar, 1995; Ackerman et al., 1995; Chabot et al., 1996; Linden et al.,1996; Thompson & Thompson,1998; Kaiser & Othmer, 2000; Keller, 2001; Thornton, 2001; Rossiter, 2002; Monastra, 2005).

However, even this well researched finding can potentially be in error in particular cognitive tasks (test anxiety situation). Beta increases (generally negatively related to delta and theta values) are generally a positive goal. However, it is unknown just how high and in what beta frequency increases should be pursued. To put the question in another way, are the relationships between beta, theta, etc., strictly linear ones (the higher the better) or do they asymptote at a certain point (reach a maximum, where on further qEEG variable increases do not produce any further clinical/cognitive improvements)?

Evidence regarding interventions on the coherence and phase re-

167

lationships have supported different perspectives depending on subject population: Epilepsy (Walker & Kozlowski, 2005) – decreasing/ increasing in reference to database, LD/ADHD/TBI (Thornton and Carmody, 2005a, 2005b) – increasing (specific frequencies) in reference to task-oriented database. Thus, applying normative group reference data (eyes-closed database) to individual cases is superior to guessing but remains problematic. There is only preliminary published (Thornton, 2000b, 2002c) research indicating what the relevant qEEG variables are for specific cognitive tasks (auditory memory and reading memory) although unpublished data has been obtained for a considerable number of additional cognitive tasks (Thornton, 2001).

4)   **Activation vs Eyes-Closed database norms.**
        Although it has been demonstrated that activation tasks provide higher reliability of data, the relationship between the values obtained in an eyes closed condition and an activation condition has not been established. Almost all of the research conducted to date on the relationship between cognition and the qEEG variables has involved an eyes-closed database comparison which then correlates the results to cognitive (IQ scores, achievement batteries, grades) measures obtained in different settings. There is certainly validity in this approach and positive relationships have been found. However, it is also certainly more desirable to know the relationships during the cognitive tasks under consideration. Therein resides the value of an activation database, as it:

        a)   bypasses the problem of the indirect relationship between eyes closed and activation values.

        b)   bypasses the problem of the indirect relationship between the qEEG variables and cognitive function.

        c)   measures directly the relationship between the qEEG variable and success at the task (to be addressed in next section).

        a. **Relationship between qEEG variables and cognitive success.**
        The eyes-closed database approach does not address the issue of the relationships of the variables to effective cognitive functioning under task conditions. The approach also doesn't address the issue of task relevant response specificity of a qEEG variable (e.g. theta isn't always a negative

frequency). For example, under auditory recall conditions in adults it is desirable to have higher levels of theta activity for memory recall (Thornton, 2001). The classic "test anxiety" situation, resulting in lowered performance is most probably the inability to "relax" the brain and produce theta, which is positively correlated with immediate recall, but instead produce high frequency beta activity (associated clinically with anxiety).

The initial question, "Does EEG biofeedback work?" seen in this context, should be phrased, "Does training qEEG cognitively relevant (and deficient from normal or optimal levels in an individual subject) variables improve the qEEG variables in the desired direction and does the related specific cognitive performance of an individual improve?"

In dealing with a systems situation where cognition involves multiple locations and connection activity in different frequencies, the only appropriate research question is one that addresses specific qEEG problems in specific individuals on specific cognitive variables. Therefore, individual case studies can be the only appropriate type of research unless similar deficits are to be found in a group of subjects, a formidable subject collection task. In other words, we can't just change the alternator in a batch of nonfunctional cars and call that an adequate research study.

5)   Do we address the absolute level of a variable or its degree of activation from an appropriate comparison condition?

Scientific research conducted in this area with modern medical technology (PET, fMRI, DTI) has approached the problem of the brain's response to cognitive tasks by examining the response on its particular measure (blood flow, etc.) in comparison to another state. The other state can be either a resting condition or another cognitive task that the authors are attempting to distinguish between. The resultant difference usually provides a single measure (blood flow, etc.). Absolute values of the measures are not reported. In addition, the relationship of the bran's response to success at the task is rarely studied.

In the qEEG activation approach it is possible to generate both the absolute level of a variable and its degree of activation from a relevant cognitive task. In addition, the relationship to success at the task is amenable to analysis. While superior to other methodologies, the relative value of addressing degree of activation variables versus absolute levels has not been addressed in research studies.

6)   **The nature of normative reference groups (sex and age considerations).**

Another issue is the use of a normative reference group that is not tied to age or sex variables. The only age discrimination employed in the activation database was between children (ages 10-14) and adults (ages 14 to 70). This cut off was due to a different patterning of successful qEEG correlates, which reflects a maturational concern (Thornton, 2001) and may relate to Piaget''s theory of formal operations. Piaget was a famous French psychologist who delineated important stages in the development of the mind's cognitive abilities.

The basic difference between the two groups (adult vs. child) was the overriding importance of relative power and magnitudes of the beta1 frequency for children and effective cognition, while for adults the predominant effective variables involved coherence relationships (Thornton, 2001). For both groups, the relative power of theta was a negative variable during the input stage of cognition. This negative theta impact was critical even when all subjects (N=250, TBI, normals, all ages, psychiatric cases, LD, ADHD) were analyzed for the relationship to successful cognition (Thornton, 2001). Delta activity was not examined due to potential artifact issues (Thornton, 2001).

The rationale behind not employing age or sex-stratified norms is that the focus of interest is success, not deviation from an age or sex-stratified reference group. An elderly person can have a superior memory if the relevant variables are functioning in a high range. This focus, in principle, allows for a smaller sample size than is generally required in database development. The clinical utility of the approach and the database has been demonstrated in the research results as well as the particular clinical case examples provided.

7)   **Assumptions regarding effect of improvement on single variables.**

An additional problem concerns assumptions behind sensor placement. If we know that a particular qEEG variable at a particular location is related to cognitive success on particular cognitive variable, the presumption would be that raising the value of that variable would result in improvement on the cognitive variable. While this may be the case, this assumption ignores the role of other qEEG variables in cognitive success and the necessity to address the problem as a system problem and not focused on a particular location or frequency. It may be critical to raise multiple variables before success becomes manifested on the cognitive measures. The author has observed this phenomenon clinically. It is evident in the example # 6, as it wasn't until the 21st session that the auditory memory score started to dramatically improve, after many variables were successfully addressed. The statement that multiple locations and connection patterns require addressing is the principle underlying a systems approach.

8)   **Lack of responsiveness of certain variables.**

Although it is clear in this case example that the qEEG variables are very amenable to operant conditioning, it is also evident that some qEEG variables in some individuals do not respond, are not as responsive as other variables, or respond in the opposite pattern to expectations. The reason for this may reside in the individual differences in the myelinated fibers(Catani et al., 2005). Catani was able to demonstrate in a DTI study that different individuals have different amounts of myelinated fibers connecting regions.

9)   **SD differences employed for reporting of significant differences.**

Many databases employ a 2 SD cut off for significance. The method employed in this research does not, but rather examines the pattern of deficits surrounding particular task relevant qEEG variables and flashlight patterns. The reasoning is not a deficit model in the traditional sense, where deficit is defined by a 2 SD difference from the norm. A move from -.50 SD to +1.5 SD on a variable is a move towards optimization as well as a "deficit" value on a variable obtaining higher levels.

10)   **What is physically happening as a result of the interventions?**

Of general concern is the question of whether the treatments are promoting physical growth of an area or of myelinated neurons or allowing the brain to employ its resources more efficiently.

Jibiki et al. (1994) were able to obtain significant negative correlations between blood flow (in group of patients with partial epilepsy) and the relative power of theta (4-7.8 Hz) and a positive correlation between blood flow and alpha (10-12.8 Hz) in the frontal, parietal and temporal regions. In the occipital regions, there was a positive correlation between blood flow and relative power of beta (13-25 Hz). The authors also noted that in previous research there was supporting evidence for the inverse relationship between delta and theta activity and blood flow (studies with cerebral infarction, Alzheimer's, and Pick's disease), as well as positive correlations between alpha power and blood flow.

By inference, but not direct research support, it might be assumed that decreasing theta and delta activity and increasing alpha and beta activity is resulting in greater blood flow to the location being addressed. It remains uncertain exactly what is physically happening when coherence and phase values are increased.

11) Question of generalization to different cognitive tasks and variables within a frequency and across frequencies.

It is unclear in the results whether the improvement of left posterior beta and theta levels during auditory memory conditions generalized to the improvement of these variables during the reading task due to the vacillating nature of the treatment interventions in a particular subject.

There was evidence in Figure 43 (case 7) of generalization of the coherence alpha improvements to phase alpha and Figure 50 (case 8), where the F8 phase beta1 values increased as a result of interventions directed towards F8 coherence alpha relationships, or Figure 53, which shows the improvement in phase beta1 and phase beta2 from F7, even though the coherence relationships were addressed. In Figure 54 (case 8), the magnitude of beta2 in left posterior locations improved, which was not the direct object of intervention, but was indirectly addressed through the RPB2 variable. Other cases have presented this type of generalization (different variable within a frequency and across beta frequency).

12) Issues of addressing variables which are not correlated with success at a task.

It has been clinically observed that if a particular variable (coherence beta2 in one example) that is particularly deficient (in SD units) is successfully addressed, unrelated cognitive variables will improve. In particular, the CB2 value from F4 is related to reading recall measures (Thornton, 2001) and was deficient in one TBI subject. When this variable was addressed under reading conditions, her auditory memory improved dramatically. While the author has not collected a significant number of these situations, this one case does make it clear that the assumption that only task relevant qEEG variables require addressing is not sufficient. The phenomena validates the necessity of addressing the brain with a systems orientation.

13)   How many sessions are required?

The literature in this area generally reports that between 30 and 40 sessions are required to obtain the results reported. Previous reports have indicated between 40-50 for LD/ADD (Thornton and Carmody, 2005a) and 54 hours (108 sessions) for the 3 SD improvement in auditory memory for the traumatic brain injured group (Thornton and Carmody, 2005b). What is important to understand from a systems viewpoint is that once the activation evaluation has been completed there is often evidence of multiple problems across different tasks. While the number of problems may appear to be overwhelming initially, there are several mitigating factors which argue against hundreds of sessions to effectively address the problems: 1) there can be generalization effects to different tasks, different locations and different frequencies and 2) a "perfect" brain is not required to obtain significant improvements in academic or cognitive performance.

In comparison, many commonly used psychoeducational methods employ many more sessions than the 30-40 reported in this research area. For example, the Orton-Gillingham method employs 350 sessions (Oakland et al., 1998), both the FastForWord and the Lindamood-Bell programs require over 100 sessions (Thornton and Carmody, 2005a) and some programs last a full year (Hunterdon learning center).

14)   Limitations of the approach.

The drawback with a cortical intervention is the possible presence of subcortical problems which could present a significant problem to cognitive improvement. The author has been involved in two cases that proved to be very recalcitrant to improvement of cognition despite improvement in the raw qEEG variables.

One case involved chemotherapy to an adolescent brain for a tumor and the other case was an adult who experienced toxic encephalopathy due to 20 plus years of exposure to toxic fumes (tetrachloroethylene, xylene). In both these cases, there was a diffuse effect upon the brain's structures with probable resultant damage to subcortical structures (areas not assessed during an evaluation or directly treated in a Neurocognitive session).

15)   Relationship to psychoeducational concepts.

Psychoeducational concepts such as auditory processing deficits are generated by psychological theory and empirical research. The relationship between specific constructs and the electrophysiology of the brain has not been specifically established in the research literature and will require decades of research to understand. The relationship between auditory processing deficits and electrophysiological function has been delineated in one research article (Thornton, 2000b).

The powerful effects of the neurocognitive approach may well override the normal scientific progression of precisely understanding these relationships prior to intervention. In addition, as the approach represents a paradigm shift in the understanding and treatment of these disorders, a new nomenclature may arise which may replace the previous categorizations employed.

Conclusion

The activation database guided qEEG Neurocognitive approach to the remediation of memory problems in the learning disabled and traumatic brain injured population (auditory and reading) has been empirically demonstrated to obtain substantially larger effect sizes in considerably less time than currently employed methods. The single case examples provide part of the reasoning of the approach with the resultant significant gains. The reasoning makes 3 assumptions:

1)   Empirically task relevant deviant values should be ad dressed until normalized or maximized.

2)   The brain should be approached as a total system.

3)   Interventions should be conducted under relevant task conditions.

While these assumptions may appear self-evident, the combination has not been the major impetus currently employed in the field. What is remarkable about the interventions is how easily the qEEG variables can be effectively addressed. Many of the deviant patterns were improved in one session. The variation in a particular memory score can be attributed to many reasons - improved qEEG values, interest, relevance to the subject, story content, story difficulty, time of day, etc. The consistency and magnitude of the improvements argue against these random variations as determining factors and supports the attribution of cognitive change to the

174

improved qEEG values.

The urgent need to employ this technology in the school system is painfully self-evident to anyone involved with these children.

Chapter 17
Implications for Society
a)   Educational system – how we rank in the world

The relevance of the technology is to more than just the learning disabled child, as improvements in brain functioning are also possible with the normal population. Three normal subjects were addressed with the procedure and averaged a 130% improvement in auditory memory. The normal brain may be more responsive to the interventions, as there are no gross genetic or physical abnormalities to overcome. However, even in a normal population there will be variations in the densities of the myelinated fibers and availability of neurons at cortical locations. Variations are inherent in any normal distribution. The following discussion is provided in the context of the technology's ability to improve normal and even supernormal brains.

The United States has the highest achieving educational system in the world if we rank universities by several indicators of academic or research performance, including alumni and staff winning Nobel Prizes and Fields Medals, highly cited researchers, articles published in Nature and Science, articles indexed in major citation indices, and the per capita academic performance of an institution. (Table 16) (Academic Ranking of World Universities, 2005)

Table 16 – US Rank in World

	Country	Top 20	Top 100	Top 200	Top 300	Top 400	Top 500
1	**USA**	17	53	90	119	140	168
2	UK	2	11	19	30	36	40
3	Japan	1	5	9	13	24	34
4	Germany		5	16	23	33	40
5	Canada		4	8	17	19	23
6	France		4	8	13	19	221
7	Sweden		4	5	9	11	11
8	Switzerland		3	6	6	7	8
9	Netherlands		2	7	9	11	12
10	Australia		2	6	9	10	14
11	Italy		1	5	9	18	23
12	Israel		1	4	4	6	7
13	Denmark		1	3	4	4	5
14	Austria		1	1	2	4	6
15	Norway		1	1	2	3	4
16	Finland		1	1	2	2	6
17	Russia		1	1	1	2	2
18	Belgium			4	6	6	7
19	China			2	6	15	18
20	Spain			2	3	4	9

The federal government has been dramatically increasing its expenditures in the area of education for the past 40 years (Figure 59). (US Government education spending)

Figure 59 - Increases in US Education Costs

US Education Costs by Year - in milions of dollars
Left Axis: Red-Year
Right Axis: Money Green - millions of dollars

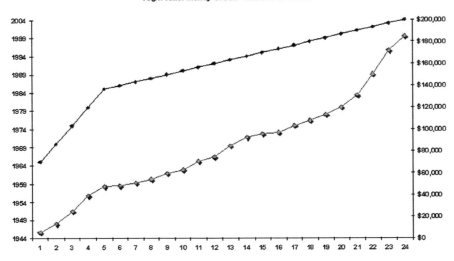

Top dashed line - year
Bottom Solid Line - Money spent

However, in comparison to other countries the achievement levels of our students are not commensurate with what we are spending (Table 17). (PISA survey, 2001)

Table 17

	Math	X	Reading	X	Science	X	P.S.	X
1	Hong Kong	550	Finland	543	Finland	548	Korea	550
2	Finland	544	Korea	534	Japan	548	Hong Kong	548
3	Korea	542	Canada	528	Hong Kong	539	Finland	548
4	Netherlands	538	Australia	525	Korea	538	Japan	547
5	Liechten-stein	536	Liechten-stein	525	Liechten-stein	525	New Zea-land	533
6	Japan	534	New Zea-land	522	Australia	525	Macao-China	532
7	Canada	532	Ireland	515	Macao - China	525	Austra-lia	530
8	Belgium	529	Sweden	514	Nether-lands	524	Liech-ten-stein	529
9	Macao-China	527	Netherlands	513	Czech Republic	523	Canada	529
10	Switzerland	527	Hong Kong China	510	New Zea-land	521	Bel-gium	525
11	Australia	524	Belgium	507	Canada	519	Swit-zerland	521
12	New Zea-land	523	Norway	500	Switzer-land	513	Nether-lands	520
13	Czech Re-public	516	Switzerland	499	France	511	France	519
14	Iceland	515	Japan	498	Belgium	509	Den-mark	517
15	Denmark	514	Macao-China	498	Sweden	506	Czech Repub-lic	516
16	France	511	Poland	497	Ireland	505	Ger-many	513
17	Sweden	509	France	496	Hungary	503	Swe-den	509
18	Austria	506	**USA**	495	Germany	502	Austria	506

	Math	X	Reading	X	Science	X	P.S.	X
19	Germany	503	Denmark	492	Poland	498	Iceland	505
20	Ireland	503	Iceland	492	Slovak	495	Hungary	501
21	Slovak Republic	498	Germany	491	Iceland	495	Ireland	498
22	Norway	495	Austria	491	**USA**	491	Luxembourg	494
23	Luxembourg	493	Latvia	491	Austria	491	Slovak	492
24	Poland	490	Czech Republic	489	Russia	489	Norway	490
25	Hungary	490	Hungary	482	Latvia	489	Poland	487
26	Spain	485	Spain	481	Spain	487	Latvia	483
27	Latvia	483	Luxembourg	479	Italy	486	Spain	482
28	**USA**	483	Portugal	478	Norway	484	Russia	479
29	Russia	468	Italy	476	Luxembourg	483	**USA**	477
30	Portugal	466	Greece	472	Greece	481	Portugal	470
31	Italy	466	Slovak Republic	469	Denmark	475	Italy	469
32	Greece	445	Russia	442	Portugal	468	Greece	448
33	Serbia	437	Turkey	441	Uruguay	438	Thailand	425
34	Turkey	423	Uruguay	434	Serbia	436	Serbia	420
35	Uruguay	422	Thailand	420	Turkey	434	Uruguay	411
36	Thailand	417	Serbia	412	Thailand	429	Turkey	408
37	Mexico	385	Brazil	403	Mexico	405	Mexico	384
38	Indonesia	360	Mexico	400	Indonesia	395	Brazil	371
39	Tunisia	359	Indonesia	382	Brazil	390	Indonesia	361
40	Brazil	356	Tunisia	375	Tunisia	385	Tunisia	345

P.S. = Problem Solving X = Mean

180

If we average the scores across nations, Finland receives the highest average (546) followed by Korea, Hong Kong and Japan while the US ranks 27th in the world with an average score of 487, 12 points below the average.

Yet we spend more on educating the student than any other county. Table 18 reflects the total average expenditure from elementary school years through college for the different countries. (Countries education cost) The table reports two values. The first on the left reports the total value from primary to the higher education level. Only the reported countries had this value available. The column on the right reports just the higher education value. As the table indicates only Switzerland spends more than us on a per student basis. Finland is the top rated country in performance and between the 10th and 12th in average cost per student.

Table 18

		Education Cost per student		Higher Education Cost per student
1	Switzerland	$29,856	Japan	$18,914
2	**USA**	$28,287	Switzerland	$16,376
3	Austria	$24,464	**USA**	$14,864
4	Sweden	$23,734	Canada	$14,816
5	Denmark	$21,492	Sweden	$12,785
6	Australia	$20,785	Australia	$11,240
7	France	$17,911	Germany	$10,108
8	Germany	$17,617	Ireland	$8,171
9	Italy	$17,329	Denmark	$7,294
10	Finland	$16,842	Finland	$7,190
11	Canada	$14,816	France	$7,058
12	Ireland	$14,610	Korea	$6,227
13	Spain	$14,281	Italy	$5,972
14	Korea	$13,463	Czech Republic	$5,478
15	Czech Republic	$11, 063	Hungary	$5,430
16	Hungary	$9,558	Spain	$5,335
17	Greece	$8,922	Mexico	$4,628
18	Mexico	$7,150	Poland	$4,395
19			Greece	$3,990
20			Turkey	$2,397

International test data tell us that we have the greatest inequities between our highest- and lowest-scoring students of any nation. In a UNICEF study, the gap between our average scorers and our low scorers gives the U.S. an abysmal ranking of 21st out of 24 industrialized nations in educational equality. (Innocenti Report Cards, no. 4, November 2002)

In conclusion, the US has the most productive university system in the world, ranks 27th in the world in overall achievement levels of its 15 year-old students, spends more per student than almost all other countries and has the largest discrepancy between average high and low scorers. We

182

could further increase our productivity, raise our overall achievement levels, and lower the discrepancy scores with the Neurocognitive intervention approach.

Chapter 18 - Education – potential effect

There have been four independent studies (Tansey, 1991; Othmer & Othmer, 1999; Linden et al., 1996; Thompson & Thompson, 1998) which have documented the gain on IQ test scores averaging 15 points. As IQ scores represent the single most powerful predictor of success in life (Brody, 1999) and have been the most intensely studied, we will need to discuss this measure and its relevance to education and success in some detail. As Table 21 will indicate a gain of 15 points on the IQ measure is equivalent to an increase in SAT scores of about 200 points and an income increase of about $30,000 a year.

Meaning of IQ test scores vs. Achievement Scores

The difference between ability measures and achievement measures is a critical one in the educational area. To put it simply, an achievement measure indicates whether a student knows a particular fact, such as 2x2. An ability measure assesses the ability of the student to learn and apply the fact appropriately. For example, How long does it take to learn the fact? Can the child employ the fact in different situations? It is more desirable to improve the student's ability, if it can be done, as the ease with which the student can learn facts and generalize is critical in the educational process as well as in life itself? Brody (1999) reported that the single best predictor of success in life is the score on an IQ test. We will need to take a close look at what the meaning of an IQ test score is on the life of an individual to fully understand the implications of Dr. Brody's statement.

Other Intelligence Constructs

Traditional IQ test scores have received criticism on a number of levels as not "truly" representative of an individual's ability and potential. For example, "practical intelligence" is not assessed in traditional IQ tests, but it is easy to measure and is involved in effective adaptation to the demands of work and daily life. Sternberg asserts that practical intelligence predicts people's future job success at least as well as, if not better than, people's scores on traditional IQ tests (e.g., see Sternberg et al., 1995). With the cooperation of the College Board, Sternberg recently directed the Rainbow Project. This research project, carried out on 15 college campuses throughout the nation, was designed to supplement the SAT by adding measures of creativity and practical intelligence. Results show that the expanded SAT predicts actual success in college more accurately than traditional SAT scores. Initial results also suggest that the ethnic differences historically observed on the math and verbal portions of the SAT are greatly reduced for tests of creativity or practical intelligence.

The concept of emotional intelligence (Goleman, 1997) has also received attention during the past decade as a relevant concept to success in life. While these concepts certainly have validity and usefulness, the availability of data on the standardized IQ test is much more prevalent in research studies. As a result, we will rely upon this type of IQ data to examine the relationship between social, economic, and employment variables; SAT scores; and international rankings.

The effect of IQ scores on social, vocational, medical, SAT, income and GDP measures

Table 19 presents the vocational effect of SD differences in IQ. (IQ and vocational effect)

Table 19

IQ Range	Frequency	Cumulative Frequency	Typical Educability	Employ-ment Options
Below 30	>1%	>1% below 30	illiterate	unemploy-able, institu-tionalized
30 to 50	>1%	>1% below 50	1st to 3rd grade	simple, non-critical household chores
50 to 60	~1%	1.5% below 60	3rd to 6th grade	very simple tasks, close supervision
60 to 74	3.5%	5% below 74	6th to 8th grade	slow, simple, supervised
74 to 89	20%	25% below 89	8th to 12th grade	asembler, food service, nurse's aide
89 to 100	25%	550% below 100	8th to 1-2 yrs. college	clerk, teller, walmart
100 to 111	50%	1 in 2 above 100	12th grade to B.A.	police offi-cer, machin-ist, sales

185

IQ Range	Frequency	Cumulative Frequency	Typical Educability	Employ-ment Op-tions
111 to 120	15%	1 in 4 above 111	B.A. to M.A.	manager, teacher, accountant
120 to 125	5%	1 in 10 above 120	B.A. to non technical PhD	manager, professor, accountant
125 to 132	3%	1 in 20 above 125	any PHD at 3rd tier	schools attorney, edi-tor, execu-tive
132 to 137	1%	1 in 50 above 132	No limita-tions	eminent pro-fessor, editor
137 to 150	.90%	1 in 100 above 127	no limita-tions	leading math, phys-ics professor
150 to 160	.10%	1 in 1,100 above 150	no limita-tions	Lincoln, Copernicus, Jefferson
160 to 174	.01%	1 in 11,000 above 160	no limita-tions	Descartes, Einstein, Spinoza
174 to 200	.01%	1 in 1,000,000 above 174	no limita-tions	Shakespeare, Goethe, Newton

Table 20 presents a social/economic view of the effect of IQ on life. (IQ and social effect)

Table 20

IQ	<75	75-90	90-110	110-125	>125
US distribution	5	20	50	20	5
Married by age 30	72	81	81	72	67
out of labor force >1 Mo./Yr.(men)	22	19	15	14	10
uemployed > 1 Mo. (men)	12	10	7	7	2
divorced in 5 years	21	22	23	15	9
% children w/IQ <75 (mothers)	39	17	6	7	-
lives in poverty	30	16	6	3	2
ever incarcerated	7	7	3	1	0
chronic welfare recipient (mothers)	31	17	8	2	0
high school dropout	55	35	6	.40	0

Table 21 documents the powerful relationships between IQ, SAT scores, quality of life and future income.

Table 21

SAT	Predicted IQ	SAT Total	Family Income
680	85		Yearly
860	98.6	864	< $10,000
900	101.5	898	$10 to $20,000
940	104.4	942	$20 to $30,000
980	107.3	976	$30 to $40,000
1000	108.7	1004	$40 to $50,000
1010	109.5	1011	$50 to $60,000
1030	110.9	1035	$60 to $70,000
1050	112.3	1049	$70 to $80,000
1070	113.8	1074	$80 to $100,000
1130	118.1	1126	>$100,000

IQ scores have also been related to death (Hart et al., 2003)."The risk of dying in 25 years was 17% higher for each standard deviation disadvantage in childhood IQ. Adjustment for social class and deprivation category accounted for some, but not all, of this higher risk, reducing it to 12%. For cancers, cause-specific mortality or cancer incidence risk was higher with decreasing IQ for all cancer, lung cancer, and stomach cancer, and lower for colorectal and female breast cancer. Cause-specific mortality or hospital admission showed higher risks with lower childhood IQ for all cardiovascular disease, coronary heart disease, stroke, and respiratory disease. These results were not statistically significant for stroke or respiratory disease."

Thus it is abundantly clear that SD differences in IQ scores have powerful effects upon an individual's life.

Effect of raising IQ scores 15 points on education
Relationship between IQ scores and Achievement scores

IQ test scores account for 40% to 50% of current expected achievement. Thus, 50% to 60% of student achievement is related to variables "beyond intelligence." Typically the range of concurrent IQ-achievement correlations is +.40 to +.70 (Reschly & Grimes, 1992). The best batteries consistently display correlations between +.60 to +.70. These correlations are statistically significant and are among the strongest predictive relations reported across all fields of psychology. Statistics employ these correlations to generate a concept called "percent of variance explained". In statistical analysis the correlation between two variables is squared to calculate the amount of variance (variation) that one variable can explain in the other. For example, one simply needs to square a correlation (e.g., .702 = .49), multiply it by 100 - .49 x 100 = 49 and then tack a percentage symbol on the end; - 49%. This value represents the amount of explained variance represented by a correlation. For example, an IQ-achievement correlation of +.70 would indicate, "the amount of achievement variance accounted for by intelligence is approximately 49%." A correlation of .60 accounts for 36 % of achievement (.602 x 100 = 36%).

On converting IQ scores to SAT scores

Table 21 employs data from two sources to estimate the predicted relationship between SAT scores and IQ scores and SAT scores to eventual income. As the table documents, there is a powerful effect of IQ on SAT scores and eventual income. (IQ to SAT) (SAT to income; SAT to IQ scores)

Effect of IQ scores on National GDP values

The IQ of a nation has been shown to have a significant relationship with the nation's gross domestic product (GDP) (Figure 60). (Lynn and Vanhanen, 2002)

Figure 60 per capita GDP vs. Avg. IQ - Linear Regression

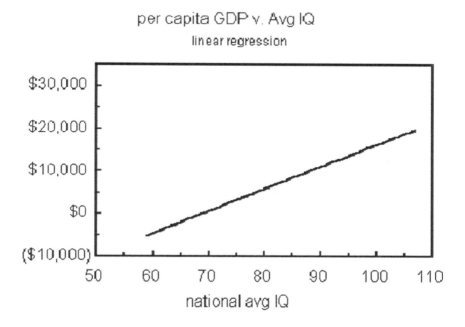

Per capita GDP vs. national average IQ. Notice how GDP is positively correlated to average IQ. The correlation coefficient is +.73. Thus IQ explains 54% of the GDP variance. Values this large are rare in social science. In the social sciences, correlations of +0.2 are said to be "low," +.4 "moderate," and +.6 "high." A correlation of +.73 is most impressive.

In conclusion, it is abundantly clear that SD differences in IQ scores have powerful effects upon an individual's life as well as the nation in which he resides. Any intervention program, which could raise an individual's IQ by 15 points would have significant repercussions on society. The neurotherapy/neurocognitive intervention program has been able to accomplish this effect.

Chapter 19 – Prisons, Drugs, and Special Education

We have a massive problem in the United States with our inability to reduce our prison population and drug abuse problem. Treatment interventions are, by and large, ineffective with these groups.

Size of the Problem

There were 2,268,000 people behind bars in the US in 2004, up 1.9% from 2003.With an incarceration rate of 724 per 100,000 inhabitants, the United States is the unchallenged world leader in both raw numbers and imprisonment per capita.

With a global prison population estimated at nine million, the US accounts for about one-quarter of all prisoners on the planet. The estimated U.S. population is 297,731,005 (population clock) or 5% of the world population, which is 6,480,917,568 and incarcerates 24% of the world's prison population.

In terms of raw numbers, only China, with almost four times the population of the US, comes close, with about 1.5 million prisoners. Our closer competitors in incarceration rates are Russia (638 per 100,000) and Belarus (554), according to the British government's World Prison Population Report. The Federal Bureau of Prisons is now the largest prison system in the land, with 180,000 inmates, followed by Texas (168,000), California (167,000), and Florida (86,000). The federal system is now at 40% over capacity. (Profile of Jail Inmates, 2002) (State Prison Expenditures, 1996)

Drugs

Criminal behavior and drug abuse behavior overlap considerably. The total number of people doing time for drugs in the United States in 2003 exceeded 530,000, according to numbers from the Bureau of Justice Statistics (Feature, 2005). People sentenced for drug crimes accounted for 21% of state prisoners and 55% of federal prisoners.

Drug abuse has a great economic impact on society-an estimated $67 billion per year. This figure includes costs related to crime, medical care, drug abuse treatment, social welfare programs, and time lost from work. Treatment of drug abuse can reduce those costs. Studies have shown that from $4 to $7 are saved for every dollar spent on treatment. It costs approximately $3,600 per month to leave a drug abuser untreated in the community, and incarceration costs approximately $3,300 per month. In contrast, methadone maintenance therapy costs about $290 per month (NIDA info facts).

LD/ED/Drop outs

The Coalition for Juvenile Justice (CJJ) report shows that between 70% and 87% of incarcerated youth suffer from learning disabilities (LD) or emotional disabilities (ED) that interfere with their education. Moreover, youth that drop out of school are three and a half times more likely to be arrested than high school graduates. In the adult criminal system, 82% of prison inmates dropped out of high school. (Leahy, 2001)

Traumatic brain injuries have been correlated with violent behavioral tendencies like those observed in the behavioral topography of perpetrators of serial homicides. (Lewis et al., 1986). A 1986 study examined the neurological histories of fifteen death row inmates and found that every member of the experimental population had experienced severe head injury prior to incarceration (Lewis et al., 1986). Galski et al., 1989) also documented the role of previous traumatic brain injuries in the violent offender. Brain damage in utero and in early childhood has been correlated with increased tendencies toward both youth and adult violence (Raine et al, 1997) (Prothow-Smith and Spivak, 1999)

Costs of Prisons

As the US has the largest prison business in the world, the costs associated with the business are also large. In its first analysis of state prison expenditures since 1990, the federal government's Bureau of Justice Statistics reports that state correctional costs rose from $12 billion in 1990 to $22 billion in 1996, an 83% increase. The state prison population rose 52% during the same time period. Federal prison expenditures rose 160% from $946 million in 1990 to $2.5 billion in 1996, an average of about 17% a year. Ninety-six percent of the state expenditures were for salaries, wages, benefits and other operating expenses. The total operating per inmate cost rose from $16,300 in 1984, to $18,400 in 1990 to $20,100 (state inmates) and $23,500 (Federal inmates) in 1996. (Stephan, 1996)

On a per capita basis, it costs every man, woman and child in the country $103 to run state prisons in 1996, up from $53 per person in 1985. California had the largest state prison expenditure in 1996, spending $3 billion and North Dakota had the smallest, $10.7 million. The figures come from an analysis of the 1996 Survey of Government Finances, conducted by the U.S. Bureau of the Census. Bureau of Justice Statistics finance specialists contacted state budget and corrections officials to ensure the numbers were accurate and then made considerable corrections to the data

In conclusion, the our drug and special education problems continue to grow in tandem with the size and cost of our prison population.

Costs to Victims

The costs of these crimes go beyond those to society's prison costs and the perpetrator's jail time. Crime victims in 1992 lost $17.6 billion in direct costs, according to the National Crime Victimization Survey. These costs included losses from property theft or damage, cash losses, medical expenses, and amount of pay lost because of injury or activities related to the crime. The crimes included in this figure are rape, robbery, assault, personal and household theft, burglary, and motor vehicle theft. Crimes include attempts as well as completed offenses. (Klaus, 1994)

Treatment – How has our society attempted to deal with these problems?

Due to the overlapping problem of criminal behavior and drug abuse, some studies have examined both of these behaviors following treatment.

The drug rehabilitation industry has been looking for effective solutions for decades. Substance Abuse and America's Prison Population revealed that 80% of the men and women behind bars in the U.S. were seriously involved with drugs and alcohol. That year, states spent nearly $30 billion on the adult corrections system, $24.1 billion of which was spent on substance-involved offenders making substance abuse the number one contributor to crime in America.

The state of Texas released a report in 2005 that examined the recidivism rate among its prisoners during 2000 and 2001. They found an average recidivism rate of about 30%, with property (35%) and drug offenders (31%) having the highest rates followed by individuals initially convicted of violent offenses (23%). The recidivism rate among other states that included California (2000- 60.5 %), Colorado (1999-47%), Pennsylvania (2000- 46%) and a national norm of 51% (1994). The Texas study also indicated that juveniles had a higher recidivism rate (about 51%). The report did not indicate whether any treatment was involved. Therefore, any intervention must be compared to the naturally occurring recidivism rate without treatment. (Statewide Criminal Justice Recidivism rates and revocation rates, 2005)

DTAP - Residential/Therapy – Alcoholism

The National Center on Addiction and Substance Abuse (CASA) conducted a five-year research study (2/2003) through Columbia University on the Drug Treatment Alternative-to-Prison (DTAP) Program and found that positive results were achieved at about half the cost of incarceration.

(DTAP, 2003)

The DTAP program provides 15 to 24 months of residential drug treatment, vocational training, and social and mental health services to drug-addicted, nonviolent repeat offenders who face mandatory punishment under New York State's second felony offender law. Participants are abusers of heroin, crack and powder cocaine, among other substances. They plead guilty to a felony, thereby ensuring a mandatory prison sentence if they abscond from the program. Sentencing is deferred upon program participation; if participants complete the program, their guilty plea is withdrawn and the charges dismissed.

The five-year CASA evaluation found that participants who completed the program and graduated were 33% less likely to be rearrested, 45% less likely to be reconvicted, and 87% less likely to return to prison than the comparable prison group.

DTAP graduates were three and one half times more likely to be employed after graduation than before their arrest. Before their arrest, 26% were working either part-time or full-time. Following successful completion of the program, 92% had found employment.

DTAP participants remain in treatment six times longer than individuals in other long-term residential treatment (a median of 17.8 months compared to three months). Retention rates are important because the longer an individual stays in treatment, the greater their chance of maintaining sobriety.

These results are achieved at about half the cost of incarceration. The average cost for each DTAP participant of residential drug treatment, vocational training, and support services was $32,975, compared to an average cost of $64,338 for the time spent in prison for DTAP participants who dropped out.

Psychotherapy – Individual / Group – Drugs and Criminal behavior

A review of treatment outcomes for drug addiction and criminality was reported by Simpson et al. (2002). Interviews were conducted at 1 and 5 years after treatment for 708 subjects (from 45 programs in 8 cities) who met DSM-III-R criteria for cocaine dependence when admitted in 1991-1993. Primary outcome measures included drug use and criminality. Self-reported cocaine use showed high overall agreement with urine (79% agreement) and hair (80% agreement) toxicology analyses. The results indicated that half (52%) had relapses to drug use: 23% to "weekly" cocaine use; 19% to "occasional" cocaine; 10% to "other drugs".

Additional conclusions noted that the percent of illegal activity declined from 40% before the intake for program participation to 25% in year 5 follow-up after discharge from the program (up slightly from 16% in year 1). The percent arrests in the past year dropped from 34% before the program intake to 18% in year 5 follow-up (down slightly from 22% in year 1). The group that received less treatment (i.e. "low treatment") did not fare as well. Low treatment usually meant less than 3-months of treatment -- considered the minimum "threshold" for an effective length of stay. In addition, poorer long-term outcomes were related to higher problem severity at treatment admission and less treatment.

We need to look at these numbers for a moment to see exactly what the result of the treatment was. If illegal activity was at the 40% figure prior the treatment, then 60% of the participants had stopped committing illegal activity, a "spontaneous cure". If the treatment program resulted in a post treatment rate of illegal activity at year 1 of 16%, then the program was effective in reducing illegal activity by another 24%. Thus, of the 40% who were still committing illegal activity, 60% (24/40) were "cured" of their illegal activities at the one year post treatment time assessment. Employing this approach to the data results in a treatment effectiveness value of 70% for cocaine abuse, 73% for heroin abuse, 73% for alcohol abuse, and 35% for any arrests (which is not the same as a recidivism number). Thus the "recidivism" rate for drug abuse was about 30% and for criminal activity between 40% (illegal activity) and 65% (arrest) if the person was engaged in the program.

EEG Biofeedback – Neurotherapy and Criminal Behavior
Initial Discovery

Dr. Von Hilsheimer and Doug Quirk reported between 1970-1995 on a series of fascinating observations and research results that are particularly relevant to the prison population (Quirk, 1995, Quirk & Von Hilsheimer). Mr. Quirk was interested in the prison population. As a psychologist he had learned to administer the Bender-Gestalt test which requires the subject to copy geometric designs. A variant of this test is the Diagnostic Differential Test (DDT).

One of the neurologists on staff where Mr. Quirk worked gave him a list of 10 patients whose serial EEGs eventually demonstrated epilepsy but who did not have seizures. He was asked what test to use to figure out how to recognize them more reliably than with the EEG. Doug found a file into which he had put the DDT's those individuals' had taken and found those particular DDT's as uninterpretable.

He had a casual conversation with a psychologist who told him of some work he had been doing with pigeons demonstrating that when an ablation was made in the region of the brain's septum the pigeons that had been trained to respond to angular signs were post operation unable to differentiate the angles from curves. The performance of his 10 puzzling patients on the DDT indicated that they couldn't handle angles as well as they could handle curves. So Quirk decided that he had found an indicator of deep diencephalic epilepsy. The first 70 patients he found with this sign on the DDT were all diagnosed by a neurologist as epileptic. All but one had typical seizure spindles on the EEG.

Quirk applied the DDT to a large number of arsonists, assaultists and rapists. Forty per cent of the serious arsonists, 30% of the assaultists, and 25% of the rapists demonstrated the sub-ictal sign on the DDT. This last group, the rapists with anomalous DDT performance, also demonstrated visible anomalies of the temporal lobe in CAT scans.

By way of contrast, fewer than 2% of the remaining 'garden varieties' of less dangerous offenders exhibited this deep-brain epileptic syndrome. In several other studies we found that there was a consistent and strong relationship between strong emotional reactivity or weak emotional control and dangerous criminal actions.

Sub-ictal Seizures

Some epilepsies whose focus lies in the deep recesses of the old brain are variously referred to as partial seizures with complex symptomatology (PSCS) or "complex partial seizures". These are non-convulsive seizures, paroxysmal events, sub-ictal states, or seizure equivalents. The behaviors associated with these sub-ictal states tend to distract the observer because they are intense, gruesome, unappetizing, and usually criminal activities. If the epileptic discharge in these seizures involves the Olds and Milner 'drive centre', the person may exhibit uncontrolled paroxysms of rage, sexual drive, hunger, satiety, alcohol use, or other excitant automatisms such as fire setting. The individual may seem perfectly normal in just a few seconds after the explosion of aberrant behavior. There is a subclass of criminal which is floridly emotional and whose emotionality is almost always associated with grotesque and extreme acting out.

The most common prodrome in deep-brain complex partial seizures seems to be heightened intensity of emotional arousal -- perhaps sometimes due to associated activation of the Olds and Milner 'drive centre'. The difficulty encountered by most people in using strong emotional arousal as a cue for behavior is that emotional arousal tends to distract attention from conscious cortical self-regulatory habits. High emotional intensity tends to disengage the subject from such moderating habits. Distracted attention and disengagement is intensified by alcohol and by recreational and medical drugs, all of which are often involved in scenes of intense emotionality. It is generally agreed that some deep-brain complex partial seizures are facilitated by alcohol ingestion.

Developing the intervention

In 1970 Quirk went to a meeting in Boston and heard Barry Sterman talk about his work with cats and human epileptics. Dr. Sternman was employing the sensori-motor rhythm (SMR) frequency (12-15 Hertz) to successfully inhibit seizure activity in cats. He was training the 13 Hertz range along the Fissure of Roland (Sensorimotor Strip or sulcus centralis – top central portion of head) which resulted in resistance to epileptic seizure - even that produced by toxins such as hydrazine (an normally infallible producer of seizures of fatal intensity). The amplitude of 13 Hz is notoriously small in epileptics over the Rolandic Fissure.

Quirk completed two preliminary studies of recidivism among Ontario Correctional Institute felons who had been discharged. He compared 55 pairs of high-risk felons, half of whom were treated by temperature biofeedback, a modified GSR technique called SCARS, and by Sterman's EEG method, and half of whom received only counseling. These felons received 33 half-hour sessions of training. These violent felons demonstrated the sub-ictal pattern on the DDT (viz., they didn't handle visual angles as well as visual curves) and on the EEG. The treatment of the 55 felons included volunteer administered temperature biofeedback training, SCARS GSR training, and EEG training of the sensorimotor rhythm at C-3 and C-4 as described by Sterman. Subsequently, he trained another group of 55 pairs of felons In the typical case, the percent of the time in which this SMR activity occurred tended to average around 10% during the first few half-hour training sessions, and to rise to 45% to 55% during the last training sessions.

Two years after his initial study of 55 pairs of felons 22 or 40% of the treated felons had been arrested again. Two years after the second study of 55 pairs of felons 11 or 20% of the treated felons had been rearrested. This rate of recidivism compared to 85% and 65% rearrested among the matched felons who were not treated by biofeedback. In other words, 60% and 80% of the treated felons were still free, while only 15% and 35% of the untreated felons had managed to remain outside of prison.

The justice system records of the offenders accepted into this bio-feedback treatment program were reviewed an average of a year and a half after release from their treatment sentences. Of the 17 offenders who received 0 to 4 half-hour training sessions (i.e., essentially no treatment), 65% had been re-convicted of criminal offenses. Of the 10 who had received 34 or more half-hour training sessions, only 2 or 20% had been re-convicted of criminal offenses. Intermediate amounts of training were found to be associated with intermediate recidivism rates. Among these subjects, neither follow-up interval nor age were related to recidivism rates.

Overall, from 1970 through 1995, Mr. Quirk trained 2776 felons by this combined method (temperature, GSR, and EEG). Of those trained, 15% were rearrested in the 3 years following release. This compares well to the range of rearrest in studies summarized by Alter et al (1996) - 42 % to 78%. In a series of reports to corrections officials, Mr. Quirk indicated that the three-year recidivism rate from the biofeedback (using these techniques) had never been more than 45%, and in some groups had fallen to 15%. Overall, the rate of recidivism was consistently close to 15%.

The common rate of recidivism in correctional institutions in the United States was generally, at the time, believed to be 98% within two years of discharge. To put the numbers in a different perspective, prisons were so bad that it could be said that we were failing to criminalize only 2% of the juvenile population enrolled in our higher institutions of learning (correctional institutes). (Quirk, 1995)

The Texas report indicated that, presently, in a normal prison population we can expect about a 51% recidivism rate presently without any form of intervention.

The effectiveness, time and cost issues for these intervention methods are summarized in Table 22 and compared to the national norm. Therefore, any intervention must be considered with reference to this base rate. An examination of the table quickly reveals that the EEG biofeedback approach is clearly the more effective mode of treatment for this condition, as well as being the least expensive.

EEG Biofeedback and Seizure Activity

EEG biofeedback originally developed out of the discoveries of B. Sterman in the application of the approach to inhibit seizure activity. It was found as early as 1969 that after training for enhanced SMR (12-15 Hz) rhythm in cats, the threshold for seizure onset was increased for chemically induced seizures (Fairchild, 1974, Sterman, 1976). Sterman and his associates (Sterman & Friar, 1972; Sterman et al., 1974) found by training epileptics to enhance the human EEG sensorimotor rhythm (SMR) of 12-15 Hertz (Hz) that their seizure management could be improved. Sterman et al. (1974) achieved an average 66% reduction in seizure incidence in four epileptics using SMR enhancement training in combination with inhibition of excessive slow-wave activity in the 6-9 Hz regime. Lubar and Bahler (1976) found similar results when they trained epileptics to enhance the SMR frequency and suppress the theta (4-7 Hz) slow wave frequency. Wyler's and Finley's studies were the first to include such pseudo-conditioning and control periods (Wyler, 1976; Finley, 1976). Such sham training was also provided in a more exhaustive, double-blind study (neither the experimenter nor the patient was aware of the contingency of reward) undertaken by Lubar, et al. in 1981. Five of 8 patients exhibited seizure reduction with respect to baseline, the reduction being 35% for the entire group.

Since the original research in this area, the evidence for the application of the technology to seizure activity has continued to amass as a reliable intervention method for seizure reduction. (Sterman, 2000) Alternate protocols to address the seizure problem have been employed by Walker & Kozlowski (2005) who reported a 100% reduction in seizure activity in a group of patients.

It has been documented that about 20% of the patients with epilepsy may exhibit ADHD symptoms. (Tan & Appelton, 2005). Electroencephalography has also been reported to be abnormal in children with ADHD, some showing epileptiform activity. The reported incidence ranges from 6.1% of 476 of children with ADHD (compared to 3.5% of 3726, normal, school age children) 18 to 30.1% of 176 children with ADHD.

As EEG seizure activity (not necessarily behavioral seizure activity) is part of the picture in the learning disabled and ADHD population, the ability of the intervention approach is self evident.

Chapter 20 – Other Clinical Applications: Alcoholism, Autism, Asperger's, etc.

When dealing with any complex system, such as the human brain, there are many deviations or aberrations in the system which could lead to "breakdowns". The first question for any system analysis is to determine where the "breakdown" occurs. Once discerned, the Neurocognitive approach can begin to effectively address the "breakdown". There is no inherent reason (other than subcortical issues) to suspect that a particular clinical condition will not respond to the operant conditioning approach of the cortical signals.

a) EEG Biofeedback and Alcoholism

Some researchers explored alpha wave biofeedback as a treatment adjunct for alcohol abuse (Passini, Watson, and Dehnel, 1977). There were two theoretical rationales: first, investigators had reported that EEGs of alcoholics were "deficient in alpha rhythms and alcohol use induced more alpha wave activity" (Pollock, Volavka, Goodwin, et al., 1983). Clinicians speculated that alcoholics might drink less if they could be taught to produce more alpha waves (Jones & Holmes, 1976). Secondly, many alcoholics and other drug abusers reported using alcohol or other drugs to relax. Thus, biofeedback training was proposed as a way to teach alcoholics an alternative to using alcohol to relax.

It was during the late 1980s and early 1990's that Peniston and Kulkosky developed an innovative therapeutic EEG alpha-theta neurofeedback protocol (Peniston & Kulkosky, 1989, 1993) for the treatment of alcoholism and the prevention of its relapse. The Peniston/Kulkosky brainwave neurofeedback therapeutic protocol combined systematic desensitization, temperature biofeedback, guided imagery, constructed visualizations, rhythmic breathing, and autogenic training incorporating alpha-theta (3-7 Hz) brainwave neurofeedback therapy (Blankenship, 1996; Peniston & Kulkosky, 1989, 1990, 1991, 1992; Saxly & Peniston, 1995).

These investigations prompted a reexamination of EEG neurofeedback as a treatment modality for alcohol abuse. Successful outcome results included increased alpha and theta brainwave production, normalized personality measures, prevention of increases in beta-endorphin levels, and prolonged prevention of relapse. These findings were shown to be significant for experimental subjects who were compared with traditionally treated alcoholic subjects and non-alcoholic control subjects. Subjects in several studies were chronic alcoholic male veterans, some of whom also suffered from combat-related posttraumatic stress disorder. Three groups were studied

a.   alcoholic alpha-theta brainwave neurofeedback therapy (NT)
b.   traditional psychotherapy, and
c.   non-alcoholic control group.

This investigation showed enhanced percentages of alpha and theta waves in the EEGs of group A (NT group) after treatment compared to pre-treatment status. The control group showed no such increase.

The NT group showed sharp reductions in self-assessed depression (Beck Depression Inventory) and sustained abstinence with significantly less relapse episodes (2/10) than the traditional therapy group (8/10) in a 36-month follow-up study. The traditional therapy group showed a significant elevation in serum beta-endorphin levels at the end of treatment compared to their own pretreatment levels, as well as the repeated measurement levels of the non-alcoholic control group. The beta-endorphins are stress-related hormones and are elevated during the experience of physical or emotional stress. Successful treatment would stabilize beta-endorphin levels, so that stress-related increases would be less likely to occur. Since elevations in serum beta-endorphin levels are associated with stress, their elevation in the traditional therapy group may indicate that this group is experiencing the stress associated with abstinence and fear of relapse. It is interesting that the NT group did not show an increase in this stress hormone after treatment, but instead showed a stabilization (Peniston & Kulkosky, 1989). The follow-up study revealed that only three of the twenty experimental patients had relapsed to alcohol by twenty-six months after NT (Peniston et al., 1989, 1995).

EEG alpha-theta brainwave neurofeedback therapy (Peniston/ Kulkosky protocol) had also been employed in a clinical study using twenty male Vietnam combat veterans with a dual diagnosis of posttraumatic stress disorder and alcohol abuse.

In addition to the aforementioned clinical studies, the Peniston/ Kulkosky protocol was employed in private group practice in the treatment of fourteen depressed alcoholic outpatients (8 males and 6 females) (Saxley & Peniston, 1995). After training, subjects showed significant improvement on BDI scores. At 21 months after NT training, only one subject was ob-served to relapse.

The recent ten year follow-up clinical evaluation of the original Peniston/Kulkosky alpha-theta brainwave neurofeedback (Peniston &

Kulkosky, 1989) clinical study confirmed the long-term effectiveness of this therapeutic intervention. Such a success rate of a treatment modality has never before been achieved.

Traditional interventions for alcohol dependency have often resulted in high attrition rates and release rates (Alford, 1980; Emrick & Hanson, 1983; Marlatt, 1983; McLachlan & Stein, 1982; Miller & Hester, 1980; Moos & Finney, 1982, 1983; Vaillant, 1983).

Gossop et al. (2002) reported a 60% relapse rate in the heroin addicts following a one year treatment program.

An additional study of the effects of Neurotherapy with the chronic alcoholic was conducted in 1997 (Kelly, 1997, 1998) in the native Indian population. There were 19 participants, 14 of whom met the DSM-IV criteria for alcohol dependence and 5 of whom met the criteria for alcohol abuse.

Participants initially were taught diaphragmatic breathing, muscle relaxation, and temperature training on a J&J I330. The participants attended two, 1-hour training sessions five days each week in addition to their regular residential treatment schedule. Within 33 days of residential treatment, the 19 participants received an average of 40 sessions of neurofeedback.

Three years later four were in sustained full remission (DSM-IV) and have had no binge drinking. Twelve participants are in sustained partial remission (DSM-IV). These 12 have had several binges (slips) in the three years but did not drink regularly and did not get into any significant difficulty because of drinking (or otherwise). One of these 12 was arrested and remained in jail for two of the three years, but was sober for the year after release. Three of the 19 remain alcohol dependent (DSM-IV). These continued to have significant problems associated with bouts of excessive drinking. One of these 3 is in prison for parole violation on a DUI conviction, and another was recently released from imprisonment for parole violation again after a DUI. Eighteen of the participants were given the Beck Depression Scale (a self rating depression scale). This scale changed from a mean of 25 (SD=9) to a mean of 4 (SD=4.6). Six of the 19 entered post training Beck scores of zero (0). It should be remarked that the nursing and other professional staff who were associated with this study all agreed that the behavioral and emotional changes in the subjects were marked, real, and positive.

Scott et al. (2005) reported a 77% abstinence rate (at 12 months) for a mixed group of 121 inpatient substance abusers (heroin, methamphetamine, crack/cocaine, alcohol; 94% multiple drug abusers) who received EEG biofeedback and the Minnesota Model 12 step program compared to 44% of the control group who received the 12 step program.

The effectiveness, time and cost issues for alternate intervention methods for the alcoholic are summarized in Table 22 and compared to the national norm. An examination of the table quickly reveals that the EEG biofeedback approach is clearly the more effective mode of treatment for this conditions, as well as being the least expensive.

Table 22

Intervention Method	Recidivism Rate - Alcohol	Recidivism Rate - Criminal Activity	Treatment Type	Treatment TIme	Cost
DTAP	13% - alcohol		residential / combined	17.8 Months	$32,975
Simpson (2002)	30% - any drug use	40%-65% - any illegal activity / arrest	psychotherapy - individual / group	3 months or more	?
Gossop (2002)	60% - heroin addicts		residential	1 year	?
Scott (2005)	23%		EEG + 12 step program	50 sessions EEG 138 days	?
Scott (2005)	56%		12 step program	110 days inpatient	?
EEG Biofeedback Quirk		15%	EEG biofeedback Quirk	40 sessions	?
Peniston & Kulkosky, 1989	15% - alcohol		EEG biofeedback		?

Dine Study	16% alchohol		EEG + residential	40 EEG + 30 days residential	$4,000 for EEG @ $100 session
Texas Report (2002) no treatment		51%	none	no treatment	$0

a) **Autism DSM IV 299.00**

The DSM IV defines both Autism and Asperger's as subcategories of Pervasive Development Disorder and applies the following criteria to the autism diagnosis.

Six or more symptoms from a, b and c.

a) impairments in social interaction, as least two of the following:

- in the use of multiple nonverbal behaviors, such as eye-to- eye gaze, facial expression, body postures, and gestures to regulate social interaction

- to develop peer relationships appropriate to developmental level

- spontaneous seeking to share enjoyment, interests, or achievements with other people

- social or emotional reciprocity

b) impairments in communication, at least one of the following:

- the development of spoken language (not accompanied by an attempt to compensate through alternative modes of communication such as gesture or mime)

- ability to initiate or sustain a conversation with others

- stereotyped and repetitive use of language or idiosyncratic language

- varied, spontaneous make-believe play or social imitative play appropriate to developmental level

c) restricted, repetitive, and stereotyped patterns of behavior, interests, and activities as manifested by at least one of the following:

- preoccupation with one or more stereotyped and restricted patterns of interest that is abnormal either in intensity or focus

- inflexible adherence to specific, nonfunctional routines or rituals

- stereotyped and repetitive motor mannerisms (e.g., hand or finger flapping or twisting or complex whole-body movements)

- persistent precoccupation with parts of objects

Additional criteria involve delays or abnormal functioning in at least one of the following areas, with onset prior to age 3 years: (1) social interaction, (2) language as used in social communication, or (3) symbolic or imaginative play and the disturbance is not better accounted for by Rett's disorder or childhood disintegrative disorder.

Prevalence

Autism has been on the rise in recent decades. Different authors have noted an increase in autism rates in the US. While some (Wing & Potter, 2002; Croen et al., 2002) have attributed the rise to improvements in detection and changes in diagnosis, other researchers (Wing, 1999) have noted a doubling of the autism rate (.5 per 1000 to 1 per 1000) in the general population.

A recent review of the special education roles in the US (Newschaffer et al., 2005) found an increase of 3.5 per 10,000 in 1982 to 18.3 per 10,000 in 1990 (a 55% change) in 10 year olds and a corresponding change in the 6 year old data (4.6 to 24.1 per 10,000) in the same time period.

A study in the United Kingdom (Chakrabarti & Fombonne, 2001) found prevalence rates of 16.8 per 10,000 for autistic disorder and 62.6 per 10,000 for the entire autistic spectrum.

A study in Brick township (New Jersey) reported rates of 40 per 10,000 in the 3-10 year old children and 67 per 10,000 within the entire autistic spectrum.

An Atlanta, Georgia study (Yeargin-Allsopp et al., 2001) found prevalence rates of 34 per 10,000 in the 3-10 year old (1996). The study noted a predominance of males (3.8 among whites, 4.3 among blacks per 1000) and a male to female rate of 4-5 to 1 per 1000.

Of the children with autism (N=9874) 62% had at least one coexisting (Metropolitan Atlanta Developmental Disabilities Surveillance Program (MADDSP)) defined disability or epilepsy. Of the children with an IQ or developmental test results (N=880), 68% had cognitive impairment (64% based on IQ data alone). Of the children with autism, 8% had epilepsy. Most (91%) of the children received special education services at some time during the 1996 school year.

The Government Accountability Office (GAO, 2005b) estimated in Jan., 2005 that the autism rate had increased by moré than 500% during the past decade with an average intervention cost of $18,000 a year (1999-2000). The prevalence figure for autism was 20,000 in 1993 and 120,000 in 2002. The average estimated cost for a special education child was $12,500.

We will not be discussing the causes of Autism which have ranged from genetic to environmental.

There have been several single case study reports of improvement (sometimes dramatic) with the application of EEG biofeedback to the autism spectrum disorder. Two group studies have been conducted to date and reported at the ISNR yearly conference. Summaries of the research are presented as follows:

Efficacy of Neurofeedback for Autistic Spectrum Disorders
Betty Jarusiewicz, Atlantic Research Institute, Atlantic Highlands, NJ

The study involved a comparison of 16 individuals trained with neurofeedback with 16 individuals who did not receive training, but continued other ongoing therapies. Eighty-eight percent of those trained reduced their levels of autistic symptoms within months, as assessed using the Autism Treatment Evaluation Checklist (ATEC) of the Autism Research Institute. The average reduction in symptoms severity was 26% compared with a control group average of less than 5%. Before and after videos were also used for comparison purposes.

There were significant improvements on average in the areas of speech (30%), socialization (34%), sleep (29%), anxiety (29%), tantrums (29%), and cognitive awareness (16%). When compared with other treatment modalities using the Rimland Treatment Effectiveness Survey, neurofeedback is rated on a par with occupational therapy, and is surpassed to date only by behavior modification and speech therapies, even in this early-stage comparison.

Assessment Guided Neurofeedback for Autistic Spectrum Disorder
Robert Coben, PhD, BCIA-EEG, D-qEEG, Neuropsychologist, Massapequa Park, New York

Dr. Coben (2005) reported the results of EEG biofeedback interventions with 37 mild autistic children. The children averaged 20 sessions. Measures included Parental Judgment, Pre and Post Autism Treatment Evaluation Checklist (ATEC), Gilliam Asperger Disorder Scale (GADS), Behavior Rating Inventory of Executive Functions (BRIEF), Personality Inventory for Children, Second Edition (PIC-2), Pre and Post Neuropsychological testing and QEEG, and Pre and Post Infrared Imaging surrounding each session.

There were 12 subjects in wait list control group who were matched for gender, age, race, handedness, other treatments, and initial Autism Treatment Evaluation Checklist (ATEC) score. The control group did not receive any new treatment during study design. Pre-post testing showed no significant change for Parental Judgment, Parent Ratings, Neuropsychological tests, Infrared Imaging for control group. The experimental group showed improvement in parents rating (33 said better, 4 said no better), a 40% reduction of symptoms on the ATEC scale, significant improvement on neuropsychological measures of attention, visual perception, language and executive function measures as well as on infrared imaging.

A Different Approach to the Autism Problem:
The Feedback Principle applied to blood flow – the HEG (hemoencephalography) system

The basic principle behind the interventions is a feedback principle. The treatment merely provides information to the subject on what is happening. This principle is applicable as a method to change behavior across a wide spectrum of human behavior.

An additional intervention strategy that has been developed in this field is blood flow biofeedback with the Hemoencephalography (HEG) system, pioneered and developed by H. Toomin. The approach has been employed successfully in Thailand with a large group of autistic disorder conditions (Limsila, P., 2001). The researchers studied a group of 180 autistic children in Thailand. After 40 sessions, the cohort's mean HEG readings increased 53%. Of the 81 subjects who were studying in public school, 86% increased their GPA by more than 0.5 (mean = 0.94) points on a 4-point scale. Only 4% decreased their GPA by more than 0.5 points (mean = 0.57).

b)   Asperger's
DSM IV 299.80 Asperger's Disorder

The diagnosis of Asperger's syndrome is rendered by use of the following criteria.

A. Impairment in social interaction, at least two of the following:

1) marked impairment in the use of multiple nonverbal behaviors, such as eye-to-eye gaze, facial expression, body postures, and gestures to regulate social interaction

2) failure to develop peer relationships appropriate to developmental level

3) a lack of spontaneous seeking to share enjoyment, interests, or achievements with other people (e.g., by a lack of showing, bringing, or pointing out objects of interest to other people)

4) lack of social or emotional reciprocity

B. Restricted, repetitive, and stereotyped patterns of behavior, interests, and activities, at least one of the following:

1) encompassing preoccupation with one or more stereotyped and restricted patterns of interest that is abnormal either in intensity or focus
2) apparently inflexible adherence to specific, nonfunctional routines or rituals
3) stereotyped and repetitive motor mannerisms (e.g., hand or finger flapping or twisting, or complex whole-body movements)
4) persistent preoccupation with parts of objects

Additional criteria involve impairment in social, occupational, or other areas of functioning, no significant delay in language, no delays in cognitive development, self help skills, adaptive behavior and curiosity.

Treatment Effect Reports

As in the case of autism clinical reports in this area have been composed of single case studies and small group studies at national conferences. Listed below are the abstracts and short descriptions of the research in this area that have presented at the annual ISNR conference.

Case Study: Ten Year Old Male with Asperger's Syndrome
Jolene Ross, PhD and James Caunt, BS, Advanced Neurotherapy, PC, Wellesley Hills, MA

After 40 sessions of neurotherapy the subject showed an approximate 2/3 improvement in behavioral ratings. The post-treatment QEEG showed significant reductions in elevated 6-9 Hz slow wave activity in the medial and central-parietal regions with eyes open. There was also a dramatic reduction in the magnitude of elevated 9-12 Hz activity in the parietal and occipital regions with eyes open while reading and while performing math.

A Comparison of QEEG Characteristics in Pediatric Asperger's Syndrome and Attention Deficit Disorder
Jolene Ross, PhD and James Caunt, BS, Advanced Neurotherapy, PC, Wellesley Hills, MA

The QEEGs of the Asperger's Syndrome subjects showed common functional features including: elevation of 4-7 Hz activity in the posterior regions, slowing at the vertex and regulatory dissociations between anterior and posterior regions of the cortex. In contrast, Attention Deficit Disorder subjects showed elevations of 4-7 Hz activity in the anterior and central regions, slowing at the vertex, and an absence of regulatory dissociations between the anterior and posterior regions of the cortex.

Asperger's and ADD Differences and Similarities- Preliminary Observations

Lynda Thompson, PhD and Michael Thompson, MD, ADD Centres, Mississauga, Ontario, Canada
Preliminary observations concerning the EEG in Asperger's appears to be showing slowing (theta and alpha) in the right parietal and temporal areas (P4, T6) and, at times, frontally at F3 and F4. There are also findings of coherence differences including hyper-coherences between P4, C4 and F4 and a hypo-coherences between the right cerebral hemisphere sites and the left frontal area. However, these children also show the characteristic patterns seen in ADD with slowing at C3, Cz and C4, and/or at F3 and Fz with a 'dip' in 13-15 Hz (SMR) across the central region (C3, Cz and C4).

d) Mental Retardation

Mental Retardation constitutes about 10% of the children eligible for special education services in the US (IDEA data tables). Table 23 presents the breakdown of the diagnostic categories employed by the Office of Special Education Programs (OSEP). There has been only one study which has addressed this group. The study was presented at a yearly conference of the European chapter of ISNR.

Table 23

Ages 6-21 (2002-3)	Number	% of Total
Total Spec.Education (IDEA)	5,946,202	
Specific LD	2,878,334	48%
TBI	21,488	.4%
Speech/Language	1,112,142	19%
Mental Retardation	593,612	10%
Developmental Delay	58,265	1%
Other		22%
Total Addressable	**4,663,841**	**78%**

Total Addressable: refers to the % of subjects who could benefit from the Neurocognitive intervention

16 Case Studies Examining the Efficacy of Neurofeedback in Mentally Retarded with the approach of Delta Down Reward
Tanju Sürmeli, Living Health Center for Research and Education,

Gayrettepe, Istanbul, Turkey

The author reported on 16 subjects ranging 6-24 years old attending private learning centers were previously diagnosed with mental retardation at various university hospitals. Sessions were completed between 40-120 depending on the case. Electrodes were placed according to QEEG analysis at posterior, central and anterior locations with inhibits set for delta (0-4 Hz) and theta (4-8 Hz) and rewards set for 12-15 Hz and 15-18 Hz. Fifteen out of sixteen patients who received NF training showed significant improvement based on parent/teacher/questionnaire/QEEG reports. One showed no progress during or after the training.

e)   Corporate America – peak performance movement – the normal brain

Sports – Golf, Archery, Markmanship

One research group (Chartier, 1998) selected, at random, golfers of different skill levels to see if helping golfers to manage their mind had a positive effect on improving their skills. The methodology blended neurofeedback technology, behavior change strategies, assessments, and coaching. The researchers wanted to see if, after training, the participants shot lower scores, struck the ball sweeter, managed the mental side of the game better, and controlled stressful situations. As measured by the Profile of Mood States (POMS), an instrument used to measure mood states of athletes, participants decreased the negative factors of tension, anxiety, depression, anger, confusion, and fatigue while increasing their levels of energy and vigor. They reduced their eighteen-hole scores by an average of eight (8) strokes. Also several golfers who shot consistently in the 90's recorded a 79 for their first time.

The skill integration practice included: sensationalization and visualization of perfect performance of a selected golf skill while maintaining targeted EEG activity and actual practice of the skill while attempting to produce the mind-body state achieved during the feedback training. Fourteen of the participants reported significant improvement in their ability to strike the ball better, more consistently, more confidently, and more accurately. They stated they were able to putt more smoothly, judge distances from the cup more accurately, and sense (feel) the putt better.

They reported an increase in their ability to both focus and concentrate. Twelve of the participants completed pre-and post training Profile of Mood States (POMS). The POMS results for 10 of those 12 subjects showed development of what is called an "Iceberg Profile", a pattern of scores that is

209

typically found in elite athletes. This is where the factors of tension, depression, anger, fatigue, and confusion are reduced below the 50th T Score and the factor of vigor is augmented above the 50th T Score. In addition to improvement in their golf game and development of mood states seen in elite athletes, a number of participants also reported significant improvement in physical and mental health. Although medical and psychological symptoms were not a focus of this study, several subjects reported remission of troubling physical symptoms including muscle spasm pain and angina. Reports of psychological changes included improved concentration and coping with stress.

Markmanship

The relevance of EEG activity to markmanship ability is inherently an interest to the military. There have been several studies which examined what is happening in the brain prior to a "good shot". Kerick et al. (2001) found that activity in the left temporal alpha (11-13 Hertz) activity was higher than that in the right temporal for the 5 second period before the shot, relative to control conditions (holding the rifle, shooting "dry" shots without aiming). This report confirmed previous report by Landers et al. (1994) with archers and other reports that have indicated the better "shooters" are the ones that produce more alpha (Haufler et al., 2000; Janelle et al, 2000; Salazar et al., 1990).

Memory

Preliminary data, employing the activation database Neurocognitive approach, on three normal subjects resulted in an average of 130% improvement of auditory memory abilities, thus providing some preliminary data that enhancing of memory abilities in normal individuals is possible. (Thornton, unpublished)

f)   The military

Stress Tolerance

For a given amount of combat exposure, people with lower intelligence are more likely to develop PTSD than are those with higher intelligence," wrote Boston researchers in the Journal of Consulting and Clinical Psychology. The research team, led by Michael L. Macklin at the Veterans Affairs Medical Center in Manchester, New Hampshire, gathered data on 90 Vietnam combat veterans -- 59 of whom had been diagnosed with PTSD. (Macklin, 1998) The inhibitory effects of raising intelligence levels would therefore have a direct effect on the emotional ability of our troops to withstand the emotional tolls of wars. As the research has indicated, raising general intelligence is a relatively easy task when employing the EEG biofeedback approach.

Lie Detection

The author (Thornton, 1994, 2006b) has conducted two preliminary studies investigating the usefulness of the qEEG in the lie detection problem. Both research results were very encouraging. However, due to problems in funding additional research, there has been no further investigation into this area.

f)   Post-Traumatic Stress, Anxiety and Depression and EEG biofeedback

There have been numerous studies regarding the effects of EEG biofeedback on PTSD, anxiety and depression and use of EEG biofeedback, generally with positive results. This book, however, will not review this area of research. Some of the results have been touched upon in the alcohol and criminal intervention sections.

Many of these reports are in the form of single case studies or small group studies at this point and have employed different criteria in their assessment of change.

The author (Thornton, unpublished) was involved in a single case study of trichotellamania, which is characterized by obsessive pulling out of the eyebrows and eyelashes. The 12-year-old child who was afflicted with this condition came to our clinic for treatment. He was engaged in psychotherapeutic interventions for about 6 months, to no avail. Many different behavioral interventions both at home and school were attempted, with no effect. Finally, it was decided to attempt the EEG biofeedback intervention. The child was hooked up to the machine and the raw signal was displayed on the computer screen. He was asked to close his eyes and indicate when he felt the impulse to pull out his eyebrows. The raw signal was observed as he intermittently noted the impulse. After several reports and the observation that there was delta activity occurring with his experiences, protocols were developed to inhibit the delta frequency over the sensorimotor strip (C3-C4). By the time the 10th session was completed, he was cured of the problem and discharged. A year later a letter was received from him that thanked the author for his help. Enclosed with the letter was his picture, with fully-grown eyebrows and eyelashes. A success.

Chapter 21 - The future of the technology – the final frontier

In their book "IQ and the Wealth of Nations", Lynn and Vanhanen (2002), the authors lay out their central tenet that the IQs of populations play a decisive role in the economic destinies of nations. The book analyses 81 countries for which direct evidence on national IQs was available. The mean national IQ correlated +.71 with per capita Gross National Product (GNP) for 1998, and +.76 with per capita Gross Domestic Product (GDP) for 1998. Other analyses consistently demonstrate national IQs predict both long term (1820-1922) and short term (1950-90; 1976-1998) economic growth rates measured variously by per capita GNP and GDP (mean R2 ~ 0.60). Regression analyses of the 81 countries, and then of 185 countries, including 104 whose national IQs are estimated by averaging those from adjoining countries, shows the national differences in wealth are explained primarily by the intelligence levels of the populations, secondarily by whether the countries have market or socialist economies; and tertiarily, by unique circumstances, such as, in the case of Qatar, the possession of valuable natural resources such as oil.

In the United States and Britain, the correlation between IQ and earnings is approximately +.35, an association the authors argue is causal because: IQs predate earnings, are moderately heritable, are stable from 5 years of age onwards, and predict not only the earnings obtained in adulthood, but educational level and many other positive outcomes along the way.

The relationship also holds for large cities. Studies carried out using the 310 administrative districts of New York City in the 1930s, found correlations of +.40 to +.70 between average IQ scores (gained from tests administered to children in schools) and measures of per capita income and educational attainment. Similar studies carried out in regions of the British Isles, France, and Spain in the 1970s have corroborated these relationships.

The evidence reported in their book reveals that there are considerable national differences in average intelligence level. The highest average IQs are found among the Oriental nations of North East Asia (IQ = 104), followed in descending order by the European nations of Europe (IQ = 98), the nations of North America and Australia (IQ = 98), the nations of South and Southwest Asia, from the Middle East through Turkey to India and Malaysia (IQ = 87), the nations of South East Asia and the Pacific Islands (IQ = 86), the nations of Latin America and the Caribbean (IQ = 85), and finally by the nations of Africa (IQ = 70).

Societal and Cost Savings Implications

There are profound economic, humanitarian, and social implications of the implementation of a Neurocognitive program into the school system, prison system and corporate America. It has been estimated (Thornton, 2005) that if the program were to be implemented into the school system on a national basis, the US would save some $327 Billion Dollars in direct educational costs. As the evidence has implied, successful interventions on the special education child during the elementary school years would have profound effects on the criminal justice system and most probably would significantly reduce our national crime rate. There would be most probably significant effects on the costs to victims, as the crime rate would decrease. The effect on our drug abusing society and prison population could also be quite profound, as successful interventions with these groups of individuals have been clinically problematic.

Corporate America could increase its productivity as much as it did with the advent of the computer.

There is also a potential effect on the acceleration of scientific discoveries. If the brains of the special education child and drug addicts are so responsive to this intervention method, there is every reason to think that the "normal" or even "super normal" brain would be equally responsive, if not more. Preliminary data on three normal subjects resulted in an average of 130% improvement of auditory memory abilities, thus providing some preliminary data that improvement of normal subjects is possible. If we interventions were conducted on a "super brain" scientist, it is quite possible that the productivity of that scientist could be improved, thus providing an acceleration of scientific discoveries.

Chapter 22
The problem of change – the politics of change and the failure of the educational system to respond
School Systems

Changing any bureaucratic system is a monstrous undertaking and should be undertaken only by another large bureaucratic organization. The following organizations have been contacted either through direct mailing of research articles, phone calls, local presentations, a CD lecture explaining the approach, or emailed articles. Despite years of marketing effort, none of these organizations have pursued the implementation of the approach and only a few ever responded, indicating that they had received the information.

Contacted Organizations
Over 6,000 schools in New Jersey and New York.

Every state special education department in the United States and many in Canada.

Almost all of the major urban cities with large numbers of special education students.

Almost all the schools in the United States which list themselves as involved in the special education area. (over 1000).

All state and federal brain injury associations as well as all Canadian brain injury organizations

The Veteran's Administration

Charles Schwab foundation, The William and Melinda Gates Foundation.

Bill Cosby, two very well know preparatory schools – in one the local psychologist refused to return the phone calls, all major and minor talk shows.

Federal Agencies
Research grants were submitted 3 times for a research study on remediation of reading disabilities. Each time the agency rejected the grant application with new reasons. The responses included such statements as "100% improvement, I'm not impressed.", "You didn't tell the parents that if they don't participate in the other program, their child will lose the benefits of the other program."

Political Contacts
Every member of the Senate Education Committee was contacted several times. A two-day trip to Washington was undertaken and presentations to the offices of 8 Senators (4 Democrat and 4 Republican) on the Senate Education Committee were conducted. No response. Every state

(New Jersey) senator and representative was contacted several times. No response.

Orton-Gillingham Society

The society was contacted several times and was not interested in hearing a presentation, despite endorsement by one of its board members.

Special Education Department

It took 6 years to get an appointment with a major northeast Board of Education. The presentation received a positive response. However, within a month the higher-level administrators rejected it and no reason was provided. The board of education preferred to stay with their current intervention program – the Orton-Gillingham method, despite its low effect size and high cost. The web site indicated that the city was spending considerable amount of monies on a program which had almost no scientific support. Over a hundred individuals involved in special education in the city were contacted via email. Only one person responded and indicated that the information on the city website was wrong.

Other Urban Educational Departments

A large Canadian metropolitan special education board was contacted and a presentation provided. Despite an initial very warm reception, there was no follow up and no request for implementation. Eventually it was learned that the rejection was based up the word "therapy" in the word Neurotherapy. Two to three years of presentations to a special education department in a large metropolitan city in the US were conducted. In the end, a few parents had a negative reaction based upon misinformation and misinterpretation and the program was not implemented.

A local neuropsychologist had made some negative comments to the parents regarding the program based upon the concept that the approach did not have a double-blind, placebo control study to support its use. When the neuropsychologist was presented with the information which contradicted his position and supplied the reference for the double-blind, placebo control condition (as well as a host of other references), he declined to further engage in the discourse. In addition, he indicated that he was engaged in writing a chapter in a book which was generally negative towards the approach. He was also unwilling to indicate to the parents what his professional opinions were regarding other programs currently being employed in the school system, which also do not have the double-blind, placebo control research study to support its use.

Unfortunately for the children, professionals involved in this area (as well as other areas) can be self-serving in their opinions and behavior. What they don't understand is the opportunity.

Local Attempts

For several years the program was presented at local schools. Not one school pursued any attempt to implement the program. The resistance was so strong that a local school board refused even to hear a call for a debate on the issue at a public meeting where open discussions were allowed. Several local parents, whose children had benefited from the program, tried to make some supportive statements about their child's involvement in the program to the school board. The parents were met with derisive comments by attendees and apathy and indifference by school officials.

Another middle to upper income school district spent an estimated $20,000 or more in legal and staff time to not provide the program to a child who had a reading problem, despite the estimated program cost of less than 25% of what was spent on legal bills.

It is difficult to understand why so many organizations, whose mission is to improve our educational system, would not jump at the chance to improve our results at a fraction of the cost currently being expended towards this goal. It is also completely unacceptable.

This book has provided the scientific evidence and the compelling logic of the need for implementation of the Neurocognitive approach across a wide spectrum of our society. It is often argued that, in an ideal world, scientific evidence needs to be thorough and convincing prior public acceptance and enactment. Scientists working in this area have been providing the evidence for decades and it continues to amass. In reality, public and educational policy appear to operate more on momentum power than reason and evidence.

There is sufficient evidence and compelling logic available at present to implement the program in a number of critical society structures (schools, prisons, drug and alcohol rehab facilities).

By far the most important focus of the implementation should be immediately into the school systems.

The problems that are facing the implementation of the Neurocognitive program into the school system are fourfold.

1)   The technology is a different, unfamiliar language. Teachers are so overwhelmed with other administrative and teaching tasks that learning a whole new technology is prohibitive.

2)   Educators may perceive the program as a threat to their positions,

as a different type of expertise will be required to administer the programs, leaving them out of a job, career and power.

3) Special education personnel may perceive the program as a threat to their careers, as they may think that the program will eventually replace them.

4) Schools specializing in the learning disabled population may perceive the program as a threat, as it will solve the LD problem too quickly and their clientele will leave, leaving their organization with financial difficulties. It is more profitable to keep the child for several years than for one year.

All of these perceived reasons have some validity to them. What will not be perceived is:

1) The inevitability of the replacement of current programs with the Neurocognitive approach, just as the car replaced the horse, the computer replaced the typewriter, or the digital camera replaced the film-based camera.

2) The long transition period which will continue to require special education personnel.

3) Though program improves the brain function; it does not teach the child anything directly. Thus special educators will be needed to continue the instruction so that the child can "catch" up.

4) Special education personnel can be retrained fairly easily. The new skills as a qEEG technician will be equally valuable to the school systems, as problems in brain functioning will always exist. In addition, job satisfaction will increase, as the staff will see greater results of their efforts in considerably less time.

5) The population which can be effectively addressed is more than just the LD or special education population. The entire student population of the United States, as well as that of other countries, can benefit.

6) There are many subtleties in brain functioning which the program does not address and which can only be addressed in a verbal interactive format.

What has not been accepted by the school systems is:

1) The responsibility to address these problems as effectively as possible in the children's interest as well as society as a whole. Political and economic reasons for avoidance of responsibility are not justification for lack of action. Would you consider a doctor competent if he prescribes a medication which is much less effective because he has a vested (political

and/or economic) interest in the less effective medication? Would you buy a car that works some of the time from a car dealer because he doesn't want to bother purchasing the better, more reliable models? His reasons are because he doesn't want to read the new manuals or he's afraid the new models will put him out of business because he won't get the repeat business.

2)   The opportunity to create a fundamental change in how we approach the educational experience and become part of that dynamic change.

Some of the responses we have heard from school systems over the years have included:

Our responses are added.

1)   Education budgets are tight and additional monies can't be afford any new programs right now.
        a. Reallocate the special education money to a different approach. The teachers just need retraining. Education budgets have always been tight, yet new programs get started and staff hired nonetheless.

2)   Current monies have been allocated to train the teachers.
        a.Why? The Chicago research study showed that teacher training doesn't improve student achievement levels. (Jacob & Lefgren, 2002)

3)   Our programs work fine. Everyone does them.
        a.Please read this book to understand the limitations.

4)   We'll look into it….or similarly…We're not interested.
        a.This is similar to the our check is in the mail response.

5)   It's an experimental program. There is no research indicating it works. There are no control groups. There are no norms.
        a.These responses indicate that the person has absolutely no knowl edge of the research in this area and arrogantly presumes that he knows everything.

6)   There are no other schools doing it. We don't want to be the first. We'll wait until the other schools do it.

a.   This is the classic sheep response.

7)   We don't want to get into an argument with anyone about it.
        a.This is the passive, "We don't want to take responsibility" argu ment.

8)   It's therapy. We don't do therapy. We're not responsible for therapy interventions.
        a.This response indicates that the person did not understand the technology or is looking for an excuse not to engage in construc-

218

tive actions. The approach has educational and therapeutic effects. An individual's self-esteem will rise if they are functioning better in life. Does this mean the intervention has only effects on self-esteem. To focus on only one aspect and reject it for that reason is a deliberate distortion of the information solely for purposes of finding a reason to reject the approach. The response is similar to rejecting chocolate ice cream because it is not ice cream.

9) We heard of a school (parent) that tried the program and said it didn't work.

a. One of the problems facing the field presently is that many practitioners are relying upon the initial research in the field to determine their protocols, which means that they are placing the electrodes on the C3-C4 area, increasing beta microvolts and decreasing theta microvolts. The problems with this approach are discussed in the questions chapter (Chapter 16). If the "program" that was tried involved this approach then it may not have "worked" for the reasons discussed in Chapter 16. There are some highly marketed programs available which employ this approach. Of the 37 subjects who have completed the full activation program, we have only had 2 subjects whose qEEG variables improved but their cognitive abilities did not, **a 95% success rate**. One case involved chemotherapy to the brain for a brain tumor and the other a case of toxic encephalopathy due to inhalation of toxic fumes over a 20-year period. Both of these cases involved massive assaults upon the cortical and subcortical brain structures. All of the other cases (100%) improved both on the qEEG variables and cognitive function measurements (memory). It is just a question of how much. However, as with any intervention approach, there are no guarantees.

Consumers of this intervention should consult with the appropriate certifying agencies to ensure that the professional they are engaging is qualified to provide the service. The Association for Applied Psychophysiology and Biofeedback (AAPB.org) provides certification in the EEG Biofeedback field. As in every field, there are various levels of expertise. The International Society for Neuronal Regulation (ISNR.org) also provides yearly conferences on current research in the field. The Quantitative EEG Certification board (Qeegboard.org) certifies professionals in the area as well as the Electrodiagnostic and Clinical Neuroscience Society (ECNS).

The following is a list of the types of questions that have been raised by an audience following the presentation of the material. Answers are provided as well.

Common Objections and/or statements

a) It's a medical intervention.

No, the Supreme Court has determined that a medical intervention can only be done by an MD. As EEG biofeedback is conducted by many different types of professionals, it is not a medical intervention.

b) It's an experimental procedure.

No. Different organizations employ different criteria to evaluate effectiveness. The "Gold Standard" has been a treatment group compared to a "sham" or placebo group and all evaluators are blind to the subject's group membership. Lower levels of scientific validation include can include control groups. The EEG biofeedback approach has 18 control group studies and one control group with the sham, placebo condition.

c) There need to be more control group studies.

If 18 independent control group studies are not enough, then what is the criteria and is this criteria being equally applied to other current models?

d) There is no double blind sham/placebo control study.

No, the DeBeus et al, 2006 study is a double blind/sham/placebo control group study.

e) The evidence is not sufficient.

If the evidence obtained to date is not sufficient, then there is no program which can qualify as sufficient.

f) You're electrocuting my child.

No, there are no signals being sent in. Like a blood pressure machine, the equipment merely reads the information coming off the brain.

g) It's dangerous.

No. The machines have received FDA approval and are safe.

h) There aren't any schools doing it now.

No. The State of Minnesota has spent some $500,000 implementing a rudimentary form of the program in its New Visions schools. In Arizona, it has been integrated into one school setting without difficulty.

i) If it is so good, why aren't more schools doing it?

They should be. I would recommend that you ask them why they are not. Your child's future is at stake.

j)   It's too good to be true.
     Maybe, but that doesn't mean it isn't true.

k)   You're going to mess up my child's brain.
     No. The approach makes your child's brain better.

l)   My doctor says it doesn't work. Therefore I don't want my child doing it. We would suggest having your doctor read this book.

m)   Most of your research is with children. Does it work with adults and old people?
     Yes. The brain doesn't stop responding to the approach just be cause it is older.

n)   You're not using any databases to design your program around.
     Yes we are. The database has about 100 normal subjects in it, ages 10-70. As the questions being asked of the database do not relate inherently to age or sex issues there is no need to stratify the sample by age or sex.

o)   Your data is fuzzy.
     This statement is fuzzy.

p)   You're going to change my child's personality.
     The procedure can change your child's abilities. Self-confidence and self-esteem should increase. Yes, indirectly the procedure will change your child's personality….for the better. Lowered impulsivity, distractibility, obsessive-compulsive behavior, etc. These are positive changes.

q)   There aren't enough subjects in the research groups.
     There are well over 1,500 subjects that have been investigated to date.

r)   The procedure affects only memory. We don't know how it affects other cognitive functions.
     Please re-read the book. It affects a diverse set of cognitive functions.

Common Questions

a)   Does it work with brain injured people?
     Yes, we have cited some of the research in this area in the beginning chapters.

b)   Do the effects hold?
     The evidence we have to date indicates a yes answer. There are two

long term (10 year follow up studies) which indicate behavioral stability in terms of grades and behavior. Sometimes it will be necessary to revisit a problem for "booster" shot purposes.

c) Does it work with brain tumor and stroke rehabilitation?
The answers are not clear or available with these conditions. There hasn't been sufficient research in these areas.

d) Why isn't the federal government funding more of the research in this area?
We don't know the answer to that question.

e) Can I do this at home?
You shouldn't because:
a. There is debate whether the machines can be purchased by non-licensed personnel.
b. There is also a large technical component to learn and master.
c. The most prohibitive problem is where are you going to put the sensors? Without a database comparison for the subject and a thorough understanding of neuroanatomy, you are essentially guessing. In the author's opinion, this would be analogous to doing brain surgery for a tumor blind, without an MRI, and hoping you got it right.
d. An additional problem for the development of the field is that your intervention will probably be ineffective, due to the problems previously discussed. The reputation of the field will then be hampered because you will report to interested others that EEG biofeedback doesn't work, without acknowledging the limitations of what was done.

f) Will it help me find my wedding ring?
Probably not. We aren't that specific yet in our knowledge.

g) Why does it take so long?
Considering that we're intervening with over 100 billion neurons, the more appropriate question would be: Why doesn't it take longer?

h) You're going to change my child's personality.
The procedure can change your child's abilities. Self-confidence and self-esteem should increase. Yes, indirectly the procedure will change your child's personality....for the better. Lowered impulsivity, distractibility, obsessive-compulsive behavior, etc. These are

positive changes.

i) Why haven't we heard of this before?

It's a relatively small field, but has been growing exponentially in the past 10 years.

j) My child cannot remember to bring his homework home. What location is responsible for that?

The knowledge base is not sufficient at this point to answer that. In addition, the brain employs relationships between locations to obtain information. The question cannot be phrased in this manner.

k) Will this cure Alzheimer's?

No. It may, however, be able to help with the normal weakening of the memory system as we get older. The left temporal area (intimately involved in memory functioning) is the last part of the brain to develop and the first to be negatively affected by the aging process.

l) Why is it so expensive?

It is considerably cheaper than almost all other programs currently available. In addition, due to its greater effectiveness, the potential life long cost savings are much more than the cost.

m) How does it work?

We know the brain responds to the reward and inhibit approach (sound and a visual image). We don't have a good answer to how the brain actually knows how to do this.

It is hoped that the questions listed have addressed all the possible concerns of the reader.

If there is an additional question, please email the author at ket@chp-neurotherapy.com. Our website is chp-neurotherapy.com. If there is any information in this book that the reader has solid, replicated scientific research indicating that the statement is either a misrepresentation or false, please immediately inform the author at the email address provided. The author acknowledges that there is always the possibility that he may have missed some relevant piece of information, despite his attempts to be thorough. However, any minor technically incorrect or missed piece of information does not negate the overwhelming evidence and logic of the approach being presented. **It is the author's opinion that the Neurocognitive approach represents the most scientifically advanced and most effective approach that we will ever have with improvement of human brain functioning.**

Chapter 23
Reports of Parents and Patients

Due to the complexity of human behavior, psychological research is often beset with the problem of what to measure. The data collected for the research reported in this book focused upon memory as the key measure. In particular, the measure was spontaneous free recall. Memory is a complex phenomenon and not a unitary concept. Memory ability can vary across different measures of memory...for smell, taste, how to do things, for where objects were placed, for a to-do list, etc. Our measures involved spontaneous free recall for auditory and reading memory. In many academic testing situations, the multiple choice format type question assesses recognition memory for information, an easier memory task. Psychological research on memory functioning invariably indicates higher scores for recognition tasks than spontaneous free recall. There were four reasons why we choose this measure as the critical measure.

1)   TBI patients report that loss of memory functioning is their most problematic deficit.

2)   Recall of a conversation is a critical cognitive skill in our modern society. A conversation is auditorily-presented information of a short length in duration. The short paragraph task reflects this situation and thus is intuitively relevant to "real-life" memory issues.

3)   Memory measures are relatively easy to administer and score.

4)   The ability of a person to comprehend and make inferences from information logically follows from a person's ability to recall the information. We can't comprehend what we can't recall.

To address the limitation of our measures, it is standard procedure to ask the parents of the individuals or the individuals who are or have participated in our program to comment on what they have observed in the behavior of themselves or their children and to provide what academic reports they have received. As is customary in these situations, we will not be providing specific names or identifying data. This type of information is not intended to be providing proof of a scientific nature.

The relationship between the qEEG variables that we are addressing and human behavior has not been delineated to the extant that we can render precise statements that this or that location or frequency is tied to this or that behavior. We are dealing with a complex system that is in constant interaction with itself and the environment. The behavior changes noted by the parents often reflect changes that we would never anticipate nor imagine to measure. We and the parents offer these comments to the reader with the understanding of the above stated limitations and problems of measurement in this area. These statements are not provided as testimonials, but as the perceptions of individuals who were involved in their children's care.

Case #1 - Clinical Update shortly after finishing program and returning to school.

I wish to express my deepest and sincere appreciation for the work that you have done for my daughter. As you know, she has suffered from multiple cognitive symptoms that are generally described as learning disabilities, but are due to her complicated medical history as a 1 pound, 15 ounce premature baby. Various medical and educational evaluations have consistently found her to be mildly retarded on standard psycho-educational and neuropsychological measures, despite an excellent vocabulary and good social skills. She has struggled with academic work since kindergarten, and has never performed at age level.

With my professional background as a pediatric and adolescent neuropsychologist and as a developmentally based psychotherapist, my husband and I have researched and tried many interventions, most without measurable results. Since your intensive treatment of her with Quantitative EEG neurotherapy for several hours a day, daily for 2 weeks, her change of abilities and feelings are incredible! She is actually reading proficiently and for sustained periods of time.

For the first time in her life, she asked me to wait a few minutes until she finished the chapter of a book she was reading. Before your intervention, it was a battle of wills to get her to read even a paragraph! Her ability to communicate her observations and articulate questions has increased dramatically. I am highly confident that she will now be able to perform much better in school in the coming year, and eventually leave her LD designation behind. As I told you, we have spent much of our savings on reading and math interventions over the years, and now with 2 concentrated weeks, everything has changed.

Her progress since we were at your clinic has brought us to the point where she can sit down and work on catching up on math for 2 and 3 hours at a time, and make real progress, and without any emotional meltdowns. Reading is still a chore for her, but she has found some books she likes, and now she reads herself to sleep most evenings.

Clinical update several months later.

The changes in her life continue to piggy-back on one another.

While it would have been nice, of course, for the neurofeedback to have filled her with content as well as solve the underlying processing issues, she is re-structuring her approach to learning and problem solving one synapse at a time. This has been difficult for her, as she has so much experience with failure, and many emotional and cognitive mechanisms in place to protect herself from the feelings that have for so long accompanied her failures, that she continues to revert to them when stressed. Her successes, however, continue to happen, and we are now at the point, 6 months after we worked with you, where she can no longer pass them off as chance occurrences. We have had some rough times during this transition, as she acclimates to a new self-appraisal, new work-habits, and the challenges that come with re-organizing an entire world-view. I had her parent-teacher conference this morning, and unlike previous conferences, which focused on her problems and resistances, this one was a catalog of successes and the pride everyone, including herself, is taking in the changes.

Today on the way to school, when still struggling with parts of the times table, Emily said that she has now made the decision to memorize them once and for all, so that she can get on to more interesting work. This is quite a change in attitude on her part. In the last 10 weeks she has covered almost an entire academic year's worth of math curriculum, including the enhancements in the program for advanced students. For the first time, we expect that she will advance beyond the basic arithmetic operations into algebra. She is already doing very well in basic geometry. Her reading fluency and comprehension continue to improve, and most of all, her ability to retrieve previously learned information has made the most dramatic turn for the better. All of this progress has now allowed us to concentrate more on broader concepts and tying individual pieces of information together to form a network of knowledge.

There has been a basic change in her ability to act as an independent, self-regulating individual in the world, which has been remarked on by everyone who has worked with her, and especially by those who have spent extended time with her. It is truly the difference between health and developmental disability. I thank you and your staff for all that you have done to help make this time in our lives come to pass. I only regret that we did not know about you and your work sooner.

Case #2 - Clinical Update #1:

I find that I am a lot less forgetful. With the ongoing medication adjustments, though, the metabolic swings make it harder for me to achieve a steady state, cognitively and otherwise, but in the last 2 days, things have finally started to feel more predictable. Still some problems with word retrieval, but overall, I notice improvement in myself.

Clinical update #2:

Since my work with you over the summer, I have noticed several areas in which my memory and learning are better than at any time in my life. This is an enormous comfort as I enter that time of life when memory and learning are said by many professionals to be on the decline. I am very much enjoying not having to work so hard to stay in the same place as before, and also to see improvements in areas I thought were destined never to improve!

Case #3

As to myself I find that I am choosing a whole different set of words to express ideas and thoughts. I felt a shift in consciousness, like shifting train tracks… a quick like a flash of light, in choosing words to express self. That was a major effect. Felt much more comfortable after that expressing self and choice of words.

Case #4

The changes are dramatic. He can now find a car in mall parking lot. He used to refuse to look for car, he would sit on curb and wouldn't even attempt to find it. Now he confidently comes out and finds it.. a major change. He is also better with driving, knowing directions (N, S, etc.), whether to turn right or left at corner. He is more oriented to where he is and where he is going, dramatic…he had no clue before. He couldn't find the lake before (Lake Michigan). He is much more aware of surroundings. Before he couldn't find something in the refrigerator. He now finds it immediately. He couldn't find things in his closet, now he can. He is not getting speeding tickets anymore, observing road conditions better and slowing down. He didn't do this before. He had 5 speeding tickets and had lost his license for 21 months. Now he is more cautious, more control of his energy and emotions. He isn't seeking thrill seeking with the car's speed. He is more of a B personality now. He has more control over his behavior. He is less caustic, more careful in saying things that will upset people. He takes less of the devil advocate attitude and goes with the flow of the situation.

Case #5

His grammar and punctuation are much better. There is much less run on sentences. His choice of words have improved dramatically. His overall writing ability has improved. He always had good ideas, but struggled be-

227

fore with word choice and getting ideas down in proper structure. His spelling is better. He got a couple of speeding tickets. Now he is not speeding anymore. He is more responsible about taking care of things that need to be done. His room is neater. There is improved perceptive about other people. He has dramatically improved his ability to read other people and tune into them. He doesn't get upset as much. He monitors where the other person is at better. He is less lazy. He stays on task better than before.

Case #6

It definitely aided him. He is now on the honor roll, but is still tutored daily. The teachers find him enjoyable. He occasional zones out. He has better attention now. I think it helped with his strabismus.

Case #7

My daughter came to you for a series of biofeedback neurotherapy sessions last summer. Her sessions were covered by the school system supplementary educational program. She had a total of ten or eleven sessions with you, which I'm sure you remember. I just wanted to write and tell you how she's doing.

I have noticed a clear and definite improvement in her academic performance. This is hard to quantify, as she has not been formally retested, and has had only one report card since then (which was overall very good). Nevertheless it is clear that she is doing much better.

Actually, there is one very clear indication of improvement: For the last few years, in the middle of every marking period, I always received a warning notice containing items such as:

Wastes time in class	Difficulty staying on task
Citizenship needs improvement	Frequent tardiness hurts progress
Creates behavior problems in class	Not listening to group instruction

And so forth. However, this past marking period, I received no warning notice! In addition, at her IEP Review meeting in December, her case manager, her guidance counselor, her study strategy teacher, history teacher and science teacher all agreed that she is an earnest and motivated student, has a good attitude, and is a pleasure to have in class!

She is now in her first year of high school, and all her teachers without exception feel that she is keeping up with the material quite well. I find this really delightful and frankly surprising, because academics have always been a major challenge. She has always tested in the low average range, combined score of around 86. But she is functioning well in the middle track —-not the basics track. She is doing Pre-algebra, which I find remarkable, since her last nationalized test score in math last year was consistent with previous years, where she tested in or around the 8th percentile! She, as I'm sure you remember, is what you might call a "character"; she has always been fun, but at times very difficult and challenging. Lately, though, we've been running into far fewer problems, and she is clearly maturing.

So, I am delighted to report that the neurocognitive sessions have had a highly beneficial and broad effect. I hope many more students will have the opportunity to receive this form of help.

Case #8

He was not very helpful although he agreed that something that has changed since June is that he keeps remembering things he said or did in the past that might have hurt someone else's feelings and feeling guilty about them. Now, this could also be related to a traumatic incident that took place at school before we left for your location. I have also noticed that he seems more physically affectionate as in putting his arm around my shoulders and allowing me to rub his back. As a small child this physical reciprocity was not a problem (hugs etc.). As he grew older he became more resistant to physical contact. He is still not very social or chatty. His speech slurs at times and spelling is a major problem. We are working on all of these. Incidentally, we saw an Imax movie yesterday, "Wired to Win." It talked about rewiring the brain through building neurological connections. They used the Tour de France as to illustrate this. It's hard to believe that doctors and other professionals are still questioning the validity of neurocognitive treatment. He has become more sociable, re-joined Scouts, went on social outings with his summer theatre troupe, and has begun to discuss his interior life more spontaneously with his mother.

Case #9

We are so happy with the results of the treatment. I am still waiting for the academic reports. We were out of town during finals and he has some incompletes that he needs to make up sometime in the next 2 weeks. He had a really awesome report card I did see part of his report card and it was awesome, he did get 2 F's but that was for gym, same teacher 2 separate classes he was an aid for gym and he just didn't get along with her.

The changes we have noticed in him are: His vocabulary has tripled. He now reads books. Before treatment he wasn't able to even read a chapter and remember what it said. He reads for pleasure now that it isn't a huge chore like it was before. His short term memory has greatly improved. I seldom have to repeat instructions to him. His self confidence levels have improved 100%. He used to be a boy who hardly spoke to anyone, now he will come up and introduce himself to strangers. He is even teaching a children's Martial Arts class. As for academic. His grades keep improving, he has gone from an F student to a C and B student. He has lots of catching up to do and I believe if we had started this treatment sooner he would be an A student by now.

Case #10:

My wife does the vast majority of the school work with him, so I asked her to write some of her observations down. My own observation is that in the activities he and I do together, he is more "with it" verbally and attentively. We went deer hunting this year and he is completely focused on that and on following my instructions relative to that. He still wanders off in his own world when things around him don't interest him. His friends say he talks too much about his video games and not much about what they do together, but enough so that he is participating in their activities more. Here is what my wife had to say: He has had a better school year this year.

He is still slow in schoolwork and homework, but the difference is that he is able to learn from drilling. (Last year, even this was an almost an impossible task.) Weaknesses still are reading comprehension, verbal attending, and keeping up with what is going on around him (classroom discussion, instruction, mealtime conversation, etc.) He still has a lack of language for his age. This is rapidly coming up to speed with the fast pace curriculum of the school he attends, but has a long way to go. Anecdotally, he seems more often in our world then he was a year ago. He still wanders off into his own imagination and "world" but not as frequently or to the extent he did last year. Hard to say if the improvement comes from the biofeedback, maturity, better classroom management, the one on one tutoring he receives from mom, or a combination of some or all. If biofeedback was locally available, I would not hesitate to incorporate it regularly in our lives.

I would add to what my wife says above, that his grades are pretty good. Still makes one C on a report card, the rest A's and B's. He's doing better than a lot of kids that don't have his issues.

Case #11

My daughter is a twenty-two year neurologically impaired female with developmental delays, sensory integration, learning disabilities, visual impairments, speech and language, anxiety and a secondary diagnosis of ADD.

She had an IEP and was "included" throughout her educational years. She has difficulties with Math however has always excelled in reading despite her learning disabilities.

I did not know what to expect when she began biofeedback but I felt confident after reading the material that she had to make some improvement. With a child like her I have and continue to try innovative treatments to boost her level of learning. When I learned about Dr. Thornton's method of biofeedback, I knew it was something she could handle since it was just a matter of sitting and listening and watching a screen.

While her expressive language is weaker then her receptive language, she has a flare to write and can express her thoughts and feelings at a higher level vs verbally.

After a few sessions subtle changes were noticed specifically with the anxiety. She graduated in June and has not had any formal educational training since. Therefore from an educational standpoint it is difficult to note whether or not any changes are occurring. However, recently, I have structured her day to include at least 30 minutes of reading and a summary of what she's read.

Before biofeedback she would tend to panic when writing her summary as she could never summarize what she's read. She's use the book to copy from the book. I have been amazed, as I have noticed that her writing ability has much improved in that it's a lot more coherent.

Case #12

I would like to provide you with an update on the progress and performance of my daughter since you treated her about a year and a half ago. In summary, the results have been outstanding and they have persisted with no apparent reversion. Prior to her treatment by you with Quantitative EEG Neurotherapy, she had great difficulty with her homework, particularly mathematics, and keeping her mind focused on her school work. This has lead to emotions of frustration, some paranoia about the teachers, and even a certain amount of suicidal thinking by her. She often stated to me that she thought she was "dumb."

Since your treatment of her with Quantitative EEG neurotherapy, her change of abilities and feelings is nothing short of phenomenal! She is completing her daily work at school in the allowed time, and she is having no great difficulty doing her homework at home. Indeed, she has even termed work "easy." This is a stunning change in behavior. She has a positive attitude, and happy and no longer complains about school or the teachers. I am certain that this is all a direct result of your intervention techniques. She is performing near the top of her class academically. In addition to her academic recovery, her social recovery has also been dramatic. Recently, she decided to run for president of her class, which she did, and she was elected! This is quite wonderful. Thank you again for your wonderful work.

Case #13

I would like to describe some of the changes that he has undergone since he started treatment at your clinic. At a very early age he was difficult to calm and soothe; was prone to temper tantrums; had difficulty playing alone and taking naps; and transitioning from one activity to another. As his mother, I began to question my ability to be an effective parent and was often exasperated and exhausted at the end of the day.

I had read various books on parenting, and found one called "The Difficult Child" by Dr. Stanley Turecki. This book was an excellent resource, and identified various in-born temperamental traits across 9 behavioral measures with corresponding behavioral strategies to help address each one. He fit into several of the following categories of temperament, such as: high activity level; distractibility; high intensity; negative persistence (i.e., stubbornness; and negotiating, etc...); and poor adaptability (i.e., difficulty with change of activity and routine).

Upon starting Kindergarten and the first and second grades, I wondered if he had ADHD, but I felt perhaps, that he just needed more time to mature physiologically and emotionally. However, with each grade he started, I would receive on-going notes from the teachers with consistent concerns : difficulty sitting still and following direction; distractibility; excessive talking; and lack of self-control. Since he is very bright, he did not suffer significantly in academics; however, his reading scores, particularly on his Terra Nova Testing fell in the lower 25th percentile.

Finally, in the middle of his second grade year, I had reached the end of my rope with teacher's notes and subtle hints of medicating him. It was then I called your clinic and had him evaluated for hyperactivity or perhaps more specifically, ADHD.

The initial screening evaluation you did confirmed that possibility and the brain mapping further indicated that he was two standard deviations off the norm for hyperactivity and distractibility. Ironically however, I felt great relief as now there seemed to be some light at the end of the tunnel, and some hope and answers to my long-standing concerns.

Approximately 8 sessions into the treatment, I began to notice a gradual decline in his reactivity and what seemed to be some delay time for him to think and then act. As treatment continued, the temper outbursts gradually decreased, and he appeared to have more of an ability to control his anger if he chose to. Additionally, his reading scores greatly improved over time with the treatment, and with supplemental help from a reading tutor for one year. Subsequently, his Terra Nova scores in reading took a jump from the lower 25th percentile to the upper 25th percentile with neurotherapy specifically addressing this area as well.

His teachers have reported much improvement in his classroom behavior over the span of time. He is an above-average student who consistently makes second honors in his class. He is well-liked by his teachers, coaches, and peers; is active in sports; and studies the piano. His self-esteem is good; he is extraverted; and often demonstrates leadership qualities.

He still requires re-direction and reminders to sit still; read directions more carefully; and to curb his socializing in the classroom. However, all that is required are reminders and re-direction, not medication and on-going consequences. Interestingly enough, he attends a structured, competitive, and conservative Catholic grammar school, and is thriving in this environment without the need thus far, for additional special services. His memory is excellent. He excels in Math, Science, and Music; and receives A's and B's in Language Arts. The treatment has been highly effective and specific; and has generalized into many areas of his life, both in and out of school. I am truly impressed with the results; and feel that I have witnessed either a small or big miracle.

Case #14:

Our daughter, when she was eight years old and attending second grade, was classified in school as a student with learning disability. Her test scores at school reveled that she was at the bottom of the class and was extremely weak in the areas of reading and writing. We were shocked and devastated when we heard the news and could not accept the fact that our child who we felt was normal and intelligent had a learning disability issue.

Due to this learning disability she was assigned to a separate special education class at school which comprised of other students who were being taught to cope with their issues. She had to split her day at school attending her regular class and special education class. This caused a lot of anxiety, nervousness, frustration, and sense of low self esteem for her as well as the family. It took us a while to accept the fact that we had to deal with this issue and we were determined to help and assist her to overcome her problem.

We were introduced to bio-feedback by my sister in law a practicing child psychologist, who mentioned to us about the treatment, technique and its effectiveness in treating children with learning issues. She referred us to your clinic and suggested that we meet you and discuss her issues. We first set up an appointment with you. We took all the evaluation papers and her test scores from the school. Having completed 15 sessions we started seeing improvement with her behavior and in her class work. She seemed to be more relaxed, focused and was able to comprehend things that were being taught to her. We were also getting positive feedback not only from her teachers at school but also from her violin teacher and her supplemental math teacher.

We had been to her school last week for a parent teacher conference and met with her special education and her third grade class teacher. They were all praise for her and mentioned to us that she has made significant progress not only in terms of academic achievement but her behavior skills as well. Their feedback was that she was doing very well in math and english and at times is the only person in class who answers the teachers correctly and is ahead of the class in certain areas. She has learnt to cope very well and is on track with other students in her regular class.

It has been a year now since she started her bio-feedback and has completed 30 sessions so far. We are extremely happy and elated with her progress and achievement and bio-feedback has certainly made a difference in her life.

Conclusion

It is hoped that this discussion has provided the necessary information and logical arguments for a basic change in our approach to several major societal problems. The most logical and important place to start is in the school systems with the special education child. Whether the educational and political system will respond is uncertain at this point. I would like to thank the reader for your time in reading this discussion.

It is the author's experienced opinion that this approach offers the best chance for a "cure" to the special education and learning disabled child's condition.

To the world a child is only one child. To a child, there is only one child. If you know how to change the mind of one child, you know how to change the world.

Academic Ranking of World Universities, 2005. http://ed.sjtu.edu.cn/rank/2005/ARWU2005TOP500list.htm

Ackerman, P.T., Dykman, R.A., Oglesby, D.M, & Newton, J.E.O. (1995). EEG Power Spectra of Dysphonetic and Nondysphonetic Poor Readers, Brain and Language, Vol. 49, 140-152.

ADHD Help http://www.adhdhelp.org/concerta.htm

Ahn H., Prichep L.S., John E.R., et al: (1980) Developmental equations reflect brain dysfunction, Science, 210,1259-1262.

Alfor, G.S. (1980). Alcoholics anonymous: An empirical outcome study. Addictive Behaviors, 5, 359-370.

Amen, D. (2004) Healing ADD, The Breakthrough Program That Allows You to See and Heal the 6 Types of ADD, Mindworks Press

Amen, D.G., Carmichael, B.D. (1997). High-resolution brain SPECT imaging in ADHD, Ann. Clin. Psychiatry, 9; 81-86.

Anastopoulos, A.D., Guevremont, D.C., Shelton, T.L., DuPaul G.J. (1992). Parenting stress among families of children with attention deficit hyperactivity disorder.J Abnorm Child Psychol. 20. 503-520.

Arfanakis, K., Haughton, V.M., Carew, J.D., Rogers, B.P., Dempsey, R.J., Meyerand, M.E. (2002). Diffusion Tensor MR Imaging in Diffuse Axonal Injury, American Journal of Neuroradiology. 23.794-802, May

August, G.J. & Garfinkel, B.D. (1990). Comorbidity of ADHD and Reading Disability among clinic-referred children. Journal of Abnormal Child Psychology, 18, 29-45.

Ayers, M. (1995). Biofeedback and Self-Regulation, 20 (# 3), Pages 309-310.

Aylward, E.E., Reiss, A.L., Reader, M.J., Singer, H.S., Brown, J.E., & Denckla,M.B. (1996). Basal ganglia volumes in children with attention-deficit hyperactivity disorder. Journal of Child Neurology, 11, 112-115.

Barker, T. A., Torgesen, J. K., & Wagner, R. K. (1992). The role of orthographic processing skills on five different reading tasks. Reading Research Quarterly, 27, 334-345.

Barkley R.A. (1998). Attention-Deficit Hyperactivity Disorder: A Handbook for Diagnosis and Treatment.2nd edition. New York, Guilford Press; 1998. Barkley RA: Accidents and Attention-Deficit/Hyperactivity Disorder.TEN 2001, 3:64-68.

Barkley R.A. (2002). Major life activity and health outcomes associated with attention-deficit/hyperactivity disorder.J Clin Psychiatry, 63 Suppl 12:10-15.

Barkley, R. A. (1990).Attention deficit hyperactivity disorder: A handbook for diagnosis and treatment.Guilford Press: New York.

Barry, R.J., Johnstone, S.J., Clarke, A.R. (2003). A review of electrophysiology in attention-deficit/hyperactivity disorder: I. Qualitative and quantitative electroencephalography. Clinical Neurophysiology, 114, 171-183.

Barry, R.J., Clarke, A. R., McCarthy, R., Selikowitz, M. (2005). Age and gender effects in EEG coherence: III. Girls with attention-deficit / hyperactivity disorder. Clinical Neurophysiology, in press, 1-9

Basar-Eroglu, C., Struber, D., Schurmann, M., Stadler, M., & Basar, E. (1996). Gamma-band responses in the brain: A short review of the psychophysiological correlates and functional significance. International Journal of Psychophysiology,24 (1-2): 110-112.

Berry, C., School Inflation, Published by the Hoover Institution © 2004 by the Board of Trustees of Leland Stanford Junior University, (http://www.educationnext.org/20044/56.html)

Biederman J, Spencer T. (2000). Non-stimulant treatments for ADHD. Eur Child Adolesc Psychiatry, 9 Suppl 1:I51-9.

Biederman J, Wilens T, Mick E, et al. (1999). Pharmacotherapy of attention-deficit/hyperactivity disorder reduces risk for substance use disorder. Pediatrics;104(2),e20.

Biederman, (2004a), unpublished http://www.maaddsg.org/news_9_9_04.htm

Biederman, J. (2004b), unpublished, http://www.medicalnewstoday.com/medicalnews.php?newsid=13307

Biederman, J. (2004c), unpublished, http://www.upliftprogram.com/h_children.html#h63

Biederman, J. Faraone, S., Keenan, K., Benjamin, J., Krifcher, B., Moore, C., Sprich-Buckminster, S., Ugaglia, K., Jellinek, M.S., Steingard, R., Spencer, T., Norman, D., Kolodny, R., Kraus, I., Perrin, J., Keller, M.B., & Tsuang, M.T.(1992). Further evidence for family-genetic risk factors in attention deficit hyperactivity disorder: Patterns of comorbidity in probands and relatives in psychiatrically and pediatrically referred samples. Archives of General Psychiatry,49, 728-738.

Biederman, J., Faraone, S.V., Mick, E., Spencer, T., Wilens, T., Kiely, K., Guite, J., Ablon, J.S., Reed, E., & Warburton, R. (1995). High risk for attention deficit hyperactivity disorder among children of parents with childhood onset of the disorder: A pilot study. American Journal of Psychiatry, 152, 431-435.

Biederman, J., Keenan, K., & Faraone, S.V. (1990). Parent-based diagnosis of attention deficit disorder predicts a diagnosis based on teacher report. Journal of the American Academy of Child and Adolescent Psychiatry, 33, 842-848.

Biederman, J., Munir, K., Knee, D., Armentano, M., Autor, S., Waternaux, C., and Tsaung, M. (1987). High rate of affective disorders in probands with attention deficit disorder and in their relatives: A controlled family study. American Journal of Psychiatry, 144(3), 330-333.

Biederman, J., Newcorn, J., & Sprich, S. (1991). Comorbidity of attention deficit hyperactivity disorder with conduct, depressive, anxiety, and other disorders. American Journal of Psychiatry, 148, 564-577

Bird B.L, Newton F,A., Sheer D.E., Ford M.R. (1978). Biofeedback training of 40 Hz EEG in humans. Biofeedback and Self-Regulation; 3 (1), 1-12.

Birnbaum H.G., Kessler R.C., Lowe S.W., Secnik K., Greenberg P.E., Leong S.A., Swensen A.R. (2005). Costs of attention deficit-hyperactivity disorder (ADHD) in the US: excess costs of persons with ADHD and their family members in 2000.Curr Med Res Opin, 21:195-206.

Birnbaum, H.G., Ben Hamadi R., Greenberg P., Cremieux P.Y., (2004). Incidence and costs of accidents among Attention-Deficit/Hyperactivity Disorder patients.J Adol Health, 35:349.e1-e9.

Birsh J. Multisensory teaching of basic language skills. Baltimore: Brookes; 1999.

Blankenship, B. (1996). Court loan approved for drug program. The Topeka Capital Journal (July).

Borman, G.D., Benson, J., Overman, L.T.,(2005). Evaluation of the Scientific Learning Corporation's Fast ForWord Computer-Based Training Program in the Baltimore City Public Schools. Submitted for publication

Boston Globe (11/20/2005), Massachusetts's efforts in the No Child Left Behind program

Boutros, N., Fraenkel, L., Feingold, A. (2005) A four-step approach for developing diagnostic tests in psychiatry: EEG in ADHD as a test case. J. Neuropsychiatry Clin Neuroscience, 17(4), 455-464.

Boyd, W.D., (2005) EEG Biofeedback in the schools: The Use of EEG biofeedback to Treat ADHD in a School Setting, reprints available William D. Boyd, Ph.D., 1385 S. Colorado Blvd., Suite 300, Denver, CO 80222

Bradley, L., & Bryant, P. E. (1978). Difficulties in auditory organization as a possible cause of reading backwardness. Nature, 271, 746-747.

Brain facts website, http://faculty.washington.edu/chudler/facts.html

Bresnahan, S.M., Barry, R.J. (2002). Specificity of quantitative EEG analysis in adults with attention-deficit hyperactivity disorder. Psych Res, 112, 133-144.

Brody, N. (1999), Intelligence (2nd edition), Academic Press, San Diego, Ca.

Bronfenbrenner U: (1979) The Ecology of Human Development.Cambridge, MA, Harvard University Press

Brown, J. L., & Moffett, C. A. (1999). The hero's journey: How educators can transform schools and improve learning. Alexandria, VA: ASCD.

Burd L, Klug M.G. Coumbe M.J., Kerbeshian J. (2003) The attention-deficit hyperactivity disorder paradox: 2. Phenotypic variability in prevalence and cost of comorbidity.J Child Neurol, 18,653-660.

Bureau of Justice Statistics (1996) State Prison Expenditures, 1996, 8/99. NCJ 172211, www.ojp.usdoj.gov/bjs/

Burke, C., Howard, L., Evangelou, T. (2005) A Project of Hope, Lindamood-Bell website 3/2005

Bush, 2003, Bush Proposes $1 Billion School Aid, MSNBC News (www. msnbc.com/news/854878.asp), 4 January 2003.

Bush, G, Whalen,P.J., Rosen, B.R., Jenike, McInerney, S.C., Rauch, S.L. (1998). The counting Stroop: an interference task specialized for functional neuroimaging--validation study with functional MRI, Hum. Brain. Mapp. 6, 270-282.

Bush, G., Frazier, J.A., Rauch, S.L., Seidman, L.J., Whalen, P.J., Jenike, M.A., Rosen, B.R., Biederman, J. (1999). Anterior cingulate cortex dysfunction in attention-deficit/hyperactivity disorder revealed by fMRI and the Counting Stroop, Biol. Psychiatry 45; 1542-1552.

Bush, G., Luu, P., Posner M.I. (2000). Cognitive and emotional influences in anterior cingulate cortex, Trends Cogn. Sci. 4; 215-222

Bush, GW. (2003) Bush Proposes $1 Billion School Aid, MSNBC News (www.msnbc.com/news/854878.asp), 4 January 2003.

Business Week -October 19, 2005 http://www.businessweek.com/magazine/content/04_22/b3885139_mz070.htm

Business Week Online MAY 31, 2004, Special Needs, Crushing Costs

Business Week Online -October 19, 2005, December 2003 Journal of the American Academy of Child & Adolescent Psychiatry, http://www.businessweek.com/magazine/content/04_22/b3885139_mz070.htm

Byers A.P. (1995). Neurofeedback therapy for a mild head injury, Journal of Neurotherapy, 1 (1), 22-37.

Byring, R.F., Salmi, T.K., Sainio, K.O., Orn, H.P. (1991). EEG in children with spelling difficulties, Electroencephalography and clinical Neurophysiogy, (79), 247-255.

California Dept. of Education AYP report (2005), (http://www.cde.ca.gov/ta/ac/ay/index.asp)

Calis,K.A., Grothe, D.R. (1990) Attention-Deficit Hyperactivity Disorder, Clinical Pharmacology, 9, 632-642.

Campbell, S.B., Werry, J.S. (1986). Attention deficit disorder (hyperactivity). In H.C. Quay & J.S. Werry (Eds.), Psychopathological disorders of childhood (3rd ed.) (pp 96-105). New York, Wiley.

Carlezon, W.A. (2003) Early Use of ADHD Drug Alters Brain, Rat Studies Show, Dec. 15 issue of Biological Psychiatry Dec. 15, vol 54: pp 1330-1337. (http://my.webmd.com/content/article/78/95700.htm)

Carmody, D. P., Radvanski, D.C., Wadhwanni, S., Sabo, M.J., & Vergara, L. (2001). EEG biofeedback training and attention-deficit/hyperactivity disorder in an elementary school setting. Journal of Neurotherapy, 43 (3), 5-27.

Carmody, D.P., Bendersky, M., Dunn, S.M., DeMarco, J.K., Hegyi, T., Hiatt, M., Lewis, M. (2006). Early risk, attention and brain activation in adolescents born preterm, in process of submission

Carnoy, M., Loeb, S., and Smith, T.L. (2001). Do higher state test scores in texas make for better high school outcomes? (Philadelphia: Consortium for Policy Research in Education, Graduate School of Education, University of Pennsylvania, CPRE Research Report Series, RR-047, November 2001).

Cartozzo, H.A., Jacobs, D., Gevirtz, R.N. (1995). EEG biofeedback and the remediation of ADHD symptomatology: a controlled treatment outcome study. Presented at the Annual Conference of the Association for Applied Psychophysiology and Biofeedback, Cincinnati, Ohio, March.

Caspi, A., McClay, J., Moffitt, T., Mill, J., Martin, J., Craig, I., Taylor, A., Poulton, R. (2002). Role of genotype in the cycle of violence in maltreated Children, Science, 297, 851–854.

Castellanos, F.X. (1997). Toward a pathophysiology of attention- deficit/hyperactivity disorder, Clinical Pediatrics, 36, 381-393.

Castellanos, F.X., Giedd, J.N., Marsh, W.L., Hamburger, S.D., Vaituzis, A.C., Dickstein, D.P., Sarfatti, S.E., Vauss, Y.C., Snell, U.W. Lange, N., Kaysen, D., Krain, A.L., Ritchie, G.F., Rajapakse, J.C., Rapoport, J.L. (1996). Quantitative brain magnetic resonance imaging in attention-deficit hyperactivity disorder, Arch. Gen. Psychiatry, 53, 607-616.

Castellanos, F.X., Giedd, J.N., Eckburg, P., Marsh, W.L., Vaituzis, A.C., Kaysen, D.,Hamburger, S.D., & Rapoport, J.L. (1994). Quantitative morphology of the caudate nucleus in attention deficit hyperactivity disorder. American Journal of Psychiatry, 151, 1791-1796.

Castellanos, F.X., Giedd, J.N., Marsh, W.L., Hamburger, S.D., Vaituzis, A.C.,Dickstein, D.P., Sarfatti,S.E., Vauss, Y.C., Snell, J.W., Rajapakse, J.C.,&Rapoport, J.L. (1996).Quantitative brain magnetic resonance imaging in attention-deficit hyperactivity disorder, Archives of General Psychiatry, 53,607-616.

Catani, M., Jones, D. K., Ffytche, D.H. (2005). Perisylvian Language Networks of the Human Brain, Ann Neurol, 57, 8-16.

Cavanaugh, C.L., Kim, A., Wanzek, J., Vaugn, S. (2004). Kindergarten reading interventions for at-risk students: twenty years of research. Learning Disabilities: A Contemporary Journal, 2 (1), 9-21.

Caviness Jr., et al. (1998). Cerebral Cortex, 8, 372-384.

CDC Report (1997-8). Prevalence of attention-deficit disorder and learning disability: United States, is based on data from the CDC's National Health Interview Survey (NHIS).

CDC report (2003). (http://www.msnbc.msn.com/id/9164588)

CDC report, 2001, Series 10, number 206, Attention deficit disorder and learning disability, 1997-1998. (http://www.cdc.gov/nchs/data/series/sr_10/sr10_206.pdf)

CDC report, 2003 (http://www.cdc.gov/mmwr/preview/mmwrhtml/mm5434a2.htm)

Center for Collaborative Education. How Are The Boston Schools Faring? An Analysis of Student Demographics, Engagement, and Performance. Boston, MA: Center for Collaborative Education, 2001. Available: http://www.ccebos.org/pubslinks.html

Chabot R.J., Serfontein G. (1996). Quantitative EEG profiles of children with attention deficit disorder. Biol Psychiatry, 40, 951-963.

Chabot, R.A., diMichele, F., Prichep, L., & John, E.R. (2001). The clinical role of computerized EEG in the evaluation and treatment of learning and attention disorders in children and adolescents. Journal of Neuropsychiatry and Clinical Neuroscience, 13, 171-186.

Chabot, R.A., Merkin, H., Wood, L.M., Davenport, T.L., & Serfontein, G. (1996). Sensitivity and specificity of QEEG in children with attention deficit or specific developmental learning disorders. Clinical Electroencephalography, 27,26-34.

Chabot, R.A., Orgill, A.A., Crawford, G., Harris, M.J., & Serfontein, G. (1999). Behavioral and electrophysiological predictors of treatment response to stimulants in children with attention disorders. Journal of Child Neurology, 14 (6), 343-351.

Chabot, R.J., Merkin, H.,Wood, L.M.,Davenport, T.L., & Serfontein, G. (1996). Sensitivity and Specificity of QEEG in Children with Attention Deficit or Specific Developmental Learning Disorders. Clinical Electroencephalograpy, 27 (1), 26-33.

Chabot, RJ, diMichele, F., Prichep, L., (2005). The Role of Quantitative Electroencephalography in Child and Adolescent Psychiatric Disorders. Child and Adolescent Psychiatric Clinics of North

America, Jan, 55-82.

Chakrabarti, S., Fombonne, E. (2001). Pervasive developmental disorders in preschool children. JAMA, 285, 3093-3099.

Chartier, D. (1998). Neurofeedback and Enhancing Golf Performance Brain Wave Training and Its Effect on Golf Performance, '98 Winter Brain Meeting Abstracts, (http://www.futurehealth. org/98BrainAbstracts.htm)

Chicago Public school report on small schools (http://smallschools.cps.k12. il.us/research.html)

Clarke, A.R., Barry, R.J., McCarthy, R., & Selikowitz, M. (2001a). Electro-encephalogram differences in two subtypes of attention-deficit/hyperactivity disorder. Psychophysiology, 38, 212-221.

Clarke, A.R., Barry, R.J., McCarthy, R., & Selikowitz, M. (2001b). EEG-defined subtypes of children with attention-deficit/hyperactivity disorder. Clinical Neurophysiology, 112, 2098-2105.

Clarke, A.R., Barry, R.J., McCarthy, R., & Selikowitz, M. (2002). EEG differences between good and poor responders to methylphenidate and dexamphetamine in children with attention-deficit/ hyperactivity disorder. Clinical Neurophysiology, 113, 194-205.

Clarke, DH (1997). How Psychiatry is making drug addicts out the America's school children (http://www.uhuh.com/education/rit-psych.htm)

Clinical Evaluation of Language Fundamentals, PsychCorp, A brand of Harcourt Assessment, Inc., 19500 Bulverde Road, San Antonio, TX 78259

Cohen, P.A., Kulik, J.A., & Kulik, C.L.C .(1982). Educational outcomes of tutoring: A meta-analysis of findings. American Educational Research Journal, 19, 237-248.

Colletti L.F. (1979). Relationship between pregnancy and birth complications and the later development of learning disabilities. J Learn Disabil. Dec 12(10), 659-63.

Comprehensive Test of Phonological Processing. PRO-ED, 8700 Shoal Creek Boulevard -- Austin, Texas 78757-6897

Cossu, G., Shankweiler, D., Liberman, I. Y., Katz, L., & Tola, G. (1988). Awareness of phonological segments and reading ability in Italian children. Applied Psycholinguistics, 9, 1-16.

Cotton, K., (1996). School Size, School Climate, and Student Performance,

School Improvement Research Series, Regional Educational Lab, (http://www.nwrel.org/scpd/sirs/10/c020.html)

Croen, L.A., Grether, J.K., Hoogstrate, J., Selvin, S. (2002). The changing prevalence of autism in California. March of Dimes Birth Defects Foundation/California Department of Health Services, California Birth Defects Monitoring Program, Oakland 94606-5226, USA., J Autism Dev Disord, 32(3), 207-15.

Darling-Hammond, L (2000). Teacher Quality and Student Achievement: A Review of State Policy Evidence, Education Policy Analysis Archives, 8 (1), January 1, 2000, ISSN 1068-2341(http://epaa.asu.edu/epaa/v8n1/)

Daschle, Tom (Democrat - South Dakota) (2004). Views on Neuroscience, presented to the American Assoc. for the Advancement of Science, April 22, 2004

Deb, S. (2000) Epidemiology and treatment of epilepsy in patients who are mentally retarded. CNS Drugs, 13, 117–128.

deBeus, R., Ball, J.D., deBeus, M.E., & Herrington, R. (2003). Attention training with ADHD children: Preliminary findings in a double-blind placebo-controlled study. Presented at the Annual Conference of the International Society for Neuronal Regulation. Houston, TX.

DeFrance J, Sheer DE. (1988) Focused arousal, 40 Hz EEG, and motor programming, In Giannitrapani D, Murri L, editors. The EEG of mental activities. Basel: Karger; p.153-169.

DeFrance J., Sheer D.E. (1988). Focused arousal, 40 Hz EEG, and motor programming, In Giannitrapani D, Murri L, editors. The EEG of mental activities. Basel: Karger; 1988,153-169.

Diagnostic and Statistical Manual of Mental Disorders - Fourth Edition (DSM-IV) (1994), American Psychiatric Association, Washington D.C.

Diller, L.H. Running on Ritalin. New York: Bantam; 1998

DTAP, (2003) White Paper, Crossing the Bridge: An Evaluation of the Drug Treatment Alternative-to-Prison (DTAP) Program, released today by The National Center on Addiction and Substance Abuse (CASA) at Columbia University, 2/2003

Duffy FH (2000), The state of EEG biofeedback therapy (EEG operant conditioning) in 2000: an editor's opinion. Clin Electroencephalogr 31(1):V-VII.

DuPaul, G.J., Barkley, R.A., & Connor, D.F. (1998). Stimulants. In R.A. Barkley (Ed.) Attention deficit hyperactivity disorder: A handbook for diagnosis and treatment (2nd ed., pp. 510-551). New York: Guilford Press.

Durston, S., Hulshoff Pol, H.E., Schnack, H.G., Buitelaar, J.K., Steenhuis, M.P., Minderaa, R.B., Kahn, R.S., van Engeland (2004). Magnetic resonance imaging of boys with attention-deficit/ hyperactivity disorder and their unaffected siblings. J. Am. Acad. Child Adolesc. Psychiatry 43; 332-340.

Dykman, R.A., Holcomb, P.J., Oglesby, D.M., & Ackerman, P.T. (1982). Electrocortical Frequencies in Hyperactive, Learning-Disabled, Mixed and Normal Children, Biological Psychiatry, 17 (6), 675-685.

El-Zein, R.A., Abdel-Rahman, S.Z., Hay, M.J., Lopez, M.S., Bondy, M.L., Morris, D.L., Legator, M.S. (2005). Cytogenetic effects in children treated with methylphenidate, Cancer Lett. 230, 1–8.

Emrick, C.D. & Hansen, J. (1983). Assertion regarding effectiveness of treatment for alcoholism: Fact or fantasy? American Psychologist, 38, 1078-1088.

Ernst, M., Liebenauer, L.L., King, A.C., Fitzgerald, G.A., Cohen, R.M.& Zametkin, A.J. (1994). Reduced brain metabolism in hyperactive girls. Journal of the American Academy of Child and Adolescent Psychiatry, 33 (6), 858-868.

Espy, K. A., Molfese, D. L, Molfese, V. J, Modglin, A. (2004). Development of Auditory Event-Related Potentials in Young Children and Relations to Word-Level Reading Abilities at Age 8 Years, Annals of Dyslexia, 54, 9-38.

Evans P.D.; Anderson J.R.; Gilbert S.L.; Malcom C.M.; Dorus S.; Lahn B.T (2004). Adaptive evolution of ASPM, a major determinant of cerebral cortical size in humans, 489-494(6).

Evans,J.R., & Park, N.S. (1996). Quantitative EEG Abnormalities in a Sample of Dyslexic Persons. Journal of Neurotherapy, 2(1), 1-5.

Fagerheim, T., Raeymaekers, P., Tonnessen, F. E., Pedersen, M., Tranebjaerg, L., & Lubs, H. (1999). A new gene (DYX3) for dyslexia is located on chromosome 2. Journal of Medical Genetics, 36, 664-669.

Fairchild, M.D., and Sterman, M.B. (1974).Unilateral Sensory-Motor-Rhythm (SMR) Training in Cats: A Basis for Testing Neurophysiological and Behavioral Effects of Monomethylhydrazine (MMH).Report to the Aerospace Medical Research Laboratory, AMRL-TR-73-123.

FastForWord Website (http://www.scilearn.com/prod2/ffwd_lb/main=home)

Feature (2005): Drug War Prisoner Count Over Half a Million, US Prison Population at All-Time High 10/28/05 (http://stopthedrugwar.org/chronicle/409/toohigh.shtml)

Fein G, Galin D, Johnstone J, et al: (1983). EEG power spectrum in normal and dyslexic children, I: reliability during passive conditions. Electroencephalogr Clin Neurophysiol, 55, 399-405.

Fein G, Galin D, Yingling CD, et al. (1986). EEG spectra in dyslexic and control boys during resting conditions. Electroencephalogr Clin Neurophysiol, 63, 87-97.

Fernandez, T., Herrera, W., Harmony, T., Diaz-Comas, L., Santiago, E., Sanchez, L., Bosch, J., Fernandez-Bouzas, A., Otero, G., Ricardo-Garcell, J., Barraza, C., Aubert, E., Galan, L., & Valdes, P. (2003). EEG and behavioral changes following neurofeedback treatment in learning disabled children. Clinical Electroencephalography, 34(3), 145-150.

Figlio, D. (2002), Aggregation and Accountability: Will No Child Truly Be Left Behind?, Fordham Foundation, Washington, D.C., 13 February 2002.

Fine, A. H., and Goldman, L. (1994). Innovative techniques in the treatment of ADHD: An analysis of the impact of EEG biofeedback training and a cognitive computer generated training. Paper presented at the 102nd Annual Convention of the American Psychological Association, Los Angeles, CA August 12-16.

Finley, W.W. (1976).Effects of Sham Feedback Following Successful SMR Training in an Epileptic: A Follow-Up Study.Biofeedback and Self-Regulation, 1, 227-235.

Finn, C.E., Rotherham, A.J., Hokanson, C.R. eds. (2001). The Rising Costs of Special Education in Massachusetts: Causes and Effects, in Finn, Rotherham, and Hokanson 2001). Rethinking Special education for a New Century, Thomas b Fordham Foundation and progressive policy institute (http://www.edexcellence.net/library/special_ed/index.html)

Fletcher, M.A. (2003). States Worry New School Law Sets Schools Up to Fail, Washington Post, 3 January 2003, p. A-1.

Flynn J.M., Deering W.M. (1989) Subtypes of dyslexia: investigation of Border's system using quantitative neurophysiology. Dev Med Child Neurol, 31, 215-223.

Foorman, B.R., Francis, D.J., Winikates, D., Mehta, P., Schatschneider, C., Fletcher, J.M. (1997). Early Interventions for Children with Reading Disabilities, Scientific Studies of Reading, 1 (3), 255-276.

Foorman, B.R.D., Francis, J, Fletcher, J.M., Schatschneider, C., Mehta, P. (1998). The role of instruction in learning to read: Preventing reading Failure in at-risk-children. Journal of Educational Psychology, 90, 3, 7-58.

Forness, S. R., Kavale, K. A., Blum, I. M., & Lloyd, J. W. (1997). What works in special education and related services: Using meta-analysis to guide practice. Teaching Exceptional Children, 29(6), 4-9.

Foster, E.M., Jones, D.E. (2005). The Conduct Problems Prevention Research Group, The High Costs of Aggression: Public Expenditures Resulting From Conduct Disorder, October, 95 (10), American Journal of Public Health 1767-1772.

Francis, D.J., Shaywitz, S.E., Stuebing, K.K., Shaywitz, B.A., and Fletcher, J.M. (1996). Developmental lag versus deficit models of reading disability: A longitudinal, individual growth curves analysis. Journal of Educational Psychology, 88(1), 3-17.

Friedkin, N., & Necochea, J. (1988). School system size and performance: A contingency perspective. Educational Evaluation and Policy Analysis, 10(3), 237-249.

Fuchs, T., Birbaumer, N., Lutzenberger, W., Gruzelier, J.H., & Kaiser, J. (2003). Neurofeedback treatment for attention-deficit/hyperactivity disorder in children: A comparison with methylphenidate. Applied Psychophysiology and Biofeedback, 28 (1), 1-12.

Galaburda, A.M., Geschwind N., Sherman G.F., Rosen, G.D., Aboitiz, F. (1985). Developmental dyslexia: four consecutive patients with cortical anomalies. Ann Neurol, 18, 222-233.

Galin, D., Raz, J., Fein, G., Johnstone, J., Herron, J., Yingling, C. (1992).

EEG Spectra in Dyslexic and Normal Readers during Oral and Silent Reading, Electroencephalography and Clinical Neurophysiology, 82, 87-101.

Galski, T., Thornton, K., and Shumski, (1991). Neuropsychology of Sex Offenders, Jan. 1991, Journal of Offender Rehabilitation

GAOa (Government Accountability Office) (2005). Charter Schools, GAO-05-5

GAOb (Government Accountability Office) (2005). Special Education, Children with autism, GAO-05-220

Gasser T., Mochs J., Lenard, H.G. et al. (1983). The EEG of mildly retarded children: developmental, classificatory and topographic aspects. Electroencephalogr Clin Neurophysiol, 55,131-144.

Gayton W.F., Bailey, C., Wagner, A., Hardesty, V.A. (1986). Relationship between childhood hyperactivity and accident proneness. Percept Mot Skills, 63, 801-802.

Gerhardstein, R., Bacon, K.D., Anthony, J., (2001). Relations between the developmental precursors of ADHD and Reading: A longitudinal study. Presented at the biennial meeting of the society for Research in Child Development, Minneapolis. MN, April, 2001, (http://www.psy.fsu.edu/~lonigan/srcd1.pdf)

Giedd, J.N., Blumenthal, J., Molloy, E.,& Castellanos, F.X. (2001). Brain imaging of attention deficit/hyperactivity disorder. Annals of the New York Academy of Sciences, 931, 33-49.

Giedd, J.N., Castellanos, F.X., Casey, B.J., Kozuch, P., King, A.C., Hamburger,S.D., Rapoport, J.L. (1994). Quantitative morphology of the corpus callosum in attention deficit hyperactivity disorder. American Journal of Psychiatry, 151, 665-669.

Gilmore A., Milne R. (2001). Methylphenidate in children with hyperactivity: review and cost-utility analysis.Pharmacoepidemiol Drug Saf; 10:85-94.

Gittelman, R., Mannuzza, S., Shenker, R., Bonagura, N. (1985). Hyperactive boys almost grown up: I. Psychiatric status. Archives of General Psychiatry, 42, 937-947.

Goldman-Fristoe Test of Articulation, AGS Publishing, 4201 Woodland Road, Circle Pines, Minnesota

Goleman, D. (1997). Emotional Intelligence: Why it Can Matter More than IQ, Daniel Goleman Bantam; Reprint edition (June 2, 1997)

Gossop, M., Marsden, J., Stewart, D. and Rolfe, A. (2000). Patterns of drinking and drinking outcomes among drug misusers 1-year followup results. Journal of Substance Abuse Treatment, 19(1), 45-50.

Gossop, M., Stewart D., Browne N., Marsden J. (2002). Factors associated with abstinence,lapse or relapse to heroin use after residentialt reatment: protective effect of coping response. Addiction, 97 (10); 1259-1267.

Grantham-McGregor,S.M., Walker,S.P., Chang, S. (2000), Nutritional deficiencies and later behavioural development. Proceedings-of-the-Nutrition-Society, Feb. 59 (1), 47-54.

Gray, P. (1998). What is behind the alarming increase in Ritalin use among US children? (http://www.wsws.org/news/1998/nov1998/rit-n04.shtml)

Greene, J.P. (2002). Effects of Funding Incentives on Special Education Enrollment, Civic Report No. 32 December 2002

Greenhill, L.L., Halperin, J.M., & Abikoff, H. (1999). Stimulant medications.Journal of the American Academy of Child and Adolescent Psychiatry, 38 (5), 503-512.

Grigorenko, E. L., Wood, F. B., Meyer, M. S., Hart, L. A., Speed, W. C., Shuster, A., & Pauls, D. L. (1997). Susceptibility loci for distinct components of developmental dyslexia on chromosomes 6 and 15. American Journal of Human Genetics, 60, 27-39.

Guevara J., Lozano P., Wickizer T., Mell L., Gephart H. (2001). Utilization and cost of health care services for children with attention-deficit/hyperactivity disorder. Pediatrics, Jul 108(1), 71-8.

Guyer, B. P., & Sabatino, D.S. (1989). The effectiveness of a multisensory alphabetic phonetic approach with college students who are learning disabled. Journal of Learning Disabilities, 22, 430-433.

Haiera, R.J., Jungb, R.E., Yeoc, R.A., Heada, K., Alkire, M.T. (2005). The neuroanatomy of general intelligence: sex matters. NeuroImage, 25 (1), 320-327.

Haney, W., (2002). Lake Woebeguaranteed: Misuse of Test Scores in Massachusetts, Part I, Education Policy Analysis Archives, vol. 10, 6 May 2002. (http://epaa.asu.edu/epaa/v10n24/)

Harmony, T., Hinojosa, G., Marosi, E., Becker, J., Rodriguez, M., Reyes, A., & Rocha, C. (1990). Correlation between EEG Spectral

Parameters and an Educational Evaluation. International Journal of Neuroscience,Vol. 54, 147-155.

Hart, C.L., Taylor, M.D., Smith, G.D., Whalley,L.J., Starr, J.M., Hole, D.J., Wilson, V., Deary, I.J. (2003). Childhood IQ, Social Class, Deprivation, and Their Relationships with Mortality and Morbidity Risk in Later Life: Prospective Observational Study Linking the Scottish Mental Survey 1932 and the Midspan Studies, Psychosomatic Medicine, 65, 877-883.

Hattie, J.A., (1992). Measuring the effects of schooling. Australian Journal of Education, 36 (1), 5-13.

Haufler, A.J., Spalding, D.L., Santa Maria, D.L., Hatfield, B.D. (2000). Neurocognitive activity during a self-paced visuospatial task: comparative EEG profiles in marksmen and novice shooters. Biol. Psychol, 53, 131-160.

Hazel, E., McBride, A., & Siegel, L. S.(1997).Learning disabilities and adolescent suicide, Journal of Learning Disabilities, November 1997, vol. 30.

Health Canada, (2005). Canadian Adverse Drug Reaction Monitoring Program (CADRMP), Marketed Health Products Directorate, HEALTH CANADA, Address Locator: 0701C, OTTAWA, Ontario, K1A 0K9, News Release, Aug. 24, 2005 (http:// www.hc-sc.gc.ca/ahc-asc/media/advisories-avis/2005/2005_ 01_e.html)

Heywood, C., & Beale, I. (2003). EEG biofeedback vs placebo treatment for attention-deficit/hyperactivity disorder: A pilot study. Journal of Attention Disorders, 7(1), 41-53

Hinshaw S.P. (1992). Externalizing behavior problems and academic underachievement in childhood and adolescence: causal relationships and underlying mechanisms. Psychol Bull, 111, 127-55.

Hohnen, B. and J. Stevenson (1999). The structure of genetic influences on general cognitive, language, phonological and reading abilities. Developmental Psychology, 35 (2), 590-603.

Holloway R.L., Broadfield, D.C., Yuan, M.S., Schwartz, J.H., Tattersall, I. (2004). Brain endocasts—The paleoneurological evidence. 3: The human fossil record. New York: Wiley-Liss. 315

Hook, P. E., Macaruso, P., & Jones, S. (2001). Efficacy of fast forward training on facilitating acquisition of reading skills by children with reading difficulties-a longitudinal study. Annals of Dyslexia, 51, 75-96.

Horwitz B, Rumsey JM, Donohue BC.(1998). Functional connectivity of the angular gyrus in normal reading and dyslexia. Proc Natl Acad Sci USA, 95, 8939-8944.

Huang, G., & Howley, C. (1993). Mitigating disadvantage: Effects of small-scale schooling on students' achievement in Alaska. Journal of Research in Rural Education, 9(3), 137-149.

Hughes J.R., John, E.R. (1999). Conventional and quantitative electroencephalography in psychiatry. J Neuropsychiatry and Clinical Neurosciences, 11 (2), 190-208.

Hughes, J.R., Deleo, A.J., Melyn, M.A.(2000). The electroencephalogram in attention deficit-hyperactivity disorder: emphasis on epileptiform discharges. Epilepsy Behav, 1,271-7.

Hughes, J.R.(1971). Electroencephalography and learning disabilities, in Progress in Learning Disabilities, edited by Myklebust HR. New York, Grune and Stratton, 18-55.

Hultquist, A. M. (1997). Orthographic processing abilities of adolescents with dyslexia. Annals of Dyslexia, 47, 89-114.

Hunterdon & Sylvan (http://www.mylearningpartners.net/compare_huntington_and_sylvan.htm)

Hynd, G.W., Hern, K.L., Novey, E.S., & Eliopulos, D. (1993). Attention deficit-hyperactivity disorder and asymmetry of the caudate nucleus. Journal of Child Neurology, 8, 339-343.

Hynd, G.W., Semrud-Clikeman, M., Lorys, A.R., & Novey, E.S. (1990). Brain morphology in developmental dyslexia and attention deficit disorder/hyperactivity. Archives of Neurology, 47, 919-926.

Inglese M; Makani S; Johnson G; Cohen BA; Silver JA; Gonen O; Grossman RI (2005). Diffuse axonal injury in mild traumatic brain injury: a diffusion tensor imaging study. Journal of neurosurgery, 103(2), 298-303.

Innocenti Report Cards, (2002) A League Table of Educational Disadvantage in Rich Nations (Florence: UNICEF Innocenti Research Center, Innocenti Report Cards, no. 4, November 2002.

International Dyslexia Society website (http://www.interdys.org/servlet/compose?section_id=8&page_id=69)

IQ and social effect (http://en.wikipedia.org/wiki/IQ)

IQ and vocational effect (http://www.netconcepts.co.za/table01.htm)

IQ to SAT (http://www.sq.4mg.com/IQ-SATchart.htm)

Jacob, B.A.,Lefgren, L. (2002). Teacher Training Doesn't Affect Chicago Students, NBER Working Paper No. 8916, Issued in April 2002

Janelle, C.M., Hillman, C.H., Apparies, R.J. et al. (2000). Expertise differences in cortical activation and gaze behavior during rifle shooting. J. Sport Exerc. Psychol, 222, 167-182.

Jenkins, L. & Brown, S.(1992) Some issues in the assessment of epilepsy occurring in the context of learning disability in adults. Seizure, 1, 49–55.

Jensen, P.S., Achenbach, T.M., Rowland, A.S. (2005). Epidemiologic Research on ADHD: What We Know and What We Need to Learn. CDC report, September 20, 2005. (http://www.cdc.gov/ncbddd/adhd/dadabepi.htm)

Jibiki, I., Kurokawa, K., Fukushima, T., Kjido, H., Yamaguchi, N., Matsuda, H., & Hisada, K. (1994). Correlations between Quantitative EEG and Regional Cerebral Blood Flow (SPECT) in Patients with Partial Epilepsy. Neuropsychobiology, Vol. 30, 46-52.

John, E.R. (1977). Functional Neuroscience, vol 2: Neurometrics: Clinical Applications of Quantitative Electrophysiology. Hillsdale, NJ, Lawrence Erlbaum

John, E.R., Prichep, L.S., Ahn, H., et a.: (1983). Neurometric evaluation of cognitive dysfunctions and neurological disorders in children. Prog Neurobiol, 21, 239-290.

Johnson, E.O., Breslau N. (2000). Increased risk of learning disabilities in low birth weight boys at age 11 years. Biol Psychiatry. Mar 15 47(6). 490-500.

Johnston, C., Mash, E.J. (2001). Families of children with attention-deficit/hyperactivity disorder: review and recommendations for future research. Clin Child Fam Psychol Rev, 4,183-207.

Jones, F.W., & Holmes, D.S. (1976). Alcoholism, alpha production, and biofeedback. Journal of Consulting and Clinical Psychology, 44, 224-228.

Joyce, M. (1997). New Visions School, Program Evaluation: EEG Neurofeedback, New Visions School - 1996-97; 3820 Emerson Ave., Minneapolis, MN 55412, (612) 521-2266 F-9647.

Juel, C., Griffith, P., Gough, P. (1986). Acquisition of literacy: a longitudinal study in first and second grade. Journal of Educational Psychology, 78, 234-255.

Juel, C. (1988). Learning to read and write: A longitudinal study of 54 children from first through fourth grades. Journal of Educational Psychology, 80, 437-447.

Kaiser, D., Othmer, S. (2000). Effect of neurofeedback on variables of attention in a large multi-center Trial. Journal of Neurotherapy, 4 (1), 5-17.

Kane, T.J., Staiger, D.O. (2002). Volatility in School Test Scores: Implications for School-Based Accountability Systems, unpublished paper, Hoover Institution, Stanford University, Stanford, Calif., April 2001; and Jaekyung Lee, Evaluating Rural Progress in Mathematics Achievement: Is 'Adequate Yearly Progress' (AYP) Feasible, Valid, Reliable, and Fair?, paper prepared for the ACCLAIM conference, SUNY-Buffalo, 3-6 November 2002.

Kashani, J.H., Cantwell, D.P., Shekim, W.D., Reid, J. (1982). Major depressive disorder in children admitted to inpatietn community mental health center. American Journal of Psychiatry, 139,671-672.

Kattlove, H. (2005). Does Ritalin Increase Cancer Risk in Children? (http://www.medicinenet.com/script/main/art.asp?articlekey=43760)

Kaye, H., John, E.R., Ahn H, et al. :(1981). Neurometric evaluation of learning disabled children. Int J Neurosci, 13, 15-25.

Kelleher, K.J., McInerny, T.K., Gardner, W.P. et al. (2000). Increasing identification of psychosocial problems: 1979-1996. Pediatrics, 1051, 1313-21.

Keller, I. (2001). Neurofeedback Therapy of Attention Deficits in Patients with Traumatic Brain Injury. J. of Neurotherapy, 5 (1/2), 19-33.

Kelly, M. J. (1997). Native Americans, neurofeedback, and substance abuse theory: Three year outcome of alpha/theta neurofeedback training in the treatment of problem drinking among Dine= (Navajo) people. Journal of Neurotherapy, 2(3), 24-60.

Kelly, M.J. (1998). Alpha/Theta Training of 19 Dine' Alcohol Drinkers - Three year Outcome Study, J. of Neurotherapy ??

Kerick, S. E., McDowell, K., Hung, T. M., Spalding, T. S., & Hatfield, B. D.

(2001). Event-related alpha power in marksmen: Motor versus integrated perceptual-motor demands of shooting. Medicine and Science in Sports and Exercise, 33(5), Supplement abstract 1013.

Kerick, S.E., Douglas, L.W., Hatfield, B.D. (2000). Cerebral Cortical Adaptation Associated with Visuomotor Practice. Medicine and Science in Sports and Exercise, 118-129.

Kim, B.N., Lee, J.S, Shin, M.S., Cho, S.C., Lee, D.S., (2002). Regional cerebral perfusion abnormalities in attention deficit/hyperactivity disorder. Statistical parametric mapping analysis, Eur. Arch. Psychiatry Clin. Neurosci. 252; 219-225.

Kim, B-N., Lee, J-S, Shin, M-S, Cho, S-C, & Lee, D-S. (2002). Regional cerebral perfusion abnormalities in attention deficit/hyperactivity disorder: Statistical parametric mapping analysis. European Archives of Psychiatry and Clinical Neuroscience, 252, 219-225.

Klassen, A.F., Miller, A., Fine, S. (2004). Health-Related Quality of Life in Children and adolescents who hae a diagnosis of attention-deficit/hyperactivity disorder. Pediatrics, 114 (5), 541-547.

Klaus, P.A. (1994). BJS Statistician, The Costs of Crime to Victims: Crime Data Brief, Bureau of Justice Statistics Crime Data Brief, U.S. Department of Justice, Office of Justice Programs, Bureau of Justice Statistics, February NCJ-145865

Klingberg, T., Hedehus, M., Temple, E., Salz, T., Gabrieli, J.D., Moseley, M.E., Poldrack, R.A. (2000). Microstructure of temporo-parietal white matter as a basis for reading ability: Evidence from diffusion tensor magnetic resonance imaging. Neuron, 25, 492-500.

Koch, C. Biophysics of Computation. Information Processing in Single Neurons, New York: Oxford Univ. Press, 1999, page 87

Kollins, S.H., McClernon, F.J., Fuemmeler, B.F. (2005). Association Between Smoking and Attention-Deficit/Hyperactivity Disorder Symptoms in a Population-Based Sample of Young Adults. Arch Gen Psychiatry, 62, 1142-1147.

Krause, K.H., Dresel, S.H., Krause, J., LaFougere, C., Brinkbaumer, K, Kung, H.F., Hahn, K., & Tatsch, K. (2000). Increased striatal dopamine transporter in adult patients with attention deficit hyperactivity disorder: Effects of methylphenidate as measured by single photon emission computed tomography. Neuroscience Letters, 285, 107-110.

Lahey, B.B., Schaughnency, E.A., Hynd, G.W. et al. (1987). Attention deficit disorder with and without hyperactivity. Comparison of behavioural characteristics of clinic-referred children. Journal of the American Academy of Child and Adolescent Psychiatry, 26(5),718-23.

Lambert, N.M. (1988). Adolescent outcomes for hyperactive children. Perspectives on general and specific patterns of childhood risk for adolescent educational, social, and mental health problems. Am Psychol, 43, 786-799.

Landers, D.M., Han, M., Walazar, W., Petruzzello, S.J., Kubitz, K.A., Gannon, T.L. (1994). Effects of learning on electroencephalographic and electrocardiagographic patterns in novice archers. Int.J. Sports Psychol, 25, 313-330.

Langlois, Rutland-Brown, & Thomas (2004). Report to Congress on Mild Traumatic Brain Injury in the United States: Steps to Prevent a Serious Public Health Problem, 2003.

Lazzaro, I., Gordon, E., Whitmont, S., et al. (1998). Quantified EEG activity in adolescent attention deficit hyperactivity disorder. Clin Electroencephalography, 29, 37-42.

Leahy, B.T. (2001). Youth aliented from the education system of ten often enter the prison system, November 29, 2001, Coalition for Juvenile Justice (http://www.juvjustice.org/media/1008. html)

Lee, J. (2002). Evaluating Rural Progress in Mathematics Achievement: Is 'Adequate Yearly Progress' (AYP) Feasible, Valid, Reliable, and Fair?, paper prepared for the ACCLAIM conference, SUNY-Buffalo, 3-6 November 2002.

Leibson, C.L., Katusic, S.K., Barbaresi, W.J., Ransom, J., O'Brien, P.C. (2001). Use and Costs of Medical Care for Children and Adolescents With and Without Attention-Deficit/Hyperactivity Disorder. JAMA, 285, 60-66.

Leibson, C.L., Long, K.H. (2003). Economic implications of attention-deficit hyperactivity disorder for healthcare systems. Pharmacoeconomics 2003, 21,1239-1262.

Lerner, J. (1989). Educational interventions in learning disabilities. Journal of the American Academy of Child and Adolescent Psychia-

try, 28, 326-331.

Lévesqu, J., Beauregard, M., Mensour, B. (2005) Effect of Neurofeedback Training on the Neural Substrates of Selective Attention in Children with Attention-Deficit/Hyperactivity Disorder: A Functional Magnetic Resonance Imaging Study, Neuroscience letters

Levy, R., Hay, D.A., McStephen, M., Wood, C., & Waldman, I. (1997). Attention deficit hyperactivity disorder: A category or a continuum? Genetic analysis of a large-scale twin study. Journal of the American Academy of Child and Adolescent Psychiatry, 36, 737-744.

Lewis, D.O., et al. (1986). Psychiatric, Neurological, and Psychoeducational Characteristics of 15 Death Row Inmates in the United States. J. Am. Psychiatry, 143, 838-845.

Liebson, C.L., Katusie, S.K., Barbaresi W.J., et al. (2001). Use and coss of medical care for children and adolescents with and without attention-deficit//hyperactivity disorder. JAMA, 285, 60-6.

Limsila, P. (2001). Intervention Program for children with Autism Spectrum Disorders in Thailand Presented at the 24th International School Psychology Colloquium 25 – 29 July, 2001, Dinan France

Lindamood-Bell website (www.Lindamood-Bell.com)

Linden, M., Habib, T., Radojevic, V. (1996). A Controlled Study of the Effects of EEG biofeedback on Cognition and Behavior of Children with Attention Deficit Disorder and Learning Disabilities. Biofeedback and Self Regulation, 21 (1)

Lloyd, J. W., Forness, S. R., & Kavale, K. A. (1998). Some methods are more effective. Intervention in School and Clinic, 33(1), 195-200.

Lord, J., Paisley, S. (2000). The Clinical Effectiveness and Cost-Effectiveness of Methylphenidate for Hyperactivity in Childhood, Version 2. London, National Institute for Clinical Excellence

Lou, H.C., Henriksen, L., Bruhn, P. (1984). Focal cerebral hypoperfusion in children with dysphasia and/or attention deficit disorder. Archives of Neurology, 41 (8), 825-829.

Lou, H.C., Henriksen, L., & Bruhn, P. (1990). Focal cerebral dysfunction in developmental disabilities. Lancet, 335 (8680), 8-11.

Lubar, J. F. (1977). Electroencephalographic biofeedback, methodology and the management of epilepsy. Pavlovian Journal of Biological Science, 12, 147-189.

Lubar, J. F. (1985). Changing EEG activity through biofeedback applications for the diagnosis and treatment of learning disabled children. Theory and Practice. Ohio State University, 24, 106-111.

Lubar, J. F., & Bahler, W. W. (1976). Behavioral management of epileptic seizures following EEG biofeedback training of the sensorimotor rhythm. Biofeedback and Self-Regulation, 1, 77-104.

Lubar, J. F., Shabsin, H. S., Natelson, S. E., Holder, G. S., Woodson, S. F., Pamplin, W. E., & Krulikowski, D. I. (1981). EEG operant conditioning in intractable epileptics. Archives of Neurology, 38, 700-704.

Lubar, J. F., Swartwood, M. O., Swartwood, J. N., & Timmermann, D. L. (1995). Quantitative EEG and auditory event-related potentials in the evaluation of Attention-Deficit/Hyperactivity disorder: Effects of methylphenid ate and implications for neurofeedback training. Journal of Psychoeducational Assessment (Monograph Series Advances in Psychoeducational Assessment) Assessment of Attention-Deficit/Hyperactivity Disorders, 143-204.

Lubar, J.F. (1991). Discourse on the development of EEG diagnostics and biofeedback for attention-deficit/hyperactivity disorders. Biofeedback and Self-Regulation, 16, 201-224.

Lubar, J.F. (2003). Neurofeedback for the management of attention deficit disorders. In M.S. Schwartz & F. Andrasik (Eds.), Biofeedback: A practitioner's guide (3rd ed., pp. 409-437. New York: Guilford Press.

Lubar, J.F., Shabsin, H.S., Natelson, S.E., Holder, G.S., Whitsett, S.F., Pamplin, W.E., and Krulikowski, D.I. (1981).EEG Operant Conditioning in Intractable Epileptics.Arch. Neurol., 38, 700-704.

Lubar, J.O., Lubar, J.F. (1984). Electroencephalographic Biofeedback of SMR and Beta for Treatment of Attention Deficit Disorders in a Clinical Setting, Biofeedback and Self-Regulation, Vol. 9 (1), 1-23.

Lundberg, I., Wall, S., & Olofsson, A. (1980). Reading and spelling skills in the first school years predicted from phonemic awareness

264

skills in kindergarten. Scandinavian Journal of Psychology, 21, 159-173.

Lynn, R. Vanhanen, T. (2002). IQ and the Wealth of Nations, Richard Lynn and Tatu Vanhanen, Westport, CT: Praeger, 256 pp., U.S. by Richard Lynn and Tatu Vanhanen

Lyon, G. R. (1995). Toward a definition of dyslexia. Annals of Dyslexia, 45, 3-27.

Lyon, G.R., Moats, L.C. (1998). Critical issues in the instruction of learning disabled. J Consult Clin Psychol, 56, 830-835.

lZhang, J. (2003). Evolution of the human ASPM gene, a major determinant of brain size. Genetics, 165, 2063-70. Abstract

M. Clay (1990) Observation Survey of Early Literacy Achievement, Hong Kong: Heinemann

Macklin, M.L., Metzger, L.J., Lasko, N.B., Orr, S.P., Pitman, R.K., Litz, B.T., McNally, R.J. (1998). Is Lower Precombat Intelligence Is a Risk Factor for Posttraumatic Stress Disorder, Journal of Consulting and Clinical Psychology, 66 (2).

Maddah, M., Mewes, A.U.J., Haker, S., Grimson, W.E.L., Warfield, S.K. (2005). Automated Atlas-Based Clustering of White Matter Fiber Tracts from DTMRI. Computer Science and Artificial Intelligence Laboratory, MIT, Cambridge, MA., 02139

Mann, C.A., Lubar, J.F., Zimmerman, A.W., Miller, C.A., & Muenchen, R.A. (1992). Quantitative Analysis of EEG in Boys with Attention-Deficit-Hyperactivity Disorder: Controlled Study with Clinical Implications. Pediatric Neurology, 8 (1), 30-36.

Mannuzza, S., Klein, R.G. (2000). Long-term prognosis in attention-deficit/ hyperactivity disorder. Child Adolesc Psychiatr Clin N Am 2000, 9, 711-726.

Mannuzza, S., Klein, R.G., Konig, P.H., Giampino, T.L. (1989). Hyperactive boys almost grown up. IV. Criminality and its relationship to psychiatric status. Arch Gen Psychiatry, 46,1073-1079.

Marchetti, A., Magar, R. Lau, H. et al. (2001). Pharmacotherapies for attention-deficit/hyperactivity disorder in children and adolescents? CMAJ 2001: 165: 1904-21.

Marchetti, A., Magar, R., Lau, H., Murphy, E.L., Jensen, P.S., Conners, C.K., Findling, R., Wineburg, E., Carotenuto, I., Einarson, T.R., Iskedjian M. (2001). Pharmacotherapies for attention-deficit/hyperactivity disorder: expected-cost analysis.Clin Ther, 23,1904-1921.

Marlatt, G.A. (1983). The controlled drinking controversy: A commentary. American Psychologist, 38, 1097-1110.

Marosi, E., Harmony, T., Sanchez, L. (1992). Maturation of the coherence of EEG activity in normal and learning-disabled children. Electroencephalogr Clin Neurophysiol, 83, 350-357.

Mathis, W.J. (2003). No Child Left Behind, Costs and Benefits. April 2003 (http://www.pdkintl.org/kappan/k0305mat.htm#38a)

Matochek, J.A., Nordahl. T.E., Gross, M., Semple, W.E., King, A.C., Cohen, R.M.,& Zametkin, R.M. (1993). Effects of acute stimulant medication on cerebral metabolism in adults with hyperactivity. Neuropsychopharmacology, 8,377-386.

Matsuura, M., Okubo, Y., Toru, M. et al. (1993). A cross-national study of children with emotional and behavioral problems: a WHO collaborative study in the Western Pacific region. Biol Psychiatry, 34, 59-65.

Matza, L.S., Secnik, K., Mannix, S., Sallee, F.R. Parent-proxy EQ-5D ratings of children with Attention Deficit/Hyperactivity Disorder in the United States and United Kingdom. Pharmacoeconomics, in press

Matza, L.S., Secnik, K., Rentz, A.M., Mannix, S., Sallee, F.R., Gilbert, D.A., Revicki, D.A. (2005). Development and assessment of health state utilities for Attention Deficit/Hyperactivity Disorder in children using parent proxy report. Qual Life Res, 14, 735-747.

McBride-Chang, C., Kail, R.V. (1996). Cross-Cultural Similarities in the Predictors of Reading Acquisition. (http://www.tau.ac.il/education/homepg/iris-levin/library/McBride%20Chang%20Kail%20reading%20prediction.doc)

McCandliss, B.D., Noble, K.G. (2003). The development of reading impairment: a cognitive neuroscience model. Ment Retard Dev Disabil Res Rev, 9, 196-205.

McEvoy, L.K., Smith, M.E., Gevins (2000). A Test-retest reliability of cognitive EEG. Clin Neurophysiol, 111, 457-463.

McGee, R., William, S., Share, D.L., Anderson, J., Silva, P. (1986), The relationship between specific reading retardation, general reading backwardness and behavioral problems in a large sample of Dunedin Boys: A Longtidinal study from 5 to 11 years, Journal of child psychology and psychiatry and allied disciplines, 27, 597-610.

McGee, R., Williams, S., Moffitt, T., & Anderson, J. (1989). A comparison of 13-year-old boys with attention deficit and/or reading disorder on neuropsychological measures. Journal of Abnormal Child Psychology, 17, 37-53.

McLachlan, J.F. & Stein, R.L. (1982). Evaluation of a day clinic for alcoholics. Journal of Studies on Alcohol, 43, 261-272.

MedWatch (http://www.ritalindeath.com)

Miller, A., Lee, S.K., Raina, P. (1998). Part 1: overview and clinical evaluation of the use of methylphenidate for attention-deficit/hyperactivity disorder. In: Miller A, Le SK, Raina P., et al., Editors. A review of therapies for attention-deficit/hyperactivity disorder. Ottawa, Canada: Candaian Coordinating Office for Health Technology Assessment (CCOHTA)

Miller, A.K., Alston, R.L. and Corsellis, J.A. (1980). Variation with age in the volumes of grey and white matter in the cerebral hemispheres of man: measurements with an image analyser. Neuropathol Appl Neurobiol., 6,119-132.

Miller, T. R., Cohen, M. A., & Wiersema, B. (1996, February). Victim Costs and Consequences: A New Look. Washington, DC: National Institute of Justice, U.S. Department of Justice

Miller, W.R. & Hester, R.K. (1980). Treating the problem drinker: Modern approaches. In Treatment of alcoholism, drug abuse, smoking, and obesity, pp. 111-141. Oxford: Pergamon.

Miltner, W.H.R., Braun, C., Arhnold, M., Witte, H., Taub, E. (1999). Coherences of gamma-band EEG activity as a basis for associative learning. Nature. 397, 434-436.

Molina, B.S.G.., Grossman, F. (2003). Childhood predictors of adolescent substance use in a longitudinal study of children with ADHD. Journal of Abnormal Psychology, Aug., 112(3), 497-507.

Molfese, D., & Molfese, V. (1979a). Infant speech perception: Learned or innate? In H. Whitaker & H. Whitaker (Eds.), Advances in neurolinguistics, (vol. 4.) (pp. 229-240). New York: Academic Press.

Molfese, D., & Molfese, V. (1979a). Hemisphere and stimulus differences as reflected in the cortical responses to newborn infants to speech stimuli. Developmental Psychology, 15, 505-511.

Molfese, D., & Molfese, V. (1985). Electrophysiological indices of auditory discrimination in newborn infants: The bases for predicting later language development. Infant Behavior and Development, 8,197-211.

Molfese, D., & Molfese, V. (1988). Right hemisphere responses from pre-school children to temporal cues contained in speech and non-speech materials: Electrophysiological correlates. Brain and Language, 33,135-156.

Molfese, D., & Molfese, V. (1997). Discrimination of language skills at five years of age using event related potentials recorded at birth. Developmental Neuropsychology, 13,133-156.

Monastra and Monastra (2005). Child & Adolescent Psychiatric Clinics of North America, Jan, 2005, 55-83.

Molfese, Dv & Molfese, V. (2000). The continuum of language development during infancy and childhood: Electrophysiological correlates. In C. Rovee-Collier, L. Lipsitt, & R. Reese (Eds.), Progress in infancy research (vol. 1) (pp. 251-287). Mahwah, NJ: Erlbaum.

Molfese, D., Molfese, V., & Kelly, S. (2001). The use of brain electrophysiology techniques to study language: A basic guide for the beginning consumer of electrophysiology information. Learning Disability Quarterly, 24,177-188.

Monastra et al. (2001). The Development of a Quantitative Electroencephalographic Scanning Process for ADHD: Reliability and Validity Studies. Neuropsychology, 15, 136-144.

Monastra, V.J. & Monastra, D.M. (2004). EEG biofeedback treatment for ADHD:An analysis of behavioral, neuropsychological, and electrophysiological response over a three-year follow-up period. Invited Address. Annual Conference of the Association for Applied Psychophysiology and Biofeedback. Colorado Springs, CO.

Monastra, V.J., Lubar, J.F., Linden, M. (2001). The development of a quantitative electroencephalographic scanning process for attention deficit-hyperactivity disorder: Reliability and validity studies. Neuropsychology, 15, 136-144.

Monastra, V.J., Lubar, J.F., Linden, M., VanDeusen, P., Green, G., Wing, W., Phillips, A. & Fenger, .N. (1999). Assessing attention deficit hyperactivity disorder via quantitative electroencephalography: An initial validation study. Neuropsychology, 13 (3), 424-433.

Monastra, V.J., Monastra, D.M., & George, S. (2002). The effects of stimulant therapy, EEG biofeedback, and parenting style on the primary symptoms of attention-deficit/hyperactivity disorder. Applied Psychophysiology and Biofeedback, 27 (4), 231-249.

Monastra, VJ, (2005). Electroencephalographic Biofeedback (Neurotherapy) as a treatment for Attention Deficit Hyperactivity Disorder; Rationale and Empirical Foundation, Child and Adolescent Psychiatric Clinics of America, Jan, 2005, 55-82.

Monastra, web site (http://www.theadhddoc.com/causes_of_adhd.php)

Moos, R., & Finney, J.W. (1983). The expanding scope of alcoholism treatment evaluation. American Psychologist, 38, 1030-1044.

Mostofsky, S.H., Cooper, K.L., Kates, W.R., Denckla, M.B., Kaufmann, W.E. (2002). Smaller prefrontal and premotor volumes in boys with attention-deficit/hyperactivity disorder. Biol. Psychiatry 52; 785-794.

Mostofsky, S.H., Reiss, A.L., Lockhart, P.,& Denckla, M.B. (1998). Evaluation of cerebellar size in attention-deficit hyperactivity disorder. Journal of Child Neurology, 13, 434-439.

Mrug, S., Hoza B., Gerdes, A.C. (2001). Children with attention-deficit/hyperactivity disorder: peer relationships and peer-oriented interventions.New Dir Child Adolesc Dev, 51-77.

MTA study, (2005), Jensen, P., Garcia, J.A., Glied, S., Crowe, M., Foster, M., Schlander, M., Hinshaw, S., Vitiello, B., Arnold, L.E., Elliott, G., Hechtman, L., Newcorn, J.H., Pelham, W.E., Swanson, J, Wells, K. (2005). Cost-Effectiveness of ADHD Treatments: Findings From the Multimodal Treatment Study of Children With ADHD. Am J Psychiatry, 162,1628-1636, September

MTA Study; Multimodal Treatment Study of Children with ADHD Cooperative Group. (1999). A 14 month randomized clinical trial of treatment strategies for attention-deficit/hyperactivity disorder. Archives of General Psychiatry, 56, 1073-1086.

MTA, 2004; National Institute of Health Multimodal Treatment study of ADHD follow-up: 24 month outcomes of treatment strategies for Attention Deficit/Hyperactivity Disorder. Pediatrics,

April 1, 2004, 2004 (113)(4), 754-761.

Murphy K., Barkley, R.A. (1996). Attention deficit hyperactivity disorder adults: comorbidities and adaptive impairments.Compr Psychiatry, 37. 393-401.

NAEP Historical Data (http://www.educationnext.org/20032/39.html)

NAEP Report (2005) (http://nces.ed.gov/pubsearch/pubsinfo.asp?pubid=2005464)

Nagy, Z., Westerberg, H. and Klingberg, T., (2004., Maturation of White Matter is Associated with the Development of Cognitive Functions during Childhood. Journal of Cognitive Neuroscience, 16, 1227-1233.

Näslund, J. C., & Schneider, W. (1996). Kindergarten letter knowledge, phonological skills, and memory processes: relative effects on early literacy. Journal of Experimental Child Psychology, 62, 30-59.

National Center for Education Statistics (NCES), US Department of Education, Federal Support for Education, Aug., 2004

National Center for Health Statistics (2004). Mean Body Weight, Height, and Body Mass Index, United States 1960-2002. Advance Data No. 347. 18 pp. (PHS 2005-1250).

National Dissemination Center for Children with Disabilities (2004),Traumatic Brain Injury, Fact Sheet 18 (FS18) January 2004

NCLB Left Behind (2005). Understanding the Growing Grassroots Rebellion Against a Controversial Law, (http://www.nclbgrassroots.org/landscape.php)

NEA Report, (2002) (http://www.nea.org/specialed/coalitionfunding2002.html)

Nelson, F.H., Rosenberg, B., VanMeter, N. (Aug.2004). Charter School Achievement on the 2003 National Assessment of Educational Progress, AFL-CIO report

New York Times (11/26/2005), Education section article

New York Times, (11/29/2005) A Victory for Education

Newschaffer, C.J., Falb, M.D., Gurney, J.G. (2005). National Autism Prevalence Trends from United States Special Education Data. Pediatrics, 115, 277-282.

NIDA InfoFacts:The National Institute on Drug Abuse (NIDA), Drug Addiction Treatment Methods (http://www.nida.nih.gov/infofacts/treatmeth.html)

Niedermeyer, E.(1987). EEG and clinical neurophysiology, in Electroencephalography: Basic Principles, Clinical Applications and Related Fields, edited by Niedermeyer E, Lopes da Silva F. Baltimore, Urban and Schwarzenberg, 1987, 97-117.

NIH (1998) Diagnosis and Treatment of Attention Deficit Hyperactivity Disorder. NIH Consens Statement 1998 Nov 16-18; 16(2): 1-37.

NIH Publication No. 01-4929, (2001) Teenage Brain: A work in progress NIH, (2004) (http://www.nimh.nih.gov/grants/rf-pds0004.pdf)

Noble, R.E. (1972). Anorexigenic acitivty of intermittent dextroamphetamine with and without meprobamate. Current Therapeutic Research, Clinical and Experimental, 14(4), 162-167.

Nolan, E.E., Gadow, K.D. (1997). Children with ADHD and tic disorder and their classmates: behavioral normalization with methylphenidate. Journal of the American Academy of Child and Adolescent Psychiatry, 36 (5), 597-604.

Northwest Evaluation Association (2005) (http://www.nea.org/specialed/index.html)

NWEA report (2005) The Impact of the No Child Left Behind Act on student Achievement and Growth: 2005 Edition. (http://www.nwea.org/research/nclbstudy.asp)

Oakes, T.R., Pizzagalli, D.A., Hendrick, A.M., Horras, K.A., Larson, C.L., Abercrombie, H.C., Schaefer, S.M., Koger, J.V., Davidson, R.J. (2004). Functional coupling of simultaneous electrical and metabolic activity in the human brain. Human Brain Mapping, 21, 257-270

Oakland, T., Black, J.L., Stanford, G., Nussbaum, N.L., Balise, R.R. (1998). An evaluation of the dyslexia training program: A multisensory method for promoting reading in students with reading disabilities. J Learn Disabil, 31 (2), 140-150.

O'Connor, J. and Wilson, B. (1995). Effectiveness of the Wilson Reading System used in public school training. In McIntyre, C. and Pickering, J. (eds.) 1995. Clinical Studies of Multisensory Structured Language Education. Salem, OR.

Office of Special Education (http://www.ed.gov/about/offices/list/osers/osep/index.html?src=mr])

Oken, B.S., Chiappa, K.H.(1988). Short-term variability in EEG frequency analysis. Electroencephalogr Clin Neurophysiol, 1988, 69,191-198.

Olson, R.K., Wise, B.W., (1992). Reading on the computer with orthographic and speech feedback: An overview of the Colorado Remedial Reading Project. Reading and Writing; An Interdisciplinary Journal, 4, 107-44.

Orlando, P. C., Rivera, R.O. (2004). EEG - Neurofeedback for Elementary Students with Identified Learning Problems. J. of Neurotherapy, 8 (2), 5-21.

OSHU Review (2005) Helfand, M., MD, MPH, McDonagh, M.S. PharmD, Peterson, K., MS, 2005, Drug Class Review on Pharmacologic Treatments for ADHD, Final Report, Sept. 2005, Oregon Evidence Based Practice Center

Othmer, S., Othmer, S., Marks, C.S. (1992). EEG Biofeedback Training for Attention Deficit Disorder, Specific Learning Disabilities, and Associated Conduct Problems, Siegfried Othmer, Susan F. Othmer, and Clifford S. Marks, Journal of the Biofeedback Society of California, September

Othmer, S., Othmer, S.F. (1992). EEG Biofeedback Training for Hyperactivity, Attention Deficit Disorder, Specific Learning Disability, and other Disorders, Handout EEG Spectrum, 16100 Ventura Blvd., Ste 100, Encino, Ca.

Othmer, S., Othmer, S.F., and Kaiser, D.A., Chapter title: EEG Biofeedback: Training for AD/HD and Related Disruptive Behavior Disorders, in Understanding, Diagnosing, and Treating AD/HD in Children and Adolescents, an Integrative Approach, edited by James A. Incorvaia, Bonnie S. Mark-Goldstein, and Donald Tessmer Aronson Press, Northvale, New Jersey, (1999)

Packard Foundation, (1996). The Center for the Future of Children, The David and Lucile Packard Foundation. (1996, Spring). Special education for students with disabilities. The Future of Children, 6(1), 4-24. Los Angeles, CA: Author.

Pakkenberg, B. and Gundersen, H.J.G. (1997). Neocortical neuron number in humans: effect of sex and age. J. Comp. Neurology, 384, 312-320, 1997.

Pakkenberg, B., Pelvig, D., Marner,L., Bundgaard, M.J., Gundersen, H.J.G., Nyengaard, J.R. and Regeur, L. (2003). Aging and the human neocortex. Exp. Gerontology, 38, 95-99.

Passini, F.T., Watson, C.B., Dehnel, L., et al. (1977). Alpha wave biofeedback training therapy in alcoholics. Journal of Clinical Psychology, 33, 292-299.

Paulesu E, Frith U, Snowling M, Gallagher A, Morton J, Frackowiak RSJ, Frith CD. (1996). Is developmental dyslexia a disconnection syndrome? Evidence from PET scanning. Brain, 119, 143-157.

Peck, M. (1985). Crisis intervention treatment with chronically and acutely suicidal adolescents. In M. Peck, N. L. Farberow, & R. E. Litman (Eds.), Youth suicide (pp. 112122). New York: Springer.

Peniston, E.G., Kulkosky, P.J. (1989). Alpha-theta brainwave training and beta endorphin levels in alcoholics. Alcoholism: Clinical and Experimental Results, 13(2), 271-279.

Peniston, E.G., Kulkosky, P.J. (1989, 1995). The Peniston/Kulkosky Brainwave Neurofeedback Therapy for Alcoholism and Posttraumatic Stress Disorders: Medical Psychotherapist Manual. Certificate of Copyright Office. The Library of Congress, 1-25.

Peniston, E.G., Kulkosky, P.J. (1990). Alcoholic personality and alpha-theta brainwave training. Medical Psychotherapy: An International Journal, 3, 37-55.

Peniston, E.G., Kulkosky, P.J. (1991). Alpha-theta brainwave neurofeedback therapy for Vietnam veterans with combat-related posttraumatic stress disorder. Medical Psychotherapy: An International Journal, 4, 47-60.

Peniston, E.G., Kulkosky, P.J. (1992). Alpha-theta EEG biofeedback training in alcoholism and posttraumatic stress disorder. The International Society for the Study of Subtle Energies and Energy Medicines, 2, 5-7.

Peniston, E.G., Marrinan, D.A., Deming, W.A., & Kulkosky, P.J. (1993). EEG alpha-theta brainwave synchronization in Vietnam theater veteran with combat-related posttraumatic stress disorder and alcohol abuse. Medical Psychotherapy: An International Journal, 6, 37-50.

Pennington, B.F. (1994). Genetics of learning disabilities. Journal of Child Neurology, 10, 69-77.

PISA Survery (2001). Knowledge and Skills for Life: First Results from

PISA 2000, Fifteen-Year-Old Students (Paris: Organisation for Economic Co-operation and Development, 2001). (http://www.oecd.org/document/28/0,2340,en_2649_201185_34010524_1_1_1_1,00.html)

Pisecco, S., Baker, D. B., Silva, P. A., & Brooke, M. (2001). Boys with reading disabilities and/or ADHD: Distinctions in early childhood. Journal of Learning Disabilities, 34, 98-106.

Pliszka, S.R. (2000). Patterns of psychiatric comorbidity with attention-deficit/hyperactivity disorder.Child Adolesc Psychiatr Clin N Am, 9, 525-40, vii.

Pollack, V.E., Valavka, J., Goodwin, D.W., et al. (1983). The EEG after alcohol in men at risk for alcoholism. Archives of General Psychiatry, 40, 857-864.

Population clock (http://www.census.gov/main/www/popclock.html)

Prior, M., Sanson, A., Smart, D., & Oberklaid, F., (1999). Relatinoships between learning difficulties and psychological problems in preadolescent children from a longitudinal sample. Journal of American Academy of Child Adolescent Psychiatry, 36, 120-1032

Profile of Jail Inmates, 2002, (NCJ-201932) (www.ojp.usdoj.gov/bjs/abstract/pji02.htm)

Prothow-Smith, D., Spivak, H. (1999). America's Tragedy. Psychiatric Times. Vol. XVI, Issue 6. June

Quirk, D., Van Helsheimer (http://www.biofeedbacklearning.com/Comp-DangO.htm)

Quirk, DA (1995).Ontario Correctional Institute, Composite Biofeedback Conditioning and Dangerous Offenders: III, Journal of Neurotherapy, (1-2)4, Number 2 - Fall

Rabin, M., Wen, L., Hepburn, M., Lubs, H. A., Feldman, E., & Duara, R. (1993). Suggestive linkage of developmental dyslexia to chromosome 1, Lancet, 342, 178, 34-36

Raine, A., Brennan, P. Mednick, S.A. (1997). Interaction between Birth Complications and Early Maternal Rejection in Predisposing Individuals to Adult Violence: Specificity to Serious, Early-Onset Violence. J. Am. Psychiatry. 154:1265-1271.

Reschly, D. J., & Grimes, J. P. (1992). State department and university co-operation: Evaluation of continuing education in consultation and curriculum-based assessment. School Psychology Review, 20(4), 522-529.

Reynolds, C., & Kamphaus, R. (1994). Behavioral assessment system for children. Circle Pines, MN: American Guidance Service.

Ridgway, S.H. (1985). The Cetacean Central Nervous System, p. 221

Ridgway, S.H. and Harrison, S., (1985) Handbook of Marine Mammals, Vol. 3, London: Academic Press

Rossiter R. (2002). Neurofeedback for AD/HD: A ratio feedback case study and tutorial. Journal of Neurotherapy, 6(3), 9-37.

Rossiter, T.R., LaVaque, T.J. (1995). A comparison of EEG biofeedback and psychostimulants in treating attention deficit/hyperactivity disorders. Journal of Neurotherapy, Summer 1995, 48-59.

Rouse, C.E., Krueger, A.B. (2004). Putting Computerized Instruction to the Test: A Randomized Evaluation of a 'Scientifically-based' Reading Program. Economics of Education Review, Vol. 23, Issue 4, August, 2004, 323.

Rumsey, J.M., Horwitz, B., Donohue, B.C., Nace, K., Maisog, J.M., Andreason, P. (1997a). Phonological and orthographic components of word recognition: A PET-rCBF study. Brain, 120:739-759.

Rumsey, J.M., Nace, K., Donohue, B., Wise, D., Maisog, J.M., Andreason, P. (1997b). A positron emission tomographic study of impaired word recognition and phonological processing in dyslexic men. Arch Neurol, 54, 562-573.[8].

Rxlist: (http://www.rxlist.com/cgi/generic3/methylin_ad.htm)

Salazar, W., Landers, D.M., Petruzzello, S.J., Han, M., Crews, D.J., Kubitz, K.A. (1990). Hemispheric asymmetry, cardiac response, and performance in elite archers, Res. Q. Exerc. Sport, 61, 351-359.

San Miguel, S.K., Forness, S.R., Kavale, K.A. (1996). Social Skills Deficits in Learning Disabilities: The Psychiatric Comorbidity Hypothesis, Learning Disability Quarterly, Volume 19, Fall.

SAT to income: (http://www.sq.4mg.com/IQincome.htm#I)

SAT to IQ scores: (http://members.shaw.ca/delajara/SATIQ.html)

Satterfield, J.H., Schel,l A. (1997). A prospective study of hyperactive boys with conduct problems and normal boys: adolescent and adult criminality.J Am Acad Child Adolesc Psychiatry, 36,1726-1735.

Sax, L., (2000). Ritalin: Better Living Through Chemistry, The World and

I.com, 287-299 http://www.worldandi.com/public/2000/No-vember/sax.html

Saxley, E. and Peniston, E.G. (1995). Alpha-theta brainwave neurofeedback training: An effective treatment for male and female alcoholics with depressive symptoms. Journal of Clinical Psychology, 51(5), 685-693.

Schachar, R. & Tannock, R. (1995). Test of four hypotheses for the comorbidity of Attention Deficit Hyperactivity Disorder and Conduct Disorder. Journal of the American Academy of Child and Adolescent Psychiatry, 34, 639-648.

Schemo, D.J. (2003). Critics Say Money for Schools Falls Short of Promises, New York Times, 4 February 2003.

Schoenberger, N. E., Shif, S. C., Esty, M. L., Ochs, L., & Matheis, R. J. (2001). Flexyx Neurotherapy System in the treatment of traumatic brain injury: an initial evaluation. Journal of Head Trauma Rehabilitation, 16(3), 260-274.

Schulte-Körne, G. (2001). Dyslexia and speech perception (Legasthenie und Sprachwahrnehmung). Münster: Waxmann Verlag.

Scott, W.C., Kaiser, D., Othmer, S., Sideroff, S.I. (2005). Effects of an EEG Biofeedback Protocol on a Mixed Substance Abusing Population, American Journal of Drug and Alcohol Abuse, 32, 455-469.

Secnik, K., Matza, L.S., Cottrell, S., Edgell, E., Tilden, D., Mannix, S. (2005b). Health state utilities for childhood attention-deficit/hyperactivity disorder based on parent preferences in the United kingdom. Med Decis Making, 25, 56-70.

Secnik, K., Swensen, A.R., Lage, M.J. (2005a). Comorbidities and costs of adult patients diagnosed with Attention-Deficit Hyperactivity Disorder. Pharmacoeconomics, 23, 93-102.

Seifert, A. R., & Lubar, J. F.l (1975). Reduction of epileptic seizures through EEG biofeedback training. Biological Psychology, 3, 157-184.

Shaywitz, S.E., Fletcher, J.M., Holahan, J.M., Schneider, A.E., Marchione, K.E., Stuebing, K.K., Francis, D.J., Pugh, K.R., and Shaywitz, B.A. (1999). Persistence of dyslexia: The Connecticut longitudinal study at adolescence. Pediatrics, 104(6), 1351-1359.

Shaywitz SE, Shaywitz BA, Fulbright RK, Skudlarski P, Mencl WE, Constable RT, et al. (2003) Neural systems for compensation and persistence: young adult outcome of childhood reading disability. Biol Psychiatry; 54: 25-33.

Shaywitz, B.A., Shaywitz, S.E., Pugh, K.R., Mencl, W.E., Fulbright, R.K., Skudlarski, P., et al. (2002). Disruption of posterior brain systems for reading in children with developmental dyslexia. Biol Psychiatry, 52, 101-110.

Shaywitz, S.E., Shaywitz, B.A., Pugh, K.R., Fulbright, R.K., Constable ,R.T., Mencl, W.E., et al. (1998). Functional disruption in the organization of the brain for reading in dyslexia. Proc Natl Acad Sci USA, 95, 2636-2641.

Sheer, D.E. (1974). Electrophysiological studies in learning disabilities. In Eichenwald H, Talbot A, editors. The learning disabled child. Austin: University of Texas Press

Sheer, D.E. (1977). Biofeedback training of 40 Hz EEG, and behavior. In Kamiya et al., Biofeedback and Self-control 1976/1977. An annual review. Chicago: Aldine; p. 435.

Sheer, D.E. (1984). Focused arousal, 40 Hz EEG and dysfunction. In Elbert J, et al., Self regulation of the brain and behavior, Berlin: Springer

Shepherd, G.M. (1998). The Synaptic Organization of the Brain, p. 6

Shin, P. (2006) Warning label on ADHD drugs sought, New York Daily News, Feb. 10, 2006, http://deseretnews.com/dn/view/0,1249,635183266,00.html

Sieg, K.G., Gaffney, G.R., Preston, D.F., & Hellings, J.A. (1995). SPECT brain imaging abnormalities in attention deficit hyperactivity disorder, Clinical Nuclear Medicine, 20 (1), 55-60.

Silberg, J., Rutter, M., Meyer, J., Maes, H., Hewitt, J., Simonoff, E., Pickles, A., Loeber, R. (1996). Genetic and environmental influences on the covariation between hyperactivity and conduct disturbance in juvenile twins. Journal of Child Psychology and Psychiatry and Allied Disciplines, 37, 803-816.

Silver, L.B. (2000). Attention-deficit/hyperactivity disorder in adult life. Child & Adolescent Psychiatric Clinics of North America 2000, 9, 511-523.

Simos, P.G., Breier, J.I. (2001). Age-related changes in regional brain activation during phonological decoding and printed word recognition. Dev Neuropsychol, 19(2), 191-210.

Simos, P.G., Breier, J.I., Fletcher, J.M., Foorman, B.R., Bergman, E., Fishbeck, K., Papanicolaou, A.C. (2000). Brain activation profiles in dyslexic children during non-word reading: a magnetic source imaging study. Neuroscience Letters, 290, 61-65.

Simos, P.G., Fletcher, J.M., Foorman, B.R., Francis, D.J., Castillo, E.M., Davis, R.N., et al. (2002). Brain activation profiles during the early stages of reading acquisition. J Child Neurol, 17, 159–163.

Simpson, D. D., Joe, G. W., & Broome, K. M. (2002). A national 5-year follow-up of treatment outcomes for cocaine dependence. Archives of General Psychiatry, 59, 538-544. (http://www. datos.org/adults/adults-5yrout.html)

Small, J.G. (1993). Psychiatric disorders and EEG, in Electroencephalography: Basic Principles, Clinical Applications, and Related Fields, edited by Niedermeyer E, Lopes da Silva F. Baltimore, Williams and Wilkins, 58; 1-596.

Smith, S. D., Kimberling, W. J., & Pennington, B. F. (1991). Screening for multiples genes influencing dyslexia. Reading and Writing: An Interdisciplinary Journal, 3, 285-298.

Smylie, M.A., Wenzel, S.A., (2003) The Chicago Annenberg Challenge: Success, Failures , and Lessions for the Future, Final Technical Report of the Chicago Annenberg Research Project, Aug., 2003   (http://www.annenbergchallenge.org/sites/chicago. html)

Solomon, M. Education News; The Problems with No Child Left Behind Monday, April 5, 2004 (http://www.educationnews.org/problems-with-no-child-left-behind.htm)

Spencer, T., Biederman, J., Wilens, T. (1999). Attention-deficit/hyperactivity disorder and comorbidity. Pediatr Clin North Am, 1999, 46:915-27, vii.

Stanovich, K., & West, R. F. (1989). Exposure to print and orthographic processing. Reading Research Quarterly, 24, 402-433.

Statewide Criminal Justice Recidivism rates and revocation rates (2005). (http://www.lbb.state.tx.us/PubSafety_CrimJustice/Recidivism_Report_2005.pdf)

Stecher, B. M., McCaffrey, D. F., Burroughs, D. Wiley, E., and Bohrnstedt, G. W. (2000). Achievement. In B. M. Stecher & G. W. Bohrnstedt (Eds.) Class size reduction in California: The 1998-99 evaluation findings. Sacramento, CA: California Department of Education.

Stecher, B. M., McCaffrey, D. M., and Burroughs, D. (1999). Achievement. In G. W. Bohrnstedt & B. M. Stecher (Eds.). Class size reduction in California: Early evaluation findings, 1996–1998. Palo Alto, CA: CSR Research Consortium.

Stecher, B. M., McCaffrey, D.F. & Bugliari, D. (2003, November 10). The relationship between exposure to class size reduction and student achievement in California. Education Policy Analysis Archives, 11(40). Retrieved [Date] from http://epaa.asu.edu/epaa/v11n40/.

Steinberg, M., Othmer, S. (2004) ADD: The 20 Hour Solution: Training Minds to Concentrate and Self-Regulate Naturally Without Medication. Brandon, OR: Robert D. Reed Publishers

Stephan, J., (1996). State Prison Expenditures, Bureau of Justice Statistics

Sterman, M. B. (1973a). Neurophysiological and clinical studies of sensorimotor EEG biofeedback training: Some effects on epilepsy. Seminars in Psychiatry, 5(4), 507-525.

Sterman, M. B. (1973b). Neurophysiological and clinical studies of sensorimotor EEG biofeedback training: Some effects on epilepsy. Chapter in L. Birk (Ed.), Biofeedback: Behavioral Medicine. New York: Grune and Stratton, 147-165.

Sterman, M. B. (1977). Sensorimotor EEG operant conditioning: Experimental and clinical effects. Pavlovian Journal of Biological Sciences, 12(2), 63-92.

Sterman, M. B. (1986). Epilepsy and its treatment with EEG feedback therapy. Annals of Behavioral Medicine, 8, 21-25.

Sterman, M. B. (2000). Basic concepts and clinical findings in the treatment of seizure disorders with EEG operant conditioning. Clinical Electroencephalography, 31(1), 45-55.

Sterman, M. B., and Friar, L. (1972). Suppression of seizures in epileptics following sensorimotor EEG feedback training. Electroencephalography and Clinical Neurophysiology, 33, 89-95.

Sterman, M. B., Macdonald, L. R., and Stone, R. K. (1974). Biofeedback training of the sensorimotor electroencephalogram rhythm in man: Effects on epilepsy. Epilepsia, 15(3), 395-416.

Sterman, M.B. (1976). Effects of brain surgery and EEG operant conditioning on seizure latency following MMH intoxication in the cat.Experimental Neurology, 50, 757-765.

Sterman, M.B. and MacDonald, L.R., (1978). Effects of Central Cortical EEG Feedback Training on Incidence of Poorly Controlled Seizures. Epilepsia, 19, 207-222.

Sterman, M.B., MacDonald, L.R., and Stone, R.K. (1974).Biofeedback training of the sensorimotor EEG rhythm in man: Effect on epilepsy.Epilepsia, 15, 395-416.

Sternberg, R. J., Wagner, R. K., Williams, W. M., Horvath, J. A., et al. (1995). Testing common sense. American Psychologist, 50, 912-927.

Stevenson, J., Graham, P., Fredman, G., & McLoughlin, V. (1987). A twin study of genetic influences on reading and spelling ability and disability. Journal of Child Psychology and Psychiatry, 28, 229-247.

Stewart MA, Cummings C, Seiger S et al (1981). The overlap between hyperactive and unsocialised aggressive children. Journal of Child Psychology and Psychiatry, 22, 35-45.

Stroop, J.R. (1935). Studies of interference in serial verbal reactions, J. Exp. Psychol. 18, 643-662.

Swensen, A.R., Birnbaum, H.G., Ben Hamadi, R., Greenberg, P., Cremieux, P.Y. (2004). Incidence and costs of accidents among Attention-Deficit/Hyperactivity Disorder patients. J Adol Health, 35, 349.e1-e9.

Swensen, A.R., Birnbaum, H.G., Secnik, K., Marynchenko, M., Greenberg, P., Claxton, A. (2003). Attention-deficit/hyperactivity disorder: increased costs for patients and their families.J Am Acad Child Adolesc Psychiatry, 42, 1415-1423.

Swensen, A.R., Secnik, K., Buesching, D.P., Barkley, R.A., Fischer, M., Fletcher, K. (2001). Young adult outcome of childhood ADHD: Cost of criminal behavior: October 23-28, Honolulu, HI., 2001.

Swets, J.A. (1988). Measuring the accuracy of diagnostic systems. Science, 240, 1285-1293.

Szatmari, P., Boyle, M., Gifford, D.R. (1989). ADDH and Conduct Disorder: degree of adequate overlap and differences among correlates. Journal of the American Academy of Child and Adolescent Psychiatry, 28, 865 - 72.

Tan, M., Appleton, R. (2005). Attention deficit and hyperactivity disorder,

methylphenidate, and epilepsy, Archives of Disease in Childhood 2005;90:57-59.

Tansey, M. (1991). Wechsler (WISC-R) Changes Following Treatment of
Learning Disabilities Via EEG Biofeedback Training in a Private Practice Setting. Australian Journal of Psychology, 43,
147-153.

Tansey, M. (1993). Ten year stability of EEG biofeedback results for a 10
year old hyperactive boy who failed in a class for the per-
ceptually impaired. Biofeedback and Self-Regulation, 18, 33-
44.

Temple, E., Deutsch, G. K., Poldrak, R. A., Miller, S. L., Tallal, P., Mer-
zenich, M. M., Gabrieli, J. D. E . (2003). Neural deficits in
children with dyslexia ameliorated by behavioral remediation: evidence form functional MRI. Proceedings of the National Academy of Sciences, 100 (5), 2860-2865.

Thapar, M., Harrington, R., McGuffin, P., (2001). Examining the comorbidity of ADHD-related behaviours and conduct problems using
a twin study design, Developmental Psychopathology Papers,
Part 2, The British Journal of Psychiatry, 179, 224-229.

Thatcher, R.W. (2000). EEG operant conditioning (biofeedback) and traumatic brain injury. Clinical Electroencephalography, 31, 38-
44.

Thatcher, R.W., Biver, C., McAlaster, R., Camacho, M., Salazar, A. (1998).
Biophysical linkage between MRI and EEG amplitude in
closed head injury. NeuroImage, 7, 352-367.

Thatcher, R.W., Cantor, D.S., McAlaster, R., Geisler, F., Krause, P. (1991).
Comprehensive predictions of outcome in closed head-in-
jured patients. The development of prognostic equations.
Ann N Y Acad Sci, 620: 82-101.

Thatcher, R. W., North, D., Biver, C., (2002). EEG discriminant analysis
of children with learning disabilities: Correlations to school
achievement and neuropsychological performance, available
at appliedneuroscience.org

The MTA Cooperative Group (1999). A 14-Month Randomized Clinical
Trial of Treatment Strategies for Attention-Deficit/Hyperac-
tivity Disorder, Arch Gen Psychiatry, 56, 1073-1086.

Thompson, K., Anthony, A., & Holtzman, A. (2001). The costs of TBI.
North Carolina Journal of Medicine, 62, 381-384.

281

Thompson, L., Thompson, M. (1998). Neurofeedback combined with training in metacognitive strategies: Effectiveness in students with ADD, Applied Psychophysiology and Biofeedback, 23 (4), 243-263.

Thomson, D., Nixey, R. (2005) Thinking to read, reading to think; Bringing meaning, reasoning and enjoyment to reading. Literacy Today, Sept., 2005

Torgesen, J.K. and Burgess, S.R. (1998). Consistency of reading-related phonological processes throughout early childhood: Evidence from longitudinal, correlational, and instructional studies. In J. Metsala & L. Ehri (Eds.), Word recognition in beginning reading (pp. 161-188). Hillsdale, N.J.: Erlbaum.

Thornton K, unpublished data

Thornton K. (1999a). Exploratory analysis: Mild head injury, discriminant analysis with high frequency bands (32-64 Hz) under attentional activation conditions & does time heal? Journal of Neurotherapy, 3(3), 1-10.

Thornton K. (1999b). Exploratory investigation into mild brain injury and discriminant analysis with high frequency bands (32-64 Hz). Brain Inj, 13 (7), 477-488.

Thornton, K, Carmody, D., (2006). White Paper on Cognitive Rehabilitation and EEG Biofeedback, in press

Thornton, K. (1994). The Anatomy of the Lie; A QEEG Investigation into Lie Detection. J. of Offender Rehabilitation, Feb.??

Thornton, K. (2000a). Exploratory Analysis: Mild Head Injury, Discriminant Analysis with High Frequency Bands (32-64 Hz) under Attentional Activation Conditions & Does Time Heal? Journal of Neurotherapy, Feb.,1-10.

Thornton, K. (2000b). Electrophysiology of Auditory Memory of Paragraphs, Journal of Neurotherapy, 4(3), 45-73.

Thornton, K. (2001). Patent # 6309361 B1 Method for Improving Memory by Identifying and Using QEEG Parameters Correlated to Specific Cognitive Functioning - issued 10-30-2001

Thornton, K. (2002a), Electrophysiology of the reasons the brain damaged subject can't recall what they hear. Archives of Clinical Neuropsychology, 17, 1-17.

Thornton, K. (2002b). Rehabilitation of Memory functioning with EEG Biofeedback. Neurorehabilitation, 17 (1), 69-81.

Thornton, K. (2002c). Electrophysiology (QEEG) of Effective Reading Memory: Towards a Generator/Activation Theory of the Mind. J. of Neurotherapy, 6(3), 37-66.

Thornton, K. (2006b). The qEEG in the Lie Detection Problem; The Localization of Guilt, submitted J. of Neurotherapy

Thornton, K.(2000c). Rehabilitation of Memory Functioning in Brain Injured Subjects with EEG Biofeedback, Journal of Head Trauma Rehabilitation, Dec., 2000, 15 (6), 1285-1296.

Thornton, K., (2004). A Cost/Benefit Analysis of Different Intervention Models for the LD/Special Education Student, Biofeedback, Winter, 2004, 9-13.

Thornton, K., Carmody, D. (2005a). EEG Biofeedback for Reading Disabilities and Traumatic Brain Injuries. Child and Adolescent Psychiatric Clinics of North America, Jan, 2005a, 137-162.

Thurman, D. J., Alverson, C., Dunn, K. A., Guerrero, J., & Sniezek, J. E. (1999). Traumatic brain injury in the United States: A public health perspective. Journal of Head Trauma Rehabilitation, 14(6), 602-615.

Tinius, T.P., Tinius, K.A. (2000). Changes after EEG biofeedback and cognitive retraining in adults with mild traumatic brain injury and attention deficit hyperactivity disorder. Journal of Neurotherapy; 4 (2): 27-44.

Token Test, Pro-Ed, PRO-ED, Inc., 8700 Shoal Creek Boulevard -- Austin, Texas 78757-6897

Torgesen, J. K., Alexander, A. W., Wagner, R. K., Rashotte, C. A., Voeller, K. K. S., & Conway, T. (2001). Intensive remedial instruction for children with severe reading disabilities: Immediate and long-term outcomes from two instructional approaches. Journal of Learning Disabilities, 34, 33-58, 78.

Trudeau, D.L., Anderson, J., Hansen, L M, Shagalov, D.N., Schmoller, J., Nugent, S., Barton, S. (1998). Findings of mild traumatic brain injury in combat veterans with PTSD and a history of blast concussion. J Neuropsychiatry Clin Neurosci, 10(3), 308-313.

Tulving, E., Markowitsch, H.J., Fergus, I.M., Craik, R.H. & Houle, S. (1996). Novelty and familiarity activations in pet studies of memory encoding and retrieval. Cerebral Cortex, 6(1), 71-79.

Ucles, P., Lorente, S. (1996). Electrophysiologic measures of delayed maturation in attention-deficit hyperactivity disorder. Clin Electroencephalography, 11, 155-6.

University of California, Irvine, Child Development Center (1998) (http://www.wsws.org/news/1998/nov1998/rit-n04.shtml)

US Government education spending (http://nces.ed.gov/programs/digest/d04/tables/dt04_364.asp)

US Surgeon General Report (2001-3) (http://www.mental-health-matters.com/articles/article.php?artID=680)

Vaillant, G.E. (1983). The natural history of alcoholism: Causes, patterns, and paths to recovery. Cambridge, MA: Harvard University Press.

vanBeijsterveldt, C.E.M., Boomsma, D.I. (2000). Genetics of the human electroencephalogram (EEG) and event-related brain potentials (ERPs): a review. Hum Genet, 94(4), 319-330,

vanBeijsterveldt, C.E.M., Molenaar, M.P.C., de Geus, E.J., Boomsma, D.I. (1996). Heritability of human brain functioning as assessed by electroencephalography, Am J Hum Genet, 58 (3), 562-573

vanbeijsterveldt, C.E.M., Molenaar, P.C., deGeus, E.J., Oomsma, D.I. (1998). Genetic and environmental influences on EEG coherence. Behav Genet, 28, 6443-53.

Vannucci, SJ, and Hagberg, H. (2994). Hypoxia-ischemia in the immature brain. Journal of Experimental Biology 207, 3149-3154.

Vellutino, F.R.D.M., Scanlon, E., Sipay, S., Small, A., Pratt, R., Chen, Denckla, M. (1996). Cognitive profiles of difficult-to-remediate and readily remediated poor readers: Early Interventions as a vehicle for distinguishing between cognitive and experiential deficits as basic causes of specific reading disability. Journal of Educational Psychology, 88, 601-638.

Vernon, D., Egner, T., Cooper, N., Compton, T., Neilands, C., Sheri, A., Gruzelier, J. (2003). The effect of training distinct neurofeedback protocols on aspects of cognitive performance. Int J Psychophysiol, Jan 47(1), 75-85.

Von Helsheimer and Quirk (http://www.biofeedbacklearning.com/CompDangO.htm)

Wagner, R. K., & Torgesen, J. K. (1987). The nature of phonological processing and its causal role in the acquisition of reading skills.

Psychological Bulletin, 101, 192-212.

Walker, J.E., Kozlowski, G.P. (2005). Neurofeedback Treatment of Epilepsy. Child and Adolescent Psychiatric Clinics of North America, 14 (1) 163-175.

Walker, J.E., Norman, C.A., Weber, R.K. (2002). Impact of qEEG-guided coherence training for patients with a mild closed head injury. J. of Neurotherapy, 6 (2), 31-45.

Wall Street Journal (Sunday, January 29, 2006)

Washington Partners LLC (2005) 1101 Vermont Avenue NW, Suite 400, Washington, DC 20005, Status on Implementation of the No Child Left Behind Act (NCLB), Article:120175, 2005 (http://www.ncte.org/about/issues/featured/120175.htm)

Washington Times, November 20, 2004 (http://www.washtimes.com/national/20041120-121240-9526r.htm)

Watkins, C., (2005). Enuresis and ADHD (http://www.ncpamd.com/adhd_and_bedwetting.htm)

Watts, R., Liston, C., Niogi, S., Ulug, A.M. (2003). Fiber tracking using magnetic resonance diffusion tensor imaging and its applications to human brain development. Mental Retardation & Developmental Disabilities Research Revies, 9, 168-177.

Web: Learning Disability Association of America website (http://www.ldanatl.org)

Web: U.S. Department of Education website: (http://www.ed.gov/index.jhtml)

Weiss, G., Milroy, T., Perlman, T. (1985). Psychiatric status of hyperactives as adults: A controlled prospective 15- year follow-up of 63 hyperactive children. Journal of the American Academy of Child and Adolescent Psychiatry, 24, 211-220.

Welner, Z., Welner, A., Stewart, M., Palkes, H., & Wish, E. (1977). A controlled study of siblings of hyperactive children. Journal of Nervous and Mental Disease, 165, 110-117.

Wender, P.H., Wolf, L.E., Wasserstein, J. (2001). Adults with ADHD. An overview. Ann N Y Acad Sci 2001, 931:1-16.

Werry, J., Elkind, G., and Reeves, J. (1987). Attention deficit, conduct, oppositional, and anxiety disorders in children. Journal of Abnormal Child Psychology, 15, 409-428.

Whitsett, S.F., Lubar, J.F., Holder, G.S., Pamplin, W.E., Shabsin, H.S. (1982). A Double-Blind Investigation of The Relationship

Between Seizure Activity and The Sleep EEG Following EEG Biofeedback Training. Biofeedback and Self-Regulation, Vol. 7, No. 2, 193-209, June

Willcut, E.G., Pennington, B.F., DeFries, J.C. (2000). Twin study of the etiology of cormorbidity between reading disability and attention-deficit/hyperactivity disorder. American Journal of Medical Genetics, 96, 293-301.

Williams, R.W., Herrup, K. (1988). Ann. Review Neuroscience, 11, 423-453.

Wilson Reading Website, (http://www.fundations.com/)

Wilson Research (http://www.ecs.org/clearinghouse/19/01/1901.htm)

Wing, L., Potter, D. (2002). The epidemiology of autistic spectrum disorders: is the prevalence rising?, Centre for Social and Communication Disorders, Elliot House, Bromley, Kent, United Kingdom. Ment Retard Dev Disabil Res Rev, 8(3),151-61.

Winter C. (1997). Learning disabilities, crime, delinquency, and special education placement. Adolescence, 1997, 32, 451-462.

Wood, R., (1998, December). The trillion-dollar sham in federal remedial education, NRRF Director of Statistical Research, The National Right to Read Foundation. Retrieved Sept. 3, 2004 from (http://www.nrrf.org/essay_Trillion_116.html)

Woodcock-Johnson Battery, Riverside Publishing, 425 Spring Lake Drive, Itasca, IL 60143-2079, USA

Wyler, A..R., Robbins, C.A., Dodrill, C.B. (1979). EEG Operant Conditioning For Control of Epilepsy. Epilepsia, 20, 279-286.

Wyler, A.R., Lockard, J.S., and Ward, A.A. (1976).Conditioned EEG Desynchronization and Seizure Occurrence in Patients. Electroencephalography and Clinical Neurophysiology, 41, 501-512..

Xiong Z, Shi S, Xu H.(2005). A controlled study of the effectiveness of EEG biofeedback training on-children with attention deficit hyperactivity disorder. J Huazhong Univ Sci Technolog Med Sci, 25(3), 368-70.

Yeargin-Allsopp, M., Rice, C., Karapurkar, T., Doernberg, N., Boyle, C., Murphy, C. (2001). Prevalence of Autism in a US Metropolitan Area, JAMA, 289 (1), 49-55.

Yule, W., Rutter, M, eds. Language Development and Disorders London: Mac Keith Press. 1987.

Zametkin, A.J., Nordahl, T.E., Gross, M., King, A.C., Semple, W.E., Rumsey, J.,Hamburger, S., & Cohen, R.M. (1990). Cerebral glucose metabolism in adults with hyperactivity of childhood onset. New England Journal of Medicine,323, 1361-1366.

Zupancic, J.A.F. Miller, A., Raina, P., Lee, S.K., Klassen, A., Olsen, L. (1998). Part 3: Economic evaluation of pharmaceutical and psychological/behavioural therapies for attention-deficit/hyperactivity disorder. In A Review of Therapies for Attention-Deficit/Hyperactivity Disorder. Edited by: Miller A, Lee SK, Raina P and et al.. Ottawa, Canada, Canadian Coordinating Office for Health Technology Assessment

Index

effect sizes 3, 10, 19, 39, 39, 41, 44, 41, 44, 98, 108, 109, 126, 139, 175
Efficacy Research 3, Intro:VI, 28
EMG 127
emotional intelligence 185
enuresis 79
Environmental 49, 50, 116
environmental factors 47, 48
epilepsy 48, 82, 171, 194, 195, 198, 204
episodic memory 135
ERP 44, 45
Evans 118, 151
event related potential 44

F

F4 64, 68, 69, 134, 153, 163, 172, 208
F7 58, 62, 63, 134, 146, 153, 157, 158, 172
F8 64, 134, 153, 161, 163, 172
Fairchild 197
family problems 84
Fast ForWord 34, 35, 36, 38, 69
federal judge 17
Fein 118
feral 6, 8, 10
financial impact 83
Finn 24
flashlight 122, 134, 135, 145, 147, 171, Figures:314, Figures:315, Figures:320, Figures:321, Figures:323, Figures:325, Figures:327
flashlight effect 122
Florida 17, 18, 19, 190
fluency 29, 30, 37, 38, 226
fMRI 8, 51, 52, 59, 60, 62, 67, 68, 69, 70, 117, 141, 143, 150, 169
Forness 41, 137
Foster 94, 95
Fp1 54
Fp2 54, 153
Franz Joseph Gall 55
Frontal 59, 147
Fuchs 126
functional magnetic resonance imaging 51
Functions 59, 60

G

Galaburda 60
Galin 167
Gamma 112

gamma 52, 120, 121, 126
gamma-band 121
GAO 15, 204
Gasser 117
Gayton 83
generalizability 163
generalization 34, 50, 137, 150, 160, 161, 164, 172, 173
Generalization effects , 46, 140
generator 122
Genetic 49
genetic 6, 7, 24, 47, 48, 50, 56, 76, 77, 116, 176, 205
George Combe 55
Georgia 12, 16, 204
Gerhardstein 81
Giedd 64
Gilmore 97, 98
Glial cells 57
Goleman 185
Gossop 201, 202
Gray 56, 58, 89, 92
gray matter 56, 57, 58, 59, 60, 66, 67, 110
Greene 18, 24
Greenhill 65
Gross Domestic Product Intro:IX, 212
Guevara 88, 89, 95
Guyer 29

H

halo effect 22
Harmony 118, 167
Hattie 31
Hawaii 12
Hawthorne Effect 125
Hazel 79
Health Canada 103, 104
HEG 206
hemisphere 44, 55, 57, 60, 61, 62, 134, 148, 155, 174, 208
Hemispheric Encoding/Retrieval Asymmetry (HERA) 135
hemoencephalography 206
heroin abuse 194
Hook 36
household incomes 85, 95
Hughes 116, 118, 120, 129
human brain Intro:II, Intro:IV, 26, 53, 54, 55, 56, 57, 121, 125, 141, 166, 199
hyperactive 66
hyperactivity 65, 71, 72, 73, 78, 80, 82, 83, 100, 103, 105, 109, 129, 132, 233

hypercoherence 118
hypoarousal 65

I

Iceberg Profile 209
IDEA 25, 26, 208
Illinois 12
impulsive 66, 72, 83
impulsivity Intro:V, 65, 66, 72, 73, 100, 105, 221, 222
inattentive 66, 131
incarcerated youth 26, 191
incarceration 190, 191, 192, 193
Indian Wolf-Girls 7
Indirect Costs 92
IDEA 25
Inglese 68, 250
inmates 26, 190, 191
Innocenti 182, 250
insurance 85, 95, 96
intelligence 2, 37, 39, 58, 81, 132, 144, 184, 185, 188, 210, 211, 212, Bib:248
international 185
International Dyslexia Society 37, 250
International Society for Neuronal Regulation (ISNR) 128
intervention programs 26, 32, 33, 39, 44
IQ Intro:IX, 2, 33, 36, 37, 58, 69, 71, 73, 74, 119, 128, 133, 142, 164, 165, 168, 174,
        184, 185, 40, 185, 184, 185, 186, 187, 188, 189, 204, 212, 213
irritability 66, 100, 101, 104, 105, 108, 109
ISNR 128, 205, 207, 208, 219

J

Jacob 43, 218, 251
Janelle 210, 251
Jenkins 82, 251
Jensen 85, 251, 265, 269
Jibiki 171, 251
Jim Doyle 17, 18
John Bib:235, Bib:241, 250, 251, 252
John, E.R Bib:241, 250, 251, 252
Johnson 48, 69, 250, 251, 286
Johnston 251
Jones 199, Bib:240, Bib:246, Bib:249, 251
Journal of Neurotherapy 134, Bib:239, Bib:244, 252, 274, 275, 282, 283
Joyce 21, 126, 251
Juel 32, 44, 251, 252

K

L

Linden 126, 128, 166, 167, 184, 263, 268
Lloyd 41, 97, 98, 137, Bib:246, 263
Loreta 53
Lou 263
Louisiana 12, 19
Lubar 109, 117, 125, 126, 128, 138, 166, 167, 198
Lundberg 31, 264
Luria-Nebraska 43
Lyon 3, 28, 265
lZhang 265

M

Macklin 210, 265
Maddah 265
magnetic resonance imaging 51, 53, 63, 70
Magnetoencephalography 51, 52
Magnitude 112
magnitude 44, 63, 150, 172, 175, 207
Maine 12, 13, 19
maltreatment 49
Manhattan Beach Unified School District 20
Manhattan Institute 18
Mann 65, 118, 167, 265
Mannuzza 78, 83, Bib:247, 265
Marchetti 92, 95, 265
Marlatt 201, 266
Marosi 118, Bib:248, 266
Massachusetts 13, 14, 19, 42
Mathis 11, 266
math difficulties 79
math disabilities Intro:III
Matochek 65, 266
Matza 91, 97, 266, 276
McCandliss 60, 266
McEvoy 116, 121, 266
McGee 81, 266, 267
McLachlan 201, 267
medical Intro:V, 8, 24, 28, 43, 48, 49, 51, 85, 87, 90, 92, 94, 95, 96, 97, 116, 129, 141,
     169, 185, 190, 192, 196, 210, 220, 225, 263
medical care 190, 263
Medical Costs 89, 92
medication 66, 82, 84, 87, 89, 92, 95, 98, 103, 105, 106, 107, 108, 109, 128, 130, 131,
     132, 137, 218, 227, 233
Medicine 92
MEG 51, 52, 53, 60, 62, 68, 117
memory Intro:I, 38, 60, 73, 43, 46, 48, 50, 59, 81, 122, 143, 123, 124, 133, 134, 135,

oppositional 66, 87
Oppositional Defiant Disorder 74, 76, 77, 81, 88
Oregon Health and Science University 106
Orlando 36, 126, 128, 272
Orthographic 31, 33, 250
Orton-Gillingham 28, 29, 37, 50, 137, 173, 215
OSHU 76, 107, 272
Othmer 109, 126, 128, 166, 167, 184
oxygen consumption 56

P

P3 49, 60, 61, 62, 63, 68, 69, 147, 151, 153, 157, 159
P4 157, 208
Packard Foundation 24, 272
Pakkenberg 57, 272
Paradigm Shift 23
Parental Choice Program 17
Parents 20, 130, 224
Parietal 59
Patent # 6309361 282
Paulesu 60, 273
Peak Amplitude 113
peak amplitude 44, 113
Peak Frequency 112, Figures:317
peak frequency 44, 113, 118, 151, 152, 153
peak performance Intro:IX, 209
Peck 79, 273
Pemoline 101, 104, 107
pemoline 100, 104, 107, 108
Peniston 199, 200, 202
Peri-Sylvian 60
Pervasive Developmental Disorder 74, 80
PET 51, 52, 60, 63, 64, 70, 99, 117, 134, 135, 141, 143, 144, 150, 169
pharmacy 88, 90
Phase 113, 124, 146, Figures:310, Figures:325, Figures:327
phase 109, 114, 122, 123, 148, 150, 156, 161, 167, 172
philosophy of science 141
phonemic awareness 29, 30, 36, 38
phonics 28, 30, 32, 33, 34, 38, 40,
phonological 28, 29, 31, 32, 33, 37, 44, 60, 62, 63, 68, 69, 81
phonological processing 31, 33, 60, 62, 63, 69, 81
physical functioning of the brain Intro:III, 10, 47, 49, 51
Physician's Desk Reference 102
physiological 132
Pisecco 82, 274
placebo-controlled 108

RCT 130, 131

reading disabilities Intro:III, 2, 33, 45, 81, 82, 129, 214

Reading memory 138

reading memory 123, 133, 137, 139, 144, 153, 154, 157, 158, 159, 161, 162, 168, 224

recidivism 192, 194, 196, 197

Rehabilitation 24, 45, Bib:247, 276, 282, 283

relationships Intro:IX, 32, 37, 76, 83, 84, 85, 113, 122, 123, 133, 134, 136, 141, 142, 147, 148, 151, 153, 157, 158, 159, 163, 167, 168, 170, 172, 173, 187, 203, 206, 212, 223

Relative Power 112, Figures:317, Figures:319, Figures:322, Figures:324, Figures:326, Figures:328

relative power 44, 65, 119, 145, 150, 151, 152, 153, 154, 157, 160, 170, 171

Reschly 274

research Intro:IV, Intro:VI, Intro:VIII, Intro:IX, 8, 10, 15, 19, 21, 22, 23, 28, 29, 31, 34, 41, 42, 33, 108, 45, 113, 42, 44, 45, 117, 46, 47, 50, 56, 58, 61, 64, 66, 70, 71, 72, 74, 76, 80, 97, 99, 106, 107, 113, 119, 32, 119, 121, 37, 120, 122, 123, 125, 128, 130, 131, 132, 133, 137, 138, 141, 142, 143, 144, 145, 148, 150, 151, 160, 161, 164, 166, 167, 168, 169, 170, 171, 173, 174, 176, 184, 185, 192, 194, 198, 205, 207, 209, 210, 211, 214, 216, 218, 219, 221, 222, 223, 224

Resource Room 36

retardation 2, 48, 56, 74, 141, 209, 266

Reynolds 132, 275

Ridgway 57, 275

Ring of Fire 66

Ritalin 65, 89, 92, 95, 97, 98, 99, 100, 101, 102, 103, 104, 105, 106, 107, 108, Bib:243, Bib:248, 252

Rossiter 126, 128, 166, 167, 275

Rouse 36, 275

Rumsey 275, 286

S

Salazar 210, 275, 281

San Miguel 77, 80, 82, 275

SAT Intro:IX, 174, 184, 185, 187, 188

Satterfield 77, 275

Saturday 6

Sax 100

Saxley 200, 275

SCARS 196

Schachar 77, 276

Schemo 11, 276

Schoenberger 276

School Choice 17

school dropouts 26

School Setting Bib:238

Schulte-Körne 31, 276

tutoring 8, 9, 13, 14, 29, 31, 38, 50, 81, 86, 231

U

V

W

X

Y

Z

RESUME

KIRTLEY E. THORNTON, PH.D.
CENTER FOR HEALTH PSYCHOLOGY, Ste. 2a
2509 PARK AVE, S. PLAINFIELD, N.J.,07080
908 -753-1800 fax-908-753-2620
Web: chp-neurotherapy.com
Email: ket@chp-neurotherapy.com

Education:

Ph.D., Clinical Psychology, New School for Social Research, Graduate Faculty Division, NY, NY, 1980, offered Hiram Halle Valedictorian Scholarship

M.A., Psychology, New School for Social Research, NY, NY 1976

B.A., Psychology, Oberlin College, Oberlin, Ohio, 1968

Professional Affiliations:

American Psychological Association

New Jersey Psychological Association

National Academy of Neuropsychology, Professional

New Jersey Learning Disability Assn, Prof. Adv.

International Neuropsychology Society

Consulting Editor; Journal of Neurotherapy

Board of Directors, qEEG Certification Board

International Society for Neuronal Regulation

Diplomate: QEEG, Neurotherapy

Research Chairman, AAPB Research Committee

Published Research

Neuropsychology of Sex Offenders. Journal of Offender Rehabilitation. Jan. 1991.

The Anatomy of The Lie: An Exploratory Investigation via the quantitative EEG, Journal of Offender Rehabilitation, 1995. 22 (3/4), 179-210.

On the Nature of Artifacting the qEEG. Journal of Neurotherapy, 1 (3), 1996, 31-40.

The Fig Technique and the Functional Structure of Memory in Head Injured and Normal Subjects. Journal of Neurotherapy, 2 (1), 1997, 23-43.

Exploratory Analysis: Mild Head Injury, Discriminant Analysis with High Frequency Bands (32-64 Hz) under Attentional Activation Conditions & Does Time Heal?. Journal of Neurotherapy, Feb., 2000,

1-10.

Exploratory Investigation into Mild Brain Injury and Discriminant Analysis with High Frequency Bands (32-64 Hz), Brain Injury, August, 1999, 477-488.

Electrophysiology of Auditory Memory of Paragraphs. Journal of Neuro therapy, 2000,Vol 4(3), 45-73.

Rehabilitation of Memory Functioning in Brain Injured Subjects with EEG Biofeedback. Journal of Head Trauma Rehabilitation, Dec., 2000, 15 (6), 1285-1296.

Rehabilitation of Memory functioning with EEG Biofeedback. Neurorehabilitation, 2002, Vol. 17 (1), 69-81.

Electrophysiology of Visual Memory for Korean Characters. Current Psychology, Spring 2002, Vol. 21, No. 1, 85-108.

Electrophysiology of the reasons the brain damaged subject can't recall what they hear. Archives of Clinical Neuropsychology, 2002, 17, 1-17.

Electrophysiology (QEEG) of Effective Reading Memory: Towards a Generator/Activation Theory of the Mind. Journal of Neurothera py, 2002, 6(3), 37-66.

EEG Biofeedback for Reading Disabilities and Traumatic Brain Injuries. Child and Adolescent Psychiatric Clinics of North America, Jan., 2005, 137-162.

A Cost/Benefit Analysis of Different Intervention Models for the LD/Spe cial Education Student, Biofeedback, Winter, 2004, 9-13.

In process of submission

The qEEG in the Lie Detection Problem; The Localization of Guilt, J. of Neurotherapy, 2006

Cognitive Rehabilitation White Paper. in review process

Book Chapters

Ch. 95, Cognitive Rehabilitation and Neuronal Plasticity, in Evidence Based Practice Manual, ed. A. Roberts & K. Yaeger, Oxford University Press, 2004

Patents

1-Patent #5564433: Method for Display, Analysis, Classification, and Correlation of Electrical Brain Function Potentials - issued 10-15-1996

2-Patent # 6309361 B1 Method for Improving Memory by Identifying and Using QEEG Parameters Correlated to Specific Cognitive Functioning – issued 10-30-2001

Nominations
1998
1-Thomas A. Edison Patent of the Year Award

June, 2002
2-Award for Distinguished Professional Contributions to Independent or Institutional Practice in the Private Sector

3-Award for Distinguished Contributions of Applications of Psychology to Education and Training

May, 2004
4-New Abilities Foundation Award for Best New Freedom Product or Technology (considered by supporters as the Nobel Peace prize award in the area of disabilities)

5-Aug., 2005 North American Brain Injury Society Innovations in Treatment Award

Figure 5 – MRI images

Courtesy of R. Leahy, Biomedical Research Engineering Lab, Univ. of
Southern California

Figure 6 - SPECT

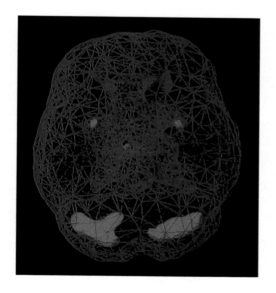

SPECT Image provided by Dr. Lisa Routh and the staff of Brainwaves
Neuroimaging Clinic

Figures:311

Figure 7 - qEEG Image

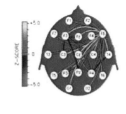

THETA/BETA

Color Coding on left figure represents deviation from normative reference group for the ratio value of theta over beta. The numbers on the scale below represents the standard deviation value for the respective colors. The figure on the right follows a similar color and standard deviation relationship. In this figure, it is the connection (coherence values) patterns which are presented in terms of their standard deviation difference from the normative reference group. The more to the yellow end of the scale indicates a higher similarity between the wave forms (coherence).

Figure 8 - Meg Image

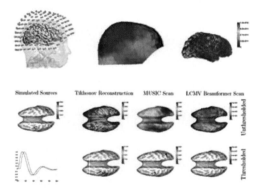

Scanning and imaging are the two approaches that have been widely used to model the position of MEG / EEG signal generators.

Figure: The imaging approaches are based on the assumption that the primary sources are intracellular currents in the dendritic trunks of cortical pyramidal neurons, that are aligned normally to the cortical surface. Various approaches can produce reconstruction / detection maps on the cortex Courtesy of R. Leahy, Biomedical Research Engineering Lab, Univ. of Southern California

Figure 9 - Loretta Image

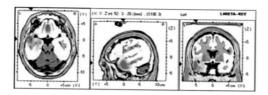

Left anterior temporal alpha focus, likely secondary to migraine ischemia (vascular changes from headache). Courtesy of Q-Metrix: Jay
Gunkelman

Reading Recall vs. Eyes Closed – Red areas indicate locations which
have higher levels of beta activations compared to the eyes closed condition. Blue areas indicated less beta activations compared to the eyes closed
condition. Images courtesy of R. Riss, PhD, Madonna Hospital, Lincoln,
Nebraska

Beta 1 - 12-16 Hertz

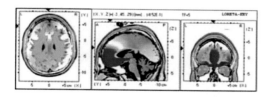

Beta2 - 16 - 24 Hertz

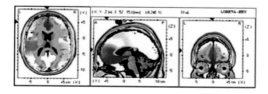

Figure 10 - Diffusion Tensor Imaging

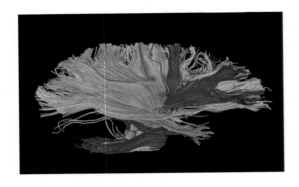

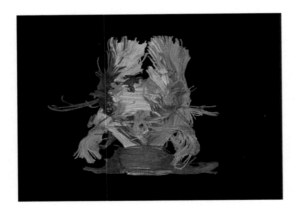

Courtesy of M. Maddah et al. (2005), MIT, Computer Science and Artificial Intelligence Lab. Boston, Mass.

Figures:314

Figure 15 – Coup-Contracoup effects in the Traumatic Brain Injured patient

Normal Brain

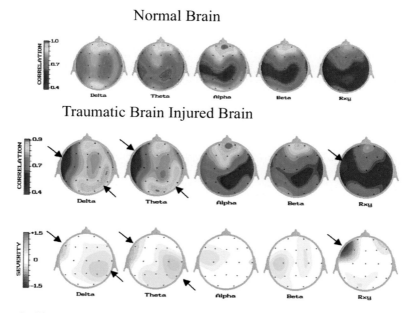

Traumatic Brain Injured Brain

Normal: Shows the relationships among EEG signals across the surface of the scalp in normal subjects.

Traumatic Brain Injured: Shows these relationships at the origin (coup) of the injury (left frontotemporal) and its effect on the contralateral (contra-coup) right temporoparietal location. The arrows pointing to the upper left position represent low relationships (i.e., disconnections) between local brain regions. The arrows that point to the lower right positions identify high relationships (i.e., leakage) within local brain regions.

The upper mappings break down the problem into measured relationships among signals in different brain regions, within five frequency bands. The lower mappings show the statistical severity of observed deviations in patient correlations from the correlations found in normal individuals.

The color-scale columns on the left show: a.) the level of intra-regional correlations and b.) the statistical severity of their deviation from the expected normal state. Statistical severity ranges between over (red) and under (blue) 'connected'. A value => +/- 0.8 has a large effect size (severity). A blue value under -.80 reflects a area with low connection values, while a red value greater than +.80 reflects an area with high connection values. Rxy figure is the combined value across all frequencies

Courtesy of W. Hudspeth, PhD

**Figure 18 - qEEG subtypes of ADD/HD 95% are Type 1 or 2
LD evenly distributed among types – blue lower than norm
– red higher than norm: 95% of ADD fall into Category 1 and 2,
while LD evenly distributed among all types - from Chabot, 2005.**

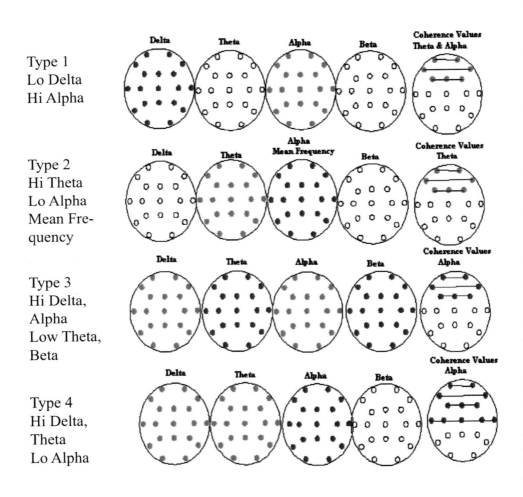

Type 1
Lo Delta
Hi Alpha

Type 2
Hi Theta
Lo Alpha
Mean Fre-
quency

Type 3
Hi Delta,
Alpha
Low Theta,
Beta

Type 4
Hi Delta,
Theta
Lo Alpha

Figures:316

Figure 26 – Traumatic Brain Injury – Case #1
Reading - Coherence and Phase Flashlight Effects from left frontal region (F7)

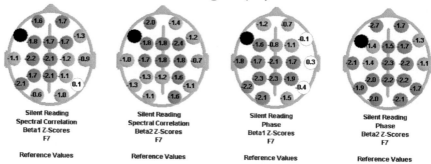

Black Circle is origin of Flashlight: Dark Blue circle represents values less than -1.50 SD below the norm; Light Blue circles represents values between -.50 SD and –1.50 SD below norm. White empty circles represent values between -.50 SD and +.50 SD around the normative value.

Figure 27 - Traumatic Brain Injured Subject – Case #1
Problem Solving
Coherence and Phase Flashlight Effects from left frontal region (F7)

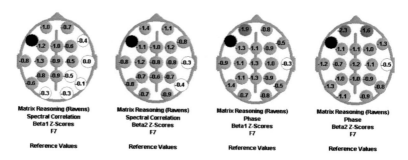

Black Circle is origin of Flashlight: Dark Blue circle represents values less than -1.50 SD below the norm; Light Blue circles represents values between -.50 SD and –1.50 SD below norm. White empty circles represent values between -.50 SD and +.50 SD around the normative value.

Figures displayed provided by software written by Altan Nahum of Lexicor Medical Technologies

Figures:317

Figure 28 – TBI Case # 2

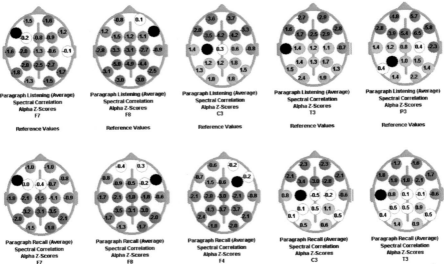

Black Circle is origin of Flashlight: Dark Blue circle represents values less than -1.50 SD below the norm; Light Blue circles represents values between -.50 SD and –1.50 SD below norm. White empty circles represent values between -.50 SD and +.50 SD around the normative value. Light orange represents values between +.50 SD and +1.50 SD. Dark orange circles represent values above +1.50 SD.

Figure 29 – Case #3 -Possible Asperger's syndrome

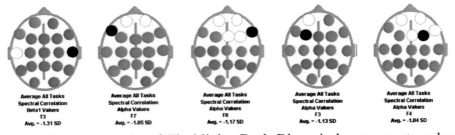

Black Circle is origin of Flashlight: Dark Blue circle represents values less than -1.50 SD below the norm; Light Blue circles represents values between -.50 SD and –1.50 SD below norm. White empty circles represent values between -.50 SD and +.50 SD around the normative value. Bottom Avg. value represents average standard deviation difference across all connnections.

Figures:318

Figure 30 – Case #4 - Normal Individual – Auditory

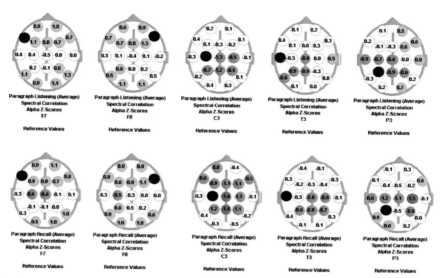

Black Circle is origin of Flashlight: Dark Blue circle represents values less than -1.50 SD below the norm; Light Blue circles represents values between -.50 SD and –1.50 SD below norm. White empty circles represent values between -.50 SD and +.50 SD around the normative value. Light orange represents values between +.50 SD and +1.50 SD. Dark orange circles represent values above +1.50 SD.

Figure 31 – Case #4 - Normal Individual - Reading

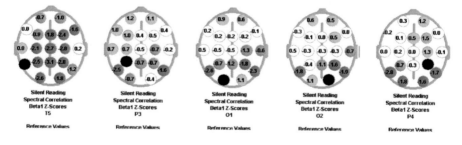

Black Circle is origin of Flashlight: Dark Blue circle represents values less than -1.50 SD below the norm; Light Blue circles represents values between -.50 SD and –1.50 SD below norm. White empty circles represent values between -.50 SD and +.50 SD around the normative value.

Figures:319

Figure 32 – Case #5 - Example of High Functioning Subject

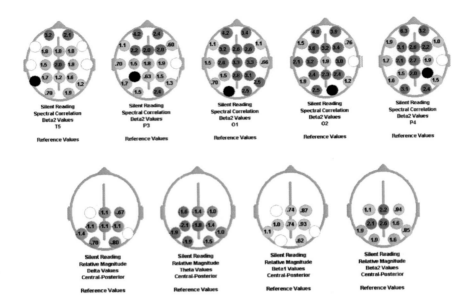

Black Circle is origin of Flashlight: Dark Blue circle represents values less than -1.50 SD below the norm; Light Blue circles represents values between -.50 SD and –1.50 SD below norm. White empty circles represent values between -.50 SD and +.50 SD around the normative value.

The red circles indicated differences of 2 standard deviations or greater than the normative value. Of some interest to note are the higher values in the left posterior region (T5-P3-O1) for the beta2 values and lower theta values in the left posterior than the right posterior. These results overlap the neuroscience research results which focus on the left posterior. Most databases would not be able to reveal this difference as their frequency range is below the 32 Hertz range.

Figure 33
An EEG biofeedback session in progress

The subject has an electrocap on the head. The electrical information is sent from the cap thru a long multicolored cable to the two boxes in
the far right corner. These boxes then send the information to the computer
where the software translates the information to qEEG parameters. The information is then presented on the screen numerically on the left and visually on the computer screen (airplane, superman, etc.). As the value of the
targeted variable increases the airplane rises. In addition, a pleasant audio
signal is generated whenever the variable obtains the target or a value above
the target. The subject listens to an audio tape (story, lecture) while their
brain is rewarded for improving its functioning. Low, negative sounds can
be programmed to occur whenever a variable obtains an undesirable value
(generally theta, delta).

The method involved is operant conditioning, the rewarding of
spontaneous behavior.

Figure 34 – Case #6
Listening to Paragraphs – Coherence Alpha Flashlight Deficits in standard deviation (SD) units

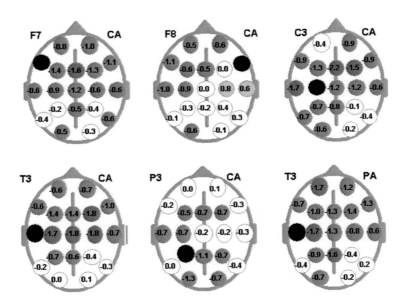

Label in upper right of head figure is origin of flashlight (i.e. F7, F8, etc.).

Dark blue circles represent connection patterns which are deviations from norm below –1.50 SD; Light blue circles are between -.50 SD and –1.50 SD; White circles are between -.50 SD and +.50 SD; Light orange circles are between +.50 SD and +1.50 SD. Dark orange circles are above +1.50 SD above norm.

Figure 35 – Case #6
Immediate Recall

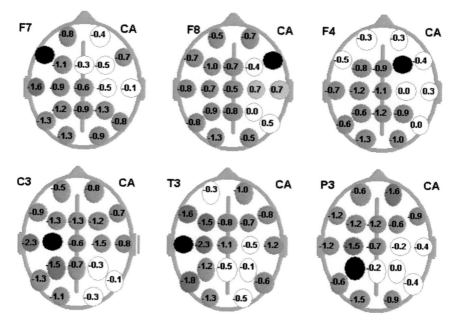

Label in upper right of head figure is origin of flashlight (i.e. F7, F8, etc.).

Dark blue circles represent connection patterns which are deviations from norm below –1.50 SD; Light blue circles are between -.50 SD and –1.50 SD; White circles are between -.50 SD and +.50 SD; Light orange circles are between +.50 SD and +1.50 SD. Dark orange circles are above +1.50 SD above norm.

Figures:323

Figure 36 Case #6
Changes in Alpha Coherence raw values as a result of treatment
Pre- Treatment

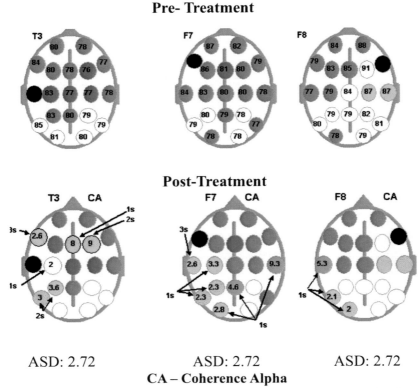

Post-Treatment

ASD: 2.72   ASD: 2.72   ASD: 2.72

CA – Coherence Alpha

ASD: average standard deviation for normative reference group for the frequency represented in the head figure. Numeric values in circles represent the change in raw values as a result of the treatment.

The numeric values outside the head figures that are followed by the s letter and have an arrow pointing to a location represent the number of sessions devoted to the particular connection. The mean of the last session, which addressed the connection pattern, is employed as the value to calculate the change figure. For example in the far left figure T3-F7 had 3 sessions devoted to the connection which resulted in a increased value during the last session of 2.6, roughly 1 SD if the average SD is employed as a reference. A circle with no arrow pointing to it indicates that the treatment did not address that connection.

Black Circle is origin of Flashlight: Dark Blue circle represents values less than -1.50 SD below the norm; Light Blue circles represents values between -.50 SD and –1.50 SD below norm. White empty circles represent values between -.50 SD and +.50 SD around the normative value.

Figure 37 – Case #6
Listening to Paragraphs – SD deficits in theta and beta RP and PKF activity

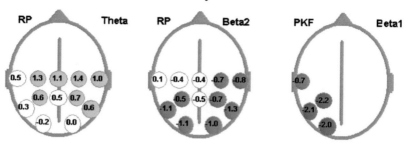

RP – Relative Power   PKF – Peak Frequency

The values in the figures presents the SD differences. Dark blue circles represent values which are deviations from norm below –1.50 SD; Light blue circles are between -.50 SD and –1.50 SD; White circles are between -.50 SD and +.50 SD; Light orange circles are between +.50 SD and +1.50 SD. Dark orange circles are above +1.50 SD above norm. Light orange circles are between +.50 SD and +1.50 SD. Dark orange circles are above +1.50 SD above norm.

Figures:325

Figure 38 – Case #6
Changes in theta and beta values as a result of treatment

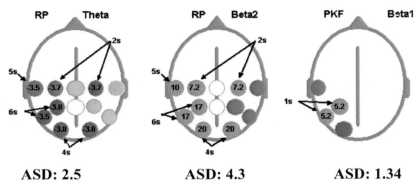

| ASD: 2.5 | ASD: 4.3 | ASD: 1.34 |

Numeric values in circles represent the change in raw values as a result of the treatment. Decreased values employ a minus sign. Positive values do not employ plus sign for presentation clarity. Circles without arrows indicate that no treatment was directed towards that location. Numeric values in circles represent the change in raw values as a result of the treatment.

The numeric values outside the head figures that are followed by the s letter and have an arrow pointing to a location represent the number of sessions devoted to the particular location. The mean of the last session, which addressed the location, is employed as the value to calculate the change figure.

Dark blue circles represent locations which have deviations from norm below −1.50 SD; Light blue circles are between -.50 SD and −1.50 SD; White circles are between -.50 SD and +.50 SD; Light orange circles are between +.50 SD and +1.50 SD. Dark orange circles are above +1.50 SD above norm.

Figure 40 – Case #6
Theta and Beta2 Z Score deficits during reading

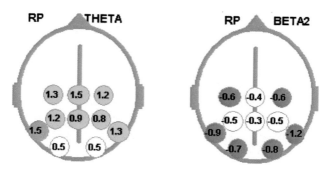

RP – Relative Power

Dark blue circles represent values which are deviations from norm below −1.50 SD; Light blue circles are between -.50 SD and −1.50 SD; White circles are between -.50 SD and +.50 SD; Light orange circles are between +.50 SD and +1.50 SD. Dark orange circles are above +1.50 SD above norm.

Figure 41 – Case #6
Results of treatment on theta and beta2 relative power raw values

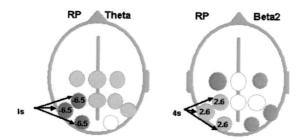

RP – Relative Power

ASD: average standard deviation for normative reference group for the frequency represented in the head figure Numeric values in circles represent the change in raw values as a result of the treatment.

Dark blue circles represent values which are deviations from norm below −1.50 SD; Light blue circles are between -.50 SD and −1.50 SD; White circles are between -.50 SD and +.50 SD; Light orange circles are between +.50 SD and +1.50 SD. Dark orange circles are above +1.50 SD above norm.

Figures:327

Figure 43 – Case #7 – Auditory Processing Problem

Pre - Treatment

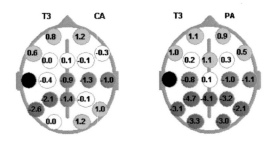

Post - Treatment

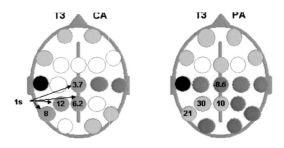

ASD= 2.72   ASD=6.3

ASD – Average Standard Deviation CA: Coherence Alpha;
Black circle represents origin of flashlight
Numeric values in circles represent the change in raw values as a result of
the treatment.

Dark blue circles represent values which are deviations from norm
below −1.50 SD; Light blue circles are between -.50 SD and −1.50 SD;
White circles are between -.50 SD and +.50 SD; Light orange circles are
between +.50 SD and +1.50 SD. Dark orange circles are above +1.50 SD
above norm.

Figures:328

Figure 44 – Case #7 – Auditory Processing Problem

Pre - Treatment

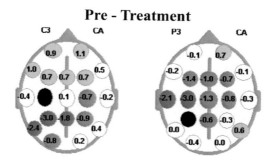

Post - Treatment

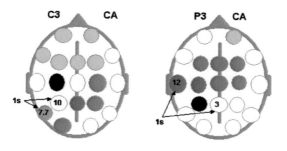

ASD = 2.72

ASD: average standard deviation for normative reference group
CA: Coherence Alpha

       Black circle indicates origin of flashlight. Values represent changes as a result of treatment.

Figure 45 – Case #7 – Auditory Processing Problem

Pre-Treatment

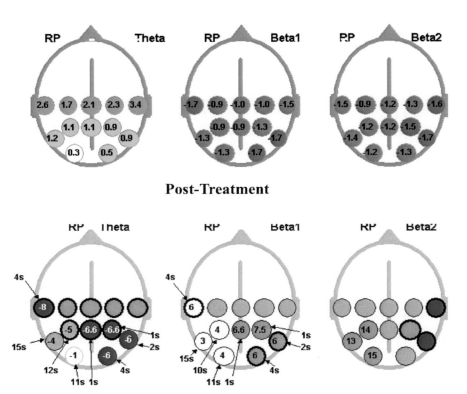

Post-Treatment

RP: Relative Power

Numeric values in circles represent the change in raw values as a result of the treatment.

Dark blue circles represent values which are deviations from norm below −1.50 SD; Light blue circles are between -.50 SD and −1.50 SD; White circles are between -.50 SD and +.50 SD; Light orange circles are between +.50 SD and +1.50 SD. Dark orange circles are above +1.50 SD above norm.

Figures:330

Figure 47 – Case #7
Reading SD Deficits - Coherence

Pre-Treatment

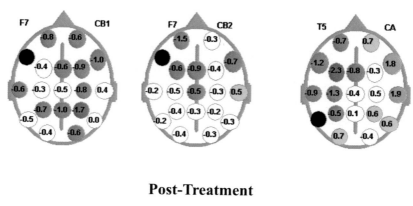

Post-Treatment

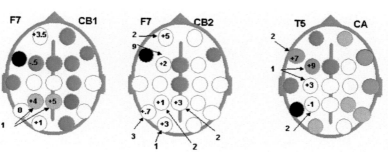

ASD: 3.7   ASD: 5.3   ASD: 2.5

CB1: Coherence Beta1; CB2: Coherence Beta2:
CA: Coherence Alpha:

Black circle represents origin of flashlight Numeric values in circles represent the change in raw values as a result of the treatment. Dark blue circles represent values which are deviations from norm below −1.50 SD; Light blue circles are between -.50 SD and −1.50 SD; White circles are between -.50 SD and +.50 SD; Light orange circles are between +.50 SD and +1.50 SD. Dark orange circles are above +1.50 SD above norm.

Figures:331

Figure 48 – Case #7 – Reading Processing Problem

Pre-Treatment

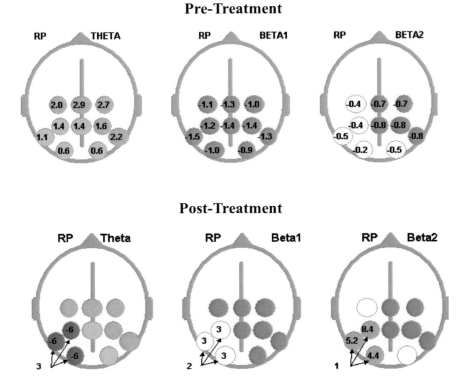

Post-Treatment

ASD: Average Standard Deviation. RP: Relative Power

Numeric values in circles represent the change in raw values as a result of the treatment.

Dark blue circles represent values which are deviations from norm below –1.50 SD; Light blue circles are between -.50 SD and –1.50 SD; White circles are between -.50 SD and +.50 SD; Light orange circles are between +.50 SD and +1.50 SD. Dark orange circles are above +1.50 SD above norm.

Figure 50 – Case #8 17 year old male – Auditory Processing

Pre-Treatment

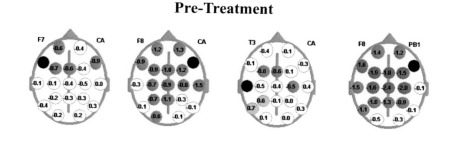

Post-Treatment

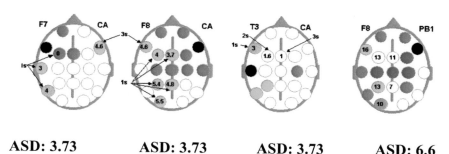

ASD: 3.73   ASD: 3.73   ASD: 3.73   ASD: 6.6

**PB1: Phase Beta1; CA: Coherence Alpha;
Black circle represents origin of flashlight**

Numeric values in circles represent the change in raw values as a result of the treatment.

Dark blue circles represent values which are deviations from norm below –1.50 SD; Light blue circles are between -.50 SD and –1.50 SD; White circles are between -.50 SD and +.50 SD; Light orange circles are between +.50 SD and +1.50 SD. Dark orange circles are above +1.50 SD above norm.

Figures:333

Figure 51 – Case #8 17 year old male - Auditory Processing

Pre-Treatment

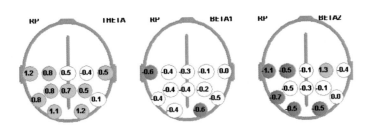

Post-Treatment

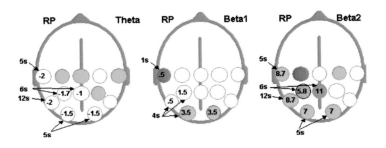

ASD: 2.3   ASD: 4.1   ASD: 5.5

RP: Relative Power ASD: average standard deviation

Numeric values in circles represent the change in raw values as a result of the treatment.

Dark blue circles represent values which are deviations from norm below –1.50 SD; Light blue circles are between -.50 SD and –1.50 SD; White circles are between -.50 SD and +.50 SD; Light orange circles are between +.50 SD and +1.50 SD. Dark orange circles are above +1.50 SD above norm.

Figure 53 – Case #8 17 year old male - Reading

Pre-Treatment

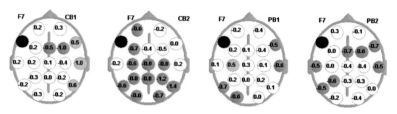

Post-Treatment

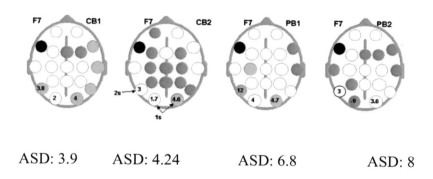

ASD: 3.9   ASD: 4.24   ASD: 6.8   ASD: 8

**CB1: Coherence Beta1; CB2: Coherence Beta1; PB1: Phase Beta1;
PB2: Phase Beta2; ASD: average standard deviation.
Black circle represents origin of flashlight.**

Numeric values in circles represent the change in raw values as a result of the treatment.

Dark blue circles represent values which are deviations from norm below −1.50 SD; Light blue circles are between -.50 SD and −1.50 SD; White circles are between -.50 SD and +.50 SD; Light orange circles are between +.50 SD and +1.50 SD. Dark orange circles are above +1.50 SD above norm.

Figure 54 – Case #8 17 year old male - Reading

Pre-Treatment

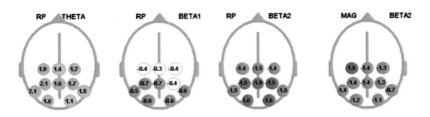

Post-Treatment

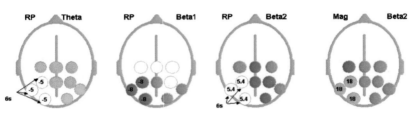

ASD: 2.4   ASD: 4   ASD: 6.1   ASD: 1.95

RP: Relative Power ASD: average standard deviation

Numeric values in circles represent the change in raw values as a result of the treatment.

Dark blue circles represent values which are deviations from norm below –1.50 SD; Light blue circles are between -.50 SD and –1.50 SD;

White circles are between -.50 SD and +.50 SD; Light orange circles are between +.50 SD and +1.50 SD. Dark orange circles are above +1.50 SD above norm.

Figure 56– Case #9 – Reading
Numeric values in Circles represent SD values.

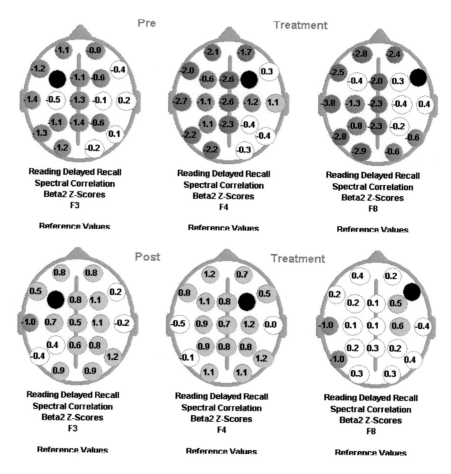

Numeric Values in circles represent standard deviation value differences from normative reference group.

Dark blue circles represent values which are deviations from norm below –1.50 SD; Light blue circles are between -.50 SD and –1.50 SD;

White circles are between -.50 SD and +.50 SD; Light orange circles are between +.50 SD and +1.50 SD. Dark orange circles are above +1.50 SD above norm.

Figures:337

Figure 57– Case #9 – Matrix Reasoning

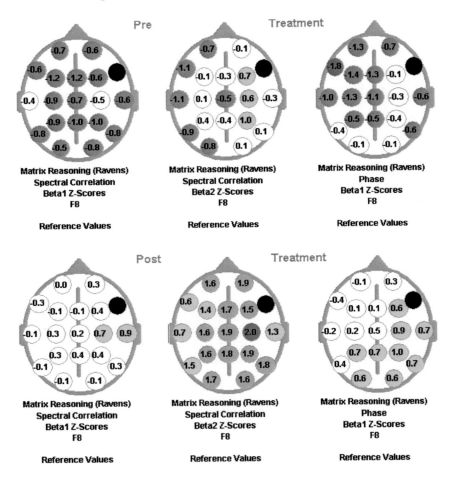

Numeric Values in circles represent standard deviation value differences from normative reference group.

Dark blue circles represent values which are deviations from norm below –1.50 SD; Light blue circles are between -.50 SD and –1.50 SD;

White circles are between -.50 SD and +.50 SD; Light orange circles are between +.50 SD and +1.50 SD. Dark orange circles are above +1.50 SD above norm.

Figure 58 - Case #9 – Matrix Reasoning

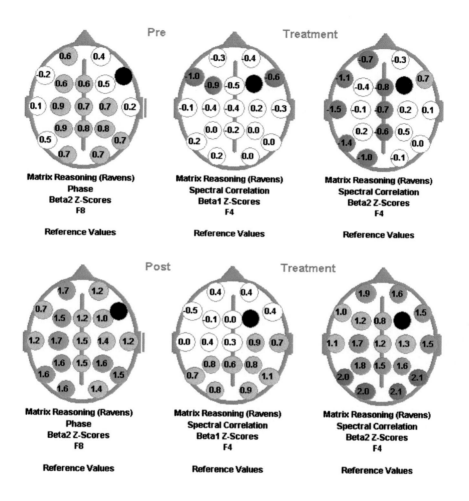

Numeric Values in circles represent standard deviation value differences from normative reference group.

Dark blue circles represent values which are deviations from norm below –1.50 SD; Light blue circles are between -.50 SD and –1.50 SD;

White circles are between -.50 SD and +.50 SD; Light orange circles are between +.50 SD and +1.50 SD. Dark orange circles are above +1.50 SD above norm.

Figures:339